T0307885

Modernism and the Orient

Edited by Zhaoming Qian

Ezra Pound Center for Literature Series: Volume 4

University of New Orleans Press

Edited by Zhaoming Qian

Modernism and the Orient

Printed in the United States of America.

ISBN: 9781608010745

Library of Congress Control Number: 2012953434

Book and cover design by Lauren Capone

University of New Orleans Press

unopress.org

The Ezra Pound Center for Literature

The Ezra Pound Center for Literature Book Series is a project dedicated to publishing a variety of scholarly and literary works relevant to Ezra Pound and Modernism, including new critical monographs on Pound and/or other Modernists, scholarly studies related to Pound and his legacy, edited collections of essays, volumes of original poetry, reissued books of importance to Pound scholarship, translations, and other works.

Series Editor: John Gery, University of New Orleans

Ezra Pound Center for Literature Book Series

Acknowledgments

I wish to thank the contributors to this volume for their enthusiasm and patience. Without the sharing of knowledge with more than a hundred colleagues from twelve countries at Hangzhou 2010, this collection would not have been so rich. Among the institutions that provided financial support were the University of New Orleans (through the efforts of Vice-Chancellor Scott Whittenburg and Dean Susan Krantz), Zhejiang University (through the efforts of Assistant President Jieping Fan and Dean Lizhen He), and Hangzhou Normal University (through the efforts of President Gaoxiang Ye and Dean Qiping Yin). Thanks are also due to my department chair Peter Schock and graduate coordinator Bob Shenk for providing superb research assistants, Mary Bamburg in fall 2010 and spring 2011 and Rich Goode in fall 2011 and spring 2012. I am grateful to Bill Lavender of the University of New Orleans Press for his faith. I am happy to thank Lauren Capone, our copy-editor. To my longtime colleague and the Ezra Pound Center for Literature Series general editor John Gery I owe special thanks for his warm and energetic roles. George Bornstein and Anne Luyat read the manuscript and commented on it. To them I am deeply indebted.

Contents

Introduction

Zhaoming Qian

An innocence, a simplicity that one does not find elsewhere in literature makes the birds and the leaves seem as near to him as they are near to children, and the changes of the seasons great events as before our thoughts had arisen between them and us. –W. B. Yeats, Introduction to Tagore's *Gitanjali*

Undoubtedly pure color is to be found in Chinese poetry, when we begin to know enough about it; indeed, a shadow of this perfection is already at hand in translations. Liu Ch'e, Chu Yuan, Chia I, and the great *vers libre* writers before the Petrarchan age of Li Po, area treasury to which the next century may look for as great a stimulus as the renaissance had from the Greeks. –Ezra Pound, *Literary Essays*

For a poet to have even a second-hand contact with China is a great matter. –Wallace Stevens, *Letters*

[O]rientalism is not a single developmental tradition but is profoundly heterogeneous. –Lisa Lowe, *Critical Terrains*

When he looked back over his experiment with Irish drama for an introduction to a 1916 collection of short plays, W. B. Yeats did not hesitate to credit the Noh drama of Japan: "I have found my first model —and in literature if we would not be parvenus we must have a model

—in the 'Noh' stage of aristocratic Japan" (*Four Plays for Dancers* 86). During the same war period, Yeats' American colleague Ezra Pound went further to list Japan and China among the crucial inspirers and teachers of Anglo-American modernists: "From Whistler and the Japanese, or Chinese . . . the fragment of the English-speaking world . . . learned to enjoy 'arrangements' of colours and masses" (*Visual Arts* 192). Yeats' and Pound's continental European contemporary Franz Kafka was no less explicit about his passion for the Far East. In 1916, he wrote in a postcard to his fiancée: "I think that if I were Chinese and were going home (at bottom, I am Chinese and am going home), I would soon have to find a way back here" (*Felice* 647).

Of the Orient, the Far East proved more productive than the Near East as a source of literary models for twentieth-century Western writers. Numerous other Euro-American modernists have acknowledged their interest in and debt to Chinese and Japanese culture as forthrightly as Yeats, Pound, and Kafka did. When interviewed in 1951 about the development of his modernist poetry, Wallace Stevens, for instance, straightforwardly told his interviewer: "Yes: I think that I have been influenced by Chinese and Japanese lyrics. But you ask whether I have ever 'tried deliberately to attain certain qualities.' That is quite possible" (*Letters* 291). Upon the publication of *O to Be a Dragon* in 1959, Marianne Moore wrote to her Chinese inspirer Mai-mai Sze, thanking her for "the fond thoughts [she] evoked – the celestial reveries for which [she was] responsible" (qtd. in Qian, *Modernist Response* 181).

Although modernist writers were entirely candid about their indebtedness to China and Japan, contemporary scholars have been strangely slow in recognizing the Orient's place in modernist studies. This bizarre non-recognition has led Christopher Bush to claim in *Idiographic Modernism* (2010): "[F]or all its talk of globalization and transnationism, contemporary modernist studies knows less and cares less about China than did many writers and thinkers in the modernist era itself" (xiv).

Contemporary scholars, however, have not been slow in recognizing modernists' extensive interchanges with China and Japan. What they hesitate to recognize is how much of a positive impact such interactions have had. Trained in the decades after the publication of Edward Said's *Orientalism* (1978), present-day literary critics are not easily convinced that the modernists could be much different from eighteenth- to nineteenth-century orientalists. Said's seminal study has substantiated that no real Islamic Orient is present in eighteenth- to nineteenth-century orientalists' representations of it. How could there then be genuine Chinese and Japanese motifs and influences in the modernists' uses of them?

The modernists, we should remember, were rebels against eighteenth- to nineteenth-century traditions. In rebelling against Romanticism and Victorianism, they tended also to rebel against their predecessors' hegemonic orientalism—what we now call Saidian orientalism. When Pound first arrived in London, it was the British Museum oriental art expert Laurence Binyon who introduced him to Chinese and Japanese aesthetics. In his review of Binyon's *The Flight of the Dragon* for *Blast* 2 (1915), Pound, however, critiqued his mentor's orientalism, ridiculing his "mind constantly hark[ing] back to some folly of nineteenth century Europe, constantly trying to justify Chinese intelligence by dragging it a little nearer to some Western precedent" (*Poetry and Prose* 3, 99). In another review published in 1918, he criticized Arthur Waley, the translator of *A Hundred and Seventy Chinese Poems* (1918), for his "touch of occidental patronage for the poor oriental" (*Poetry and Prose* 3, 126).

Admittedly, the modernists were not completely devoid of the influence of Saidian orientalism, but with a broadened global view and with what Pound called "the new historic sense of our time" (*Guide to Kulchur* 30), they could hardly believe in Western cultural superiority. To varying degrees, they were repelled by old-fashioned Euro-centralism. Take the French modernist Marcel Proust. His Orient in *À la Recherche du Temps Perdu*, according to Andrè Benhaïm (95) and Christine Froula, functions actually to "disorient" Eurocentric France and Frenchness. While Proust's disgust with Saidian orientalism was implicit, Marianne Moore's was not. In a 1928 review of *Guide-posts to Chinese Painting* by British art historian Louise Wallace Hackney, the American modernist poet reprimanded its "writing and thinking" as "occidentally 'prompt'" making "a delighted consideration of [Chinese] art . . . less than delightful" (*Complete Prose* 255). Stevens who shared with Moore an interest in oriental art is known to have said that "I hate orientalism." The statement was made in 1953 with regard to the French painter Roger Bezombes, whom Stevens found to endorse painting "neither eastern nor western, but a conglomeration of both, a kind of syncretism" (*Letters* 797). Clearly Moore and Stevens distinguished between orientalism and the Orient. They passionately admired things genuinely Chinese or Japanese while at the same time detesting hegemonic orientalism.

As I have noted elsewhere, "instinctive affinity is the ground of all appreciation and influence" (*Orientalism and Modernism* 6). At the turn of the past century as internationalism began, the modernists' horizon was expanded to reach beyond the borders of Europe and America. In their attempts to break away from nineteenth-century traditions, making it new, they frequently found their modernist Self like the oriental Other. Yeats described his discovery of the Self in the Other in a 1913 speech in praise of the Bengali poet Rabindranath Tagore: "A whole people, a whole civilization, immeasurably strange to us seems to have been taken up into this imagination; and yet we are not moved because of its strangeness, but because we have met our own image" (Introduction to Tagore's *Gitanjali* 5). John Gould Fletcher in Pound's Imagist circle echoed Yeats when reminiscing about a visit to the Boston Museum of Fine Art's Oriental Wing: "The hours I spent then in the Oriental Wing, seeing the Sung or Kamakura masterpieces with new eyes, re-educated me in regard to the purposes of a pictorial art close in spirit to my own poetry, and to the function of the poetic artist in reshaping the world. They rededicated me to the vital instinct, and to the soul of nature" (*Life Is My Song* 185).

Not all modernists tried deliberately to infuse their work with Chinese and Japanese motifs and methods, only a few. Far-Eastern ethics of pictorial presentation, reverence for objectivity, and style that includes ellipsis, allusion, and juxtaposition, however, appeared attractive to all of them. T. S. Eliot made no conscious effort to learn from China and Japan. Yet we are certain of his admiration for Pound's *Cathay* and belief in the glory of Chinese civilization. In a 1933 essay he declared: "I have the highest respect for the Chinese mind and for Chinese civilization; and I am willing to believe that Chinese civilization at its highest has graces and excellences which may make Europe seem crude" (*After Strange Gods* 43). Researchers are still trying to find hard proof for a direct Chinese influence on Robert Frost whose poetry strikes us as especially Taoist-like. Indeed, modernism's interest in and interchanges with China and Japan are far more intricate and multifaceted than have been generally suspected. No single model of orientalism can be appropriated to account for all modernism-Orient relationships. Indeed, there are as many orientalisms as are modernists and modernisms. East/West interconnections in the modernist movement must be interpreted case by case and interval by interval.

This collection of essays, gathered from the third International Conference on Modernism and the Orient (Hangzhou 2010), seeks to investigate diverse roles China and Japan (in the case of T. S. Eliot India, China, and Japan) played in the development of Euro-American literary modernism. The twelve essays gathered in this volume fall into three groups. The two essays in the first section examine the Orient in late nineteenth-century precursors to modernism – the Irish playwright and critic Oscar Wilde, who, as Wyndham Lewis puts it, "'electrified' the art world" (*Wyndham Lewis on Art* 335), and the American poet Emily Dickinson, whom William Carlos Williams thought of as his "patron saint" ("Interview with Stanley Koehler" 12). The contributions in the second group deal with early twentieth century modernists—Yeats, Pound, Proust, Frost, Woolf, Joyce, and Eliot—and the Orient. The four essays in the last section explore post-World War II modernism and China/Japan. The poets discussed in this group include late Pound, late Moore, Zukofsky, Harry Guest, and Lee Harwood.

In his contribution, Longxi Zhang redresses an overlooked aspect of Oscar Wilde's work – his reading of the Taoist philosopher Zhuangzi in 1890 and the impact of Taoism on his philosophy. Zhang examines the particular perspective from which Wilde understood Zhuangzi and allowed Zhuangzi to impact his social and political views, his conviction of personal freedom, and his rejection of all forms of government. Wilde recognized in Zhuangzi's works a philosophy with which he later sympathized in his essay, "The Soul of Man under Socialism." Wilde's interest in Zhuangzi, Zhang concludes, anticipated a similar interest many Euro-American modernists had well into the twentieth century.

Sabine Sielke in her essay focuses on how Emily Dickinson and Marianne Moore – as paradigmatic figures in American modernism –

have been recontextualized by current critical perspectives emerging in the larger field of postcolonial studies. Wondering what we remember of modernism as we "orientalize" its cultural practices, Sielke explores the politics and desire informing revisionary approaches to the poets' work that waver between yet another attempt at othering modernism and a domestication of the Orient.

Daniel Albright begins his essay by recounting archaeological discoveries, a 33,000-year-old flute made of the bone of a griffon vulture found in southern Germany and a 9,000-year-old flute made of the bone of a red-crowned crane found in central China. Taking off from the modernist sense that "the most profound art comes from the innermost recesses of the body," he playfully examines this notion in his reinterpretation of Yeats' *The Herne's Egg* concerning a flute made from a heron's thigh-bone. Albright also discusses Pound's opera *Le Testament*, in which flute music accompanies a brothel scene, as well as selections of Pound's translations of Noh plays and Chinese poems in which flutes figure prominently. Exploring how in the work of Yeats and Pound the flute interweaves the celestial and unearthly with the outright carnal and sexual, Albright's essay shows how, at the crossroads of literature and music, modernist texts made Orient and Occident collide.

In her chapter Christine Froula discusses Marcel Proust's *À la Recherche du Temps Perdu* and its complex allusions to cultures of the Near, Middle, and Far East. In the spirit of André Benhaïm's argument that Proust's Orient "owes little to Orientalism: rather it shows a desire to disorient Frenchness" by registering residues of influences from beyond France's geographical borders (95), Froula's essay approaches Proust's evocations of Eastern cultures through allusions to the seventeenth-century Dutch master Vermeer. Appropriating for Bergotte's death scene a French art critic's 1921 claim that Vermeer's craft had a Chinese patience otherwise to be found only in paintings from the Far East, Proust opened France's borders, Froula argues, to a historically-grounded cultural imagination resonating throughout his *Recherche*.

Qiping Yin begins his contribution by addressing an imbalance in Robert Frost criticism: many critics argue that the common ground between Frost's poetry and Taoism lies in "a quest for a thorough freedom" from self, society, and nature. Yin counters this somewhat reductive view by bringing to light Frost's impulse at once to renounce the world and to accept the world, which corresponds precisely to the Taoist insistence on a balance between *Ru Shi* (renouncing the world) and *Chu Shi* (accepting the world). Frost's "West-Running Brook" with its central symbol of a brook alluding to water and road, two key Taoist images, offers itself as a good point of entry into Frost-Taoist affinities. On this ground Yin examines Frost's poetry from "Mending Wall" to "Directive" and prose from "The Figure a Poem Makes" to "A Monument to After-Thought Unveiled," finding aspects of *Chu Shi* and juxtaposed moments of *Ru Shi*.

Showing that elements of and allusions to Chinese culture permeate James Joyce's *Ulysses* and *Finnegan's Wake*, the essay by Ira Nadel focuses on the oriental touches in Joyce's graphic design – in particular, the ways in which Joyce's typography and visual forms echo Chinese writing. Joyce's choices in diction and punctuation shape meaning through visual form in a manner reminiscent of ideogrammic methods. Nadel attributes this practice to the impact of Ernest Fenollosa whose work Joyce knew by way of Pound's revision and publication of Fenollosa's *The Chinese Written Character as a Medium for Poetry*.

In her essay, Fen Gao examines Virginia Woolf's critique of traditional western poetic's binary criteria of truth and falsehood, noting that her notion of literary truth as on an equilibrium between the truth of life and the illusion of art corresponds to the Chinese concept of *zhenhuan*, which holds that literary truth is a fusion of the thing, the spirit, and the poetic. Both concepts break through a linear replacement of a literary criterion from the thing through the spirit to the symbol and convey an integral perception of literary truth. Tracing the development of Woolf's writing through works including "Monday or Tuesday," *To the Lighthouse*, and *A Room of One's Own*, Gao finds in each a different facet of this proximity.

Every critic of Pound's *Cathay* will refer to Eliot's statement that "Pound is the inventor of Chinese poetry for our time" ("Introduction" 14). While most will hasten to conclude that Pound, therefore, was an orientalist manipulator of Chinese poetry, Christian Kloeckner alerts us to Eliot's admiration for both Pound's creativity and his faithfulness to Far-Eastern texts. "When the writing is most like Mr. Pound," Eliot is cited as declaring: "it also presents the appearance of being most faithful to the original" ("Noh" 103). From Eliot's enthusiasm for *Cathay*, Kloeckner moves on to his theory of impersonality, which he believes to be obtained both through his study of Brahminist and Buddhism texts and through his embrace of Far East/West cultural exchanges. Highlighting impersonality's ethical and political pliability, Kloeckner rejects interpretations that either reduce Eliot's concept to its culturally imperialist appropriations or praise it for its provision of empathetic space for the Other. By focusing on Eliot's essays and the Eastern voices in *The Waste Land*, he suggests that precisely because impersonality is such an aesthetically and politically contested concept, our reexamination can tell us much about the ways in which modernist writers explored Eastern "alternative aesthetic space." Furthermore, the history of how scholars have read and judged impersonality reveals much about our field's changing critical concerns and their respective blind spots.

Ronald Bush centers his essay on Ezra Pound and Guanyin. Excised references in Pound's unpublished Italian and English avant-texts confirm the central importance of the Buddhist bodhisattva that Pound called "Kuanon of all delights" in the *Pisan Cantos*. Echoing commentary on Asian art by Laurence Binyon and Ernest Fenollosa, Pound applied a poet's imagination to the figure's traditional iconographic associations with the moon, a vessel of pure water, the lotus, and the willow to create a powerful composite representation of heaven's compassionate intercession and the healing power of nature. For Bush, Pound's drafts make Guanyin function as a bridge between Buddhist spirit and Confucian thought. Closely associated with the trope of the willow, Guanyin amplified Pound's account of the power of compassionate nature to rescue the poet from the depths of his despair.

My contribution to the volume is based on a newly discovered recording of Marianne Moore's 1957 lecture on the Tao. This lecture, entitled "Tedium and Integrity in Poetry," proves to be at once a tribute to Chinese painter and writer Mai-mai Sze's *The Tao of Painting* ("Integrity") and a critique of contemporary American poetry ("Tedium"). Moore's lecture along with other archival material reveals that her encounter with *The Tao of Painting* and its author Sze channeled a new surge of creativity in Moore, resulting in astonishing experimental modernism in her late lyrics. Poems such as "To a Giraffe" and "Blue Bug" in *Tell Me, Tell Me* (1966) display Moore's renewed confidence in the modernist ideal of impersonality during the postmodern era.

Richard Parker addresses Louis Zukofsky's late approach towards Zen Buddhism. The appearance of Zen images and themes in the final stretches of "A" and the sequences that would follow—*80 Flowers* and "Gamut"—is a crucial moment of realignment. Parker contends that Zen offered Zukofsky (via Cid Corman, Will Petersen, and Robert Duncan) a way of countering the constraining Confucian inheritance of Pound and reciprocating his seminal influence on the New American Poets. Parker analyses Zen's tentative presence in Zukofsky's late short poems. His essay concludes with archival material that points to the forms his orientalism would have taken had "Gamut," Zukofsky's last project, been completed.

Tony Lopez focuses on particular poems by two contemporary British poets, Harry Guest and Lee Harwood, who began to be published in the 1960s, and considers how their allegiance to Poundian poetics and international modernism extends the literary representation of the Orient into a still developing modernist strand in contemporary literary culture. Guest's substantial engagement with Japanese aesthetics and landscape and Harwood's direct reference to Pound, Confucius, and the *Yijing* (*I Ching*) demonstrate how late modernism revises and re-presents the earlier Orient, respected for spiritual perception and strength.

This volume, like the 3rd international Conference on Modernism and the Orient where early versions of the twelve presentations were first delivered, is an attempt to carry on the exciting exchanges on the theme begun at Yale 1996 and Cambridge 2004.[1] Fenollosa, Yeats, Stein, Stevens, Pound, and Fletcher (subjects at Yale 1996) with their fruitful reactions to Japan and China offered six illustrations of modernism's heterogeneous Orient—its intensity as well as its intricacy.[2] Similarly impressive cases (including Yeats/Pound/Asian music and post-World War II Pound) with newly unearthed archival materials and fresh insights presented in a single volume will reinforce this point yet to be given the centrality it deserves. While this book aims to expand exploration of Euro-American modernism's Orient both in historic time and in interdisciplinary areas, it is not intended to be comprehensive or definitive. Modernism's dialogue with the Orient constantly challenges scholars with its variations, contradictions, and ambivalences. These contributions not only reflect this but hope to advance ongoing research and debate on this critical topic.

Notes

1. Yale 1996, or the Conference on Modernism and the Orient held at Yale 18-19 October 1996, was organized by Patricia Willis of the Beinecke Rare Book and Manuscript Library, Yale University. Cambridge 2004, or the Conference on Orientalism and Modernism held at Cambridge 17-19 June 2004, was organized by Judith Green of King's College, University of Cambridge. Hangzhou 2010, or the 3rd International Conference on Modernism and the Orient held in Hangzhou, China 4-7 June 2010, was co-directed by myself and Fen Gao of Zhejiang University.

2. For expanded versions of some of the papers delivered at the 1996 Yale conference, see Zhaoming Qian, *The Modernist Response to Chinese Art: Pound, Moore, Stevens*, Chapter 6 "Stevens's 'Six Significant Landscapes'"; Mary Paterson Cheadle, *Ezra Pound's Confucian Translations*, Chapter 2: "Translating Chinese"; and Richard Taylor, "Noh Drama and its Assimilation in the West: Weil – Britten - Yeats – Pound," www.richard-dean-taylor.de. For revised versions of some of the papers delivered at the 2004 Cambridge conference, see Eric Hayot, ed. "Modernisms' Chinas," a special issue of *Modern Chinese Literature and Culture*, 2006.

Works Cited

Benhaïm, André. "From Baalbek to Baghdad and Beyond: Marcel Proust's Foreign Memories of France." *Journal of European Studies* 35 (2005): 87-110.

Binyon, Laurence. *The Flight of the Dragon: An Essay on the Theory and Practice of Art in China and Japan, Based on Original Sources*. London: Murray, 1911.

Bush, Christopher. *Idiographic Modernism: China, Writing, Media*. New York: Oxford UP, 2010.

Cheadle, Mary Paterson. *Ezra Pound's Confucian Translations*. Ann Arbor: U of Michigan P, 1997.

Eliot, T. S. *After Strange Gods: A Primer of Modern Heresy.* New York: Harcourt, Brace, 1933.

___. Introduction. *Selected Poems of Ezra Pound.* 1928. London: Faber and Faber, 1956. 7-21.

___. "The Noh and the Image." *The Egoist* 4.7 (August 1917): 102-03.

Fletcher, John Gould. *Life Is My Song: The Autobiography of John Gould Fletcher.* New York: Farrar and Rinehart, 1937.

Kafka, Franz. *Briefe an Felice und andere Korrespondenz aus der Verlobungzeit.* Ed. Erich Heller and Jurgen Born. Frankfurt: Fischer, 1967.

Lewis, Wyndham. *Wyndham Lewis on Art.* Ed. W. Michel and C. J. Fox. New York: Fund and Wagnalls, 1969.

Lowe, Lisa. *Critical Terrains: French and British Orientalisms.* Ithaca: Cornell University Press, 1994.

Moore, Marianne. *Complete Prose of Marianne Moore.* Ed. Patricia C. Willis. New York: Viking, 1986.

Pound, Ezra. *Ezra Pound and the Visual Arts.* Ed. Harriet Zinnes. New York: New Directions, 1980.

___. *Ezra Pound's Poetry and Prose Contributions to Periodicals.* 11 vols. Ed. Lea Baechler, A. Walton Litz, and James Longenbach. New York: Garland, 1991.

___. *Guide to Kulchur.* New York: New Directions, 1970.

___. *Literary Essays.* Ed. T. S. Eliot. New York: New Directions, 1968.

Qian, Zhaoming. *The Modernist Response to Chinese Art: Pound, Moore, Stevens.* Charlottesville: U of Virginia P, 2003.

___. *Orientalism and Modernism: The Legacy of China in Pound and Williams.* Durham: Duke UP, 1995.

Said, Edward. *Orientalism.* New York: Random House, 1978.

Stevens, Wallace. *Letters of Wallace Stevens.* Ed. Holly Stevens. New York: Knopf, 1966.

Williams, William Carlos. Interview with Stanley Koehler. 1962. *Writers at Work: The 'Paris Review' Interviews.* 3rd series. New York: Viking, 1967. 3-30.

Yeats, William Butler. *Four Plays for Dancers.* 1916. New York: Macmillan, 1921.

___. Introduction. *Gitanjali: Song Offerings.* By Rabindranath Tagore. 1913.

Boston: Branden Books, 1979. 1-7.

Modernism and the Orient

Elective Affinities? On Wilde's Reading of Zhuangzi

Zhang Longxi

At the beginning of his famous novel, *The Picture of Dorian Gray*, Oscar Wilde describes Lord Henry Wotton as lying on some Persian saddle-bags in a divan and smoking his cigarettes, while the silhouette of some birds in flight, a veritable show of *ombres chinoises*, is unfolding itself in front of his eyes: "and now and then the fantastic shadows of birds in flight flitted across the long tussore-silk curtains that were stretched in front of the huge window, producing a kind of momentary Japanese effect, and making him think of those pallid jade-faced painters of Tokyo who, through the medium of an art that is necessarily immobile, seek to convey the sense of swiftness and motion" (*Dorian Gray* 1). Here, Wilde is portraying what would be an exotic and fascinating Oriental effect in the Victorian English imagination, though at the same time he is perfectly aware that this effect owes more to the fantasy of exoticism than to the reality of an Oriental country. "The Japanese people are the deliberate self-conscious creation of certain individual artists," as Wilde puts it in his essay "The Decay of Lying" in an unsentimental, sober-minded vein. "The actual people who live in Japan are not unlike the general run of English people; that is to say, they are extremely commonplace, and have nothing curious or extraordinary about them. In fact the whole of Japan is a pure invention" ("Decay" 46-47). For Wilde, of course, art and imagination are far more important than the banality of life, and it is artistic creation that gives us beauty and meaning in life. He certainly prefers the artistic invention of Japan to the banal reality of Japan, but he knows the difference between imagination and reality.

Wilde articulates these important ideas in the critical essays collected in the volume entitled *Intentions*. As I have argued elsewhere, the "dialogues on art and criticism in *Intentions* have a coherent and symmetrical structure" (Zhang 160). First, "The Decay of Lying" puts forward the bold creed of the new aesthetics of art for art's sake: that "Life imitates art far more than Art imitates life"; and that "Life holds the Mirror up to Art, and either reproduces some strange type imagined by painter or sculptor, or realizes in fact what has been dreamed in fiction" ("Decay" 32, 39). Then "The Critic as Artist" establishes a similarly structured relationship between criticism and art as that between art and life, arguing that if we understand life through art, then we understand art through criticism, for "the critic occupies the same relation to the work of art that he criticises as the artist does to the visible world of form and colour, or the unseen world of passion and of thought" ("Critic" 136-37). Wilde claims that "the highest Criticism, being the purest form of personal impression, is in its way more creative than creation"; that it is "the only civilised form of autobiography" ("Critic" 138, 139). In his concept of creative criticism, Wilde fully acknowledges the critic's subjectivity, the specific insight into the nature of life and art from the critic's own perspective and imaginative vision.

Such an idea or, rather, a distorted form of it, may have gone to the extreme in more recent literary theory and criticism. Terry Eagleton calls Oscar Wilde "a proto-post-structuralist" ("Wilde" 49), while Ronán McDonald acknowledges that "Wilde's critical essays in *Intentions* (1899) anticipate emphasis on the constitutive powers of language and human perception" (73). Eagleton talks about Wilde's language as a deliberate twist of English, "as the colonial's revenge on the imperialist father-tongue," "a subaltern's strike at the bland heartiness of his English betters" ("Wilde" 49). But what a world of difference between Wilde's style of writing and that of contemporary postmodern and postcolonial critics! Eagleton speculates that "there must exist somewhere a secret handbook for post-colonial critics," of which an important rule reads: "'Be as obscurantist as you can decently get away with.' Post-colonial theorists are often to be found agonizing about the gap between their own intellectual discourse and the natives of whom they speak; but the gap might look rather less awesome if they did not speak a discourse which most intellectuals, too, find unintelligible" (Eagleton, "Spivak" 158). "Post-colonial theory makes heavy weather of a respect for the Other," Eagleton continues, "but its most immediate Other, the reader, is apparently dispensed from this sensitivity" (159). While the contemporary cultural critic or theorist is often more interested in any number of social or political issues than literature as such, for Wilde, artistic creation is always the focus of critical attention, and his witty and delightful essays are so much greater a joy to read than the obscurantist and jargon-ridden academese that we find in some of the contemporary writings that masquerade as literary or cultural criticism.

Against such a background I wish to comment on Wilde's review of the Chinese philosopher Zhuangzi (or Chuang Tzŭ) as translated by the English Sinologist Herbert Giles and published in London in 1889. Though the book of Zhuangzi is not a literary work—but again, Zhuangzi's language is probably more literary and poetic than most poets and writers, and his ideas are expressed in far more subtle paradoxes and striking metaphors than most literary writings— Wilde's long review published in *Speaker* on 8 February 1890, is certainly infused with the creative spirit as he argued for in "The Critic as Artist." If the mention of a "momentary Japanese effect" in *Dorian Gray* can be seen as a decorative motif that embellishes the opening of the novel with an Oriental flavor, Wilde's review entitled "A Chinese Sage" is a serious engagement with the philosophy of Zhuangzi, whom Giles presented as a "mystic, moralist, and social reformer." Wilde's review is an important piece that not only gives us a rare opportunity to catch a glimpse of his interest in the thought of an ancient philosopher from the East, but also provides an example of Wilde's criticism as he reads Zhuangzi from the perspective of a Victorian critic and uses the Chinese philosopher's ideas to comment on the English society of his own time. Wilde's review is also important because it shows how much interest there was in Taoist philosophy and mysticism at the turn of the century in the late 1890s and the early 1900s. Because that review is not included in most modern editions of Wilde's works, it is not readily available and has not received the critical attention it deserves, and that is all the more reason for us to examine it as an important aspect of Wilde's oeuvre often neglected even by Wilde scholars.

In his introduction to the translation, Giles describes Zhuangzi as an enemy of the Confucian school and a follower of the mysteries of

Laozi (Lao Tzŭ), and as a great debater whose "literary and dialectic skill was such that the best scholars of the age proved unable to refute his destructive criticism of the Confucian and Mohist schools" (*Chuang Tzŭ* vi). Giles portrays Zhuangzi as a fiercely independent and free spirit, and he tells the story of the Chinese philosopher refusing to accept the position of Prime Minister of the State of Chu by saying: "I would rather disport myself to my own enjoyment in the mire than be slave to the ruler of a State. I will never take office. Thus I shall remain free to follow my own inclinations" (*Chuang Tzŭ* vi-vii). Both Laozi and Zhuangzi are great masters of paradoxical expressions, and Giles samples some of these that articulate what he calls "the wondrous doctrine of *Inaction*." For example, "Do nothing, and all things will be done"; "The weak overcomes the strong, the soft overcomes the hard"; "The softest things in the world override the hardest. That which has no substance enters where there is no fissure. And so I know that there is advantage in *Inaction*" (*Chuang Tzŭ* viii-ix). By a strange coincidence, these short and paradoxical sayings sound very much like the epigrammatic expressions we typically relate to Wilde's style, the kind of witty expressions found in the preface to *Dorian Gray* or in the essays in *Intentions*. Wilde himself must have realized this when he read Giles's translation and found in Zhuangzi a kindred spirit.

Of course, Wilde did not know much about Chinese philosophy or Taoism, and it would be unrealistic to expect from him much expert discussion of Zhuangzi as a Taoist philosopher. What is of interest in Wilde's review, however, is the way in which he read Zhuangzi and found in the Chinese philosopher a congenial style and a sympathetic mind that influenced his own social and political ideas, his conviction of personal freedom and the rejection of all forms of government. In fact, reading Wilde's review and his presentation of Zhuangzi, one may feel confused whether Wilde is quoting Zhuangzi or is speaking for himself; but that reminds us of one of the most famous passages in the *Zhuangzi*, where the philosopher woke up from a dream in which he had become a butterfly, and was not sure which was real: whether the dream was reality or the reality was a dream, whether he was a man dreaming of being a butterfly or he was a butterfly dreaming of being Zhuangzi the philosopher (Guo Qingfan 3: 53-54). Such effacing of differences, as Isabelle Robinet observes, characterizes a Taoist sage when he is liberated from "all internal and external conflict, and all wants and desires, his spirit is free and lives in perfect unity with himself and with everything" (32). The way Wilde speaks is in perfect keeping with that spirit, and when we read his review, sometimes we may feel uncertain whether Zhuangzi or Wilde is speaking. Wilde finds Zhuangzi an anti-social philosopher, and he declares that "the most caustic criticism of modern life I have met with for some time is that contained in the writings of the learned Chuang Tzǔ" ("A Chinese Sage" 177). The English middle class might have seen the portraits of the Chinese sage on porcelain or Chinese screens and found them amusing, but, says Wilde, "If they really knew who he was, they would tremble. Chuang Tzǔ spent his life in preaching the great creed of Inaction, and in pointing out the uselessness of all useful things. 'Do nothing, and everything will be done,' was the doctrine which he inherited from his great master Lao Tzǔ. To resolve action into thought, and thought into abstraction, was his wicked transcendental aim" ("A Chinese Sage" 178). Wilde compares Zhuangzi to Western philosophers and mystics from Plato and Philo to Master Eckhart, Jacob Böhme, and Hegel, claiming that "Chuang Tzǔ may be said to have summed up in himself almost every mood of European metaphysical or mystical thought, from Heraclitus down to Hegel." But he was far more radical than his European counterparts, for "Chuang Tzǔ was something more than a metaphysician and an illuminist. He sought to destroy society, as we know it, as the middle classes know it; and the sad thing is that he combines with the passionate eloquence of a Rousseau the scientific reasoning of a Herbert Spencer" ("Chinese Sage" 178, 179). Bringing the ancient Chinese philosopher closer to the modern world, Wilde's Zhuangzi sounds more and more like Vivian in "The Decay of Lying" or Gilbert in "The Critic as Artist," that is to say, personae or mouthpieces of Wilde's own ideas, speaking in typically Wildean paradoxical epigrams. Zhuangzi, says Wilde, is not a sentimentalist:

> He pities the rich more than the poor, if he ever pities at all, and prosperity seems to him as tragic as suffering. He has nothing of the modern sympathy with failures, nor does he propose that the prizes should always be given on moral grounds to those who come in last in the race. It is the

race that he objects to; and as for active sympathy, which has become the profession of so many worthy people in our own day, he thinks that trying to make others good is as silly an occupation as 'beating a drum in a forest in order to find a fugitive.' It is a mere waste of energy. That is all. While, as for a thoroughly sympathetic man, he is, in the eyes of Chuang Tzǔ, simply a man who is always trying to be somebody else, and so misses the only possible excuse for his own existence. ("Chinese Sage" 179)

Zhuangzi's ideal of a Golden Age, says Wilde, is of a time "when there were no competitive examinations, no wearisome educational systems, no missionaries, no penny dinners for the people, no Established Churches, no Humanitarian Societies, no dull lectures about one's duty to one's neighbour, and no tedious sermons about any subject at all. In those ideal days, he tells us, people loved each other without being conscious of charity, or writing to the newspapers about it"("Chinese Sage" 179-80).

These are obviously Wilde's own ideas disguised as the Chinese philosopher's, but surprisingly they show a remarkably accurate grasp of the core ideas of the Taoist philosophy, its argument against the kind of human intervention, as represented by Confucian teachings, in the natural course of things. The great Taoist philosopher Laozi famously said, "When the great *tao* becomes defunct, benevolence and righteousness arise; when cleverness comes out, great hypocrisy appears; when the six kinship relations are not in harmony, filial piety and parental grace emerge; when the state is in chaos, loyal ministers become visible" (Wang Bi 3:10). As Chen Guying, a specialist of Taoist philosophy, well observes, this is Laozi's "description of the morbid social condition at the time, and also his sarcastic commentary on the ideas of benevolence, righteousness, loyalty, and filial piety as the Confucians advocated" (135). The Taoist philosophy Laozi and Zhuangzi taught is a kind of naturalism, with its emphasis on non-action over Confucian activism and social intervention. "To maintain the natural, original condition of human nature is a basic idea of the book of *Zhuangzi*," writes another Chinese scholar in commenting on the "external chapters" of the *Zhuangzi*, "As the Confucian concepts of 'benevolence and righteousness' represent an aggression on the original human nature, it is not surprising that Zhuangzi put them in question and critique" (Chen Yinchi 172). As opposed to the Confucian moral and political philosophy, Zhuangzi and the Taoist philosophy he represents advocate naturalism and quietism over different forms of human action, intervention, and government.

In this regard, we may say that Wilde was quite insightful in representing Zhuangzi as an enemy of social intervention and government, and a champion for individual freedom. Wilde's Zhuangzi argues for "leaving mankind alone," for "there has never been such a thing as governing mankind" ("Chinese Sage" 180).

In Wilde's review, Zhuangzi's philosophy becomes mainly a critique of modern life and modern political institutions. "And what would be the fate of governments and professional politicians if we came to the conclusion that there is no such thing as governing mankind at all?" Wilde continues to say. "It is clear that Chuang Tzǔ is a very dangerous writer, and the publication of his book in English, two thousand years after his death, is obviously premature, and may cause a great deal of pain to many thoroughly respectable and industrious persons" ("Chinese Sage" 186). That may be hyperbole typical of Wilde, but that does not mean it is not sincere, for here we find some basic ideas Wilde develops further in his political essay *The Soul of Man under Socialism*.

As a man of artistic sensibility and a Victorian aesthete, Wilde's idea of socialism strikes us today as fundamentally mistaken and peculiarly quixotic, but it has its connections with the kind of English socialist fantasies of a William Morris, and it is more of a plea for individualism and artistic freedom than a socialist theory. Reading *The Soul of Man* together with his review of Zhuangzi, the connections of ideas become inescapable. The very beginning of the essay reads: "The chief advantage that would result from the establishment of Socialism is, undoubtedly, the fact that Socialism would relieve us from that sordid necessity of living for others which, in the present condition of things, presses so hardly upon almost everybody. In fact, scarcely anyone at all escapes" (*Soul of Man* 1). That sounds very much like Zhuangzi's Golden Age when, as Wilde describes it, there were "no Humanitarian Societies, no dull lectures about one's duty to one's neighbour"; and "There was no chattering about clever men, and no laudation of good men. The intolerable sense of obligation was unknown" ("Chinese Sage" 180). In

Wilde's somewhat idiosyncratic understanding, socialism is valuable
because "it will lead to Individualism" (*Soul of Man* 2). It will be the
condition of free individuals who follow whatever comes naturally
without imposing on others, including for the benefit of others. The
personality of man, says Wilde, "will grow naturally and simply, flower-
like, or as a tree grows," and "it will not be always meddling with others,
or asking them to be like itself. It will love them because they will be
different. And yet while it will not meddle with others it will help all,
as a beautiful thing helps us, by being what it is" (*Soul of Man* 9). This
reminds us of what Wilde says about Zhuangzi's philosophy in his
review, and in another passage, he more directly refers to Zhuangzi the
Chinese philosopher: "Individualism, then, is what through Socialism
we are to attain. As a natural result the State must give up all idea
of government. It must give it up because, as a wise man once said
many centuries before Christ, there is such a thing as leaving mankind
alone; there is no such thing as governing mankind. All modes of
government are failures" (*Soul of Man* 13). For Wilde, Zhuangzi is a
radical thinker that negates all forms of government, a predecessor of
modern anarchism.

This idea of leaving others alone and not meddling with them can
find no better exemplification than Zhuangzi's fable of Hundun and his
unexpected death. Hundun, says Zhuangzi, was emperor of the center,
and he always treated kindly Shu, emperor of the south sea, and Hu,
emperor of the north sea. "Shu and Hu wanted to repay Hundun for
his kindness, and they said: 'everyone has seven orifices to see, to listen,
to eat, and to breathe, but he alone doesn't have any. Let's try to poke
holes for him.' So they poked one hole each day, and by the seventh
day Hundun died" (Guo Qingfan 3: 139). The point is clear—imposing
on others what you think best, even with good intentions and meant
to benefit others, may result in such tragic destruction of the original
nature of things. Without eyes, ears, nostrils or mouth, Hundun is the
symbolic figure for the natural, primordial, undifferentiated condition
of things, while Shu and Hu, whose names imply moving and acting
quickly, represent human action from a distinctly human perspective.
For Zhuangzi, as Wilde rightly argued, it is best to leave others alone in
their original, natural condition.

Indeed, as Sos Eltis remarks, "Wilde's individualist doctrine also presented many parallels with Taoist philosophy, a philosophy which itself provided one of the earliest bases for anarchist thought." He goes on to mention Wilde's review of Zhuangzi and observes that "The relevance of this doctrine to 'The Soul of Man under Socialism' is clear" (Eltis 22-23). If we read Zhuangzi, his witticism and paradoxical expressions indeed suggest some stylistic affinities with Wilde's epigrams in addition to the kind of retrogressive criticism of modern life that Wilde finds attractive and inspiring. Although there are many more ideas and insights in Zhuangzi's philosophy that Wilde did not touch on, the emphasis he put on freedom and individuality in his reading of Zhuangzi does reveal a very important aspect of the Taoist philosopher that deserves our critical attention.

Wilde died as the world moved into the twentieth century, but his interest in Zhuangzi anticipated a similar interest many modernist poets had well into the twentieth century. Both Ezra Pound and William Carlos Williams owned copies of Giles' *A History of Chinese Literature* (1901) with a section rehearsing illustrative extracts from *Chuang Tzŭ: Mystic, Moralist, and Social Reformer* (*History* 60-68). Giles' *History* was popular at the time with the modernists, and "his version of Zhuangzi's parable about how he dreamed of being a butterfly," as Zhaoming Qian argues, "may well have appealed to Williams as it had appealed to Pound," as both admired "the Chinese sage's refusal to make distinctions among worldly things" (Qian 146). Zhuangzi and his predecessor Laozi, along with the Chinese written language and Chinese culture, proved to be a great inspiration for the modernist poets, but they were read differently with different focuses and interpretations. What Wilde found in Zhuangzi in the 1890s was a radical critique of middle-class values and modern political institutions and an advocacy for individual freedom, but what Pound and Williams saw in "the Chinese sage's refusal to make distinctions" led to an understanding of the Chinese language as a medium that eschewed logical connections and abstract conceptualizations in favor of images and concrete *things* themselves, thus a medium specifically suited to the modernist poetics of immediacy and concreteness. We may also be reminded that roughly at the same time in the 1920s, in the fin-de-siècle Vienna, Fritz Mauthner appreciated Laozi and Zhuangzi and "discovered in Tao a primeval critique of language (*in Tao eine uralte Sprachkritik zu entdecken)*" (Mauthner 2:468). Understanding of Zhuangzi or Taoism or the Chinese language and culture changes all the time, and Wilde is certainly different from Pound, Williams, and others. The point is, however, that when we put the different readings and interpretations in perspective, we may realize that the intellectual connections of Western modernism with the East are serious and deep, and that Oscar Wilde is one of the predecessors in this respect that still needs to be recognized and appreciated in our understanding of modernist literature.

Works Cited

Chen Guying. *Laozi zhushi ji pingjie [Laozi with Notes and Critical Evaluations]*. Beijing: Zhonghua, 1984.

Chen Yinchi. *Zhuangzi jingdu [Close Readings of the Zhuangzi]*. Shanghai: Fudan UP, 2005.

Eagleton, Terry. "Gayatri Spivak." *Figures of Dissent: Critical Essays on Fish, Spivak, Žižek and Others*. London: Verso, 2005. 159-67.

___."Oscar Wilde." *Figures of Dissent: Critical Essays on Fish, Spivak, Žižek and Others*. London: Verso, 2005. 48-51.

Eltis, Sos. *Revising Wilde: Society and Subversion in the Plays of Oscar Wilde*. Oxford: Oxford UP, 1996.

Giles, Herbert A., trans. *Chuang Tzŭ: Mystic, Moralist, and Social Reformer*. London: Bernard Quaritch, 1889.

___. *A History of Chinese Literature*. New York: Appleton, 1910.

Guo Qingfan (1844 - 95?), ed. *Zhuangzi jishi [The Variorum Edition of the Zhuangzi]*. *Zhuzi jicheng [Collection of Master Writings]*. Vol. 3. Beijing: Zhonghua, 1954. 1-481.

Mauthner, Fritz. *Wörterbuch der Philosophie: Neue Beiträge zu einer Kritik der Sprach*. 2 vols. Munich: Georg Müller, 1910.

McDonald, Ronán. *The Death of the Critic*. London: Continuum, 2007.

Qian Zhaoming. *Orientalism and Modernism: The Legacy of China in Pound and Williams*. Durham: Duke UP, 1995.

Robinet, Isabelle. *Taoism: Growth of a Religion*. Trans. Phyllis Brooks. Stanford UP, 1997.

Wang Bi (226-249). *Laozi zhu [Laozi with Annotations]*. *Zhuzi jicheng*

[*Collection of Master Writings*] Vol. 3. Beijing: Zhonghua, 1954. 1-60.

Wilde, Oscar. "A Chinese Sage." *A Critic in Pall Mall: Being Extracts from Reviews and Miscellanies.* London: Methuen, 1919. 177-87.

___. "The Critic as Artist." *Intentions.* New York: Bretano's, 1905. 87-198.

___. "The Decay of Lying: An Observation." *Intentions.* New York: Bretano's, 1905. 3-52.

___. *The Picture of Dorian Gray.* New York: Modern Library, 1992.

___. "The Soul of Man." *The Soul of Man and Prison Writings.* Ed. Isobel Murray. Oxford: Oxford UP, 1990. 1-37.

Zhang Longxi. "The Critical Legacy of Oscar Wilde." Regenia Gagnier, ed. *Critical Essays on Oscar Wilde.* New York: G. K. Hall, 1991. 157-71.

"Orientalizing" Emily Dickinson and Marianne Moore— Complicating Modernism?

Sabine Sielke

After decades of marginalization, Emily Dickinson and Marianne Moore have now starred, for decades, as central canonized figures in the study of U.S.-American modernisms. What their single-minded poetry and poetics have perhaps most vigorously inspired in this grand-scale revisionary enterprise is the emergence of manifold analyses on how modernist poetics participate in the ongoing (de- and re-) constructions of gender. Meanwhile, however, the particular interventions of Dickinson and Moore into US-American modernist imaginaries have been taken into new geo-political directions which focus on the 'Eastern drift' in the poets' work and engage matters of race, ethnicity, and class. Current explorations of their texts, evolving, in part, in the larger force field of postcolonial studies, project Dickinson as "Post-Colonial Feminist" (Pencak) and Moore as "Subversive Orientalist" (Stamy) and thereby propose a radical recontexualization of their poetic enterprise.

What, however, is the goal of this remapping of modernist terrain by way of the Orient? What motivates our interest in how Orient and Orientalisms figure in the poetry of Dickinson and Moore? What vistas do these supposedly new approaches to Dickinson and Moore open up to us? In what ways, I wonder, do they transform our sense of what modernism was? What do we remember of modernism as we "orientalize" its cultural practices? And what do we forget about modernism in the process of resituating its poetic practices in the cultural politics of global geo-political and economic processes? I fear, I am not going to answer all of these questions sufficiently, but I do think this is the right moment to raise them. First and foremost, my contribution here aims at exploring the politics of and the desire informing our current critical perspectives. My argument evolves in three parts: In part one, I recall, briefly, what for me aligns Dickinson and Moore in the first place, drawing on, yet also revising, the argument I made in my book *Fashioning the Female Subject: The Intertextual Networking of Dickinson, Moore, and Rich* (1997). In part two, I review some ways in which concepts of Orient and Orientalism(s) have so far informed revisions of Dickinson's and Moore's work. Making no claim for comprehensiveness, I wonder how some of these readings add to or challenge our understanding of the two poets' work. In part three, finally, I reflect on the implicit effects of our desire to orientalize modernist poetry and of modernism in general. Interestingly enough, current rereadings of Dickinson and Moore may celebrate the poets' recognition of the Orient and its cultures as both ethically and aesthetically valuable, yet they also hesitate to contextualize or theorize this turn in critical approach. Such reluctance may result in part from the fact that these readings risk to reproduce both tendencies to re-exoticize early modernism (which strongly inform revisions of Dickinson) and a domestication of Oriental cultures to subsume the unfamiliar under the familiar (which Moore's poetry, in particular, seems to invite).

Part One: Engendered Modernism(s)

Due in part to feminist criticism and gender studies, our general sense of what (American) modernism was has changed dramatically during the last 30 to 40 years, and what follows can be but a very short version of a much more complex debate. Until the 1970s, what we had come to call American "high modernism" appeared a boys' network in which the work of Moore, H. D., and Amy Lowell formed a somewhat derivative periphery and from which Gertrude Stein was significantly absent or outcast. What we have witnessed since then is an ongoing attempt to reposition female modernist poets (and Dickinson as their "foremother") in their relation to this supposed center (whose position necessarily shifted in the process) while retaining for them a certain degree of otherness (and thus a proximity to a variety of other others, including Oriental cultures). The general effect of these revisions was a transformation of a canonized concept of modernism into several versions of distinct modernisms.

My own work engaged French poststructuralism, especially the work of Julia Kristeva, Luce Irigaray, and Hélène Cixous, and associated Dickinson and Moore on the basis of their texts' aesthetic disruptiveness and the challenge their work posed to traditional concepts of subject constitution. At the same time I argued that both poets retained single-minded, yet flexible formal frames, such as Dickinson's hymn stanza and Moore's syllabics, as a mode of authority – a view that took issue and opposed the notion that female poets primarily question and dismiss marks of authority. While I interpreted the poets' "inbetween" position, their oscillation between rejecting and claiming authority, in terms of gender – that is in relation to the different versions of subject constitution we encounter in Walt Whitman, Stéphane Mallarmé, Ezra Pound, T. S. Eliot, and William Carlos Williams, among others –, I now wonder what new spin this argument takes as we renegotiate the poets' interrogation of Oriental cultures. And I do assume, by the way, that there is no other way for Dickinson and Moore to encounter Far Eastern cultures than by way of an "Oriental vision" (Kang); no other views were available to them and remain even more rare for us now, even if we meanwhile inhabit a "global village" (McLuhan). Yet, since Far Eastern cultures, seen from Western perspectives, have always been gendered feminine, I do wonder how our engagement of Dickinson's and Moore's visions may affect our assessment of the gender of modernism. Can we call Dickinson's and Moore's interest in these cultures "Orientalisms," and, if so, are they gendered versions of Orientalism? What difference do we detect in the poets' distinct perspectives on the far-away places they travelled in their minds[1] and encountered in art objects only? And how does our sense of the evolution of American modernism shift as we move from Dickinson's to Moore's Orientalisms?

Part Two: "Fabrics of the East" and "Certain Ming Products": Orient and Orientalisms in Dickinson and Moore

First, let's be fair: The study of orientalist exoticisms and far Eastern places in Dickinson's and Moore's poetry is still in its infancy. It is motivated in part by a scholarly interest in biographical matters (which still dominate a large part of Dickinson and Moore scholarship); and it depends on the professional turns that scholars of modernism take, traveling to events such as the conferences on "Modernism and the Orient" in Hangzhou in 2010 and on "Emily Dickinson in Japan: Like Fabrics of the East," organized by the Emily Dickinson International Society in Kyoto in August 2007. First and foremost, of course, it evolves with the agenda of postcolonial criticism central to current British and Canadian studies and still somewhat peripheral to American studies.

One of the few notable exceptions—among which I also count *Orient and Orientalisms in US-American Poetry and Poetics*, edited by Christian Klöckner and me in 2009—is certainly Malini Johar Schueller's book *U.S. Orientalisms* (1998). Situated at the crossroads of post-colonial and gender studies, Schueller's study stripped eighteenth- and nineteenth-century American literature from its (global) insularity in literary criticism and read it in the context of an "anxiety-ridden" "imperial self-definition" of 'American' nationhood based on "raced and gendered distinctions" (4). Accordingly, in his review essay "Orientalizing American Studies" (2008), Schueller underlines the "continuing importance of Orientalism as a paradigm [...] for conceptions of national and local identities" (488). Therefore, a focus on Orientalisms allows us to interrogate how in the poetry of Dickinson and Moore subjectivity is constituted as an interplay between America|self and Orient|other (and I am well aware that I am reducing a rather complex process to a set of debatable terms here). What function then does the Orient take in that interplay? Any answer to this question needs to account for two moments of cultural history: While in the U.S., 'the Orient' has constituted an arena of poetic experimentation, mapped out an "alternative aesthetic space" (Haddad 2), and become central to the evolution of U.S.-American poetry and poetics from Romanticism to modernism and post-modernism, thereby transforming the cultural topography of the Orient itself, U.S.-American poetry in turn has been inscribed by nationally specific processes of colonization, modernization, and decolonization.

These intricate interrelations between poetry and—cultural as well as colonial—politics show even in the work of Emily Dickinson who saw "New Englandly" (*Poems* 256), as she famously claimed, never laid eyes on a desert nor on an exotic country, and considered a move "around the corner in Amherst" a long journey (Benfey 81). In the light of this complexity, what do we make of the renewed interest in Dickinson's "encounter with the East" (Uno 43) which risks to subsume the conflicting historical and economic dynamics on which such encounters are built under the emergent paradigm of a modernist aesthetics? Hiroko Uno, for instance, speculates on how "the long history of Chinese trade in New England" (45) affected Dickinson's family and what the poet made of her visit to the Boston China Museum in 1846, an institution that opened in the wake of the first trade agreement between the U.S. and China in 1844 (cf. Uno 47-48); Christopher Benfey remains rather vague as he claims that Dickinson's retreat from society "reminds us of the Chinese and Japanese tradition of the scholarly recluse" (82), that "Dickinson's literary forms […] remind us of Asian writers" (83), and that one "is tempted […] to regard Emily Dickinson as a sort of honorary Japanese citizen, a Japanese poet in exile on Main Street" (83). Considering Benfey's debatable alliances between Japanese tearooms and New England cottages or Japanese tea ceremonies and Calvinism, I am tempted to read his essay as the extreme example of a tendency to "defamiliarize" Dickinson and strip her work off its local insularity, while at the same time diminishing geopolitical distance and cultural difference, thereby turning Asia into a familiar place next door.

And yet, even if parts of Asia were close to home—Katsura trees, gingos, and Japanese larches were planted in Amherst's streets, and Dickinson not only observed "Flowers like Asia" (L650, qtd. in Benfey 82) grow in her garden, but also used chinaware—the poet was (as Benfey knows perfectly well) a traveler of a different variety: "Vermont or Asia," she wrote in a late letter to her friend Elizabeth Holland, "[m]any of us go farther" (L685, qtd. in Benfey 82), suggesting that distances don't matter. Along these lines Dickinson came to evolve a poetics which, as Gudrun Grabher argued thirty years ago, shares moments of Zen Buddhism and is proximate to the Japanese haiku (172-234).[2]

It is of particular interest, in this context, to remember Grabher's original work. Interrogating the poet's take on idealism, Grabher's 1981 study *Emily Dickinson: Das transzendentale Ich* also corrected, as Roland Hagenbüchle noted, the overt "(gender-specific) bias" ("Dickinson and Literary Theory" 357) of critics including Allen Tate who (in)famously claimed that Dickinson was not philosophically inclined, in fact "cannot reason at all" (87). Grabher's argument, by contrast, triangulates Dickinson's poetry and poetics in its relation to German idealism (especially Fichte, Schelling, and Hegel), American transcendentalism, and East-Asian philosophy. And this was by no means a small achievement. For whereas the interrelation between idealism, Transcendentalism and Zen Buddhism as well as the impact of Eastern, Asian, or "Oriental" philosophy on the American romanticists, in general, and the Transcendentalists, in particular, had received thorough scholarly attention, the proximity of Dickinson's sense of the "transcendental I," German idealist philosophy, and notions of how subject and world interrelate in Asian philosophy, particularly in Zen Buddhism, had not yet been explored; nor had the crossroads between Dickinson's poetics and the Japanese tradition of the haiku made any significant mark on Dickinson studies prior to Grabher's work (cf. 172-234). What, according to Grabher, Dickinson's transcendentalism, Fichte's idealism, and Zen Buddhism have in common is that they affirm the primacy of the subject and of perception in a process aimed at overcoming the dualism of subject and object; for each one of these philosophies the "transcendental I" is the starting point of both this process and "a new constitution of the world" (237).

Philosophically inclined, Dickinson explores the primacy of the subject and of perception in a genre—poetry—which in itself she considered an outlandish potion. In her poem "It would never be Common - more - I said -" (1862, *Poems* 388), for instance, the speaker refers to the pleasures of a particular poetic practice as, "my moment of Brocade," "My - drop - of India":

It would never be Common - more - I said -
Difference - had begun -
Many a bitterness - had been -
But that old sort - was done -
I put my pleasure all abroad -
I dealt a word of Gold
To every Creature - that I met -
And Dowered - all the World -

When - suddenly - my Riches shrank -
A Goblin - drank my Dew -

My Palaces – dropped tenantless –
Myself – was beggared – too –

I clutched at sounds –
I groped at shapes –
I touched the tops of Films –
I felt the Wilderness roll back
Along my Golden lines –

The Sackcloth – hangs upon the nail –
The Frock I used to wear –
But where my moment of Brocade –
My – drop – of India?

The "Orientalist" trope on which this poem rests ("drop – of India")
strongly resonates with dear memories of "indulgence" ("Difference")
and "riches" ("Palaces," "Gold," "Golden lines," "Brocade"). At the
same time, these pleasures are highly precarious. In fact, this—first
and foremost poetological—text advertises a poetics that many other
of Dickinson's poems explicitly critique and call into question on
grounds of epistemology and (gender) politics:[3] the Adamic practice
of naming which puts into poetic practice the Transcendentalist belief
that poetry can bridge the gap between self and other or nature, an
idealist position Dickinson resisted. For her, "Perception of an object
cost / Precise the object's loss –" (*Poems* 1103). Otherness – be it the
alterity, or "Wilderness," of nature or that of another person or territory
– cannot be domesticated, appropriated, and thus be negated; rather,
it remains a mystery. One may thus perhaps call Dickinson's poetry
anti-imperialist and anti-colonial, in its own indeterminate manner.
For Dickinson, any kind of poetics that conquers otherness is fleeting,
an unsustainable reward ("Brocade"); the poetics Dickinson cherished
was proximate to infinity:

To pile like Thunder to its close
Then crumble grand away
While Everything created his
This – would be Poetry –

Or Love – the two coeval come –

We both and neither prove –
Experience either and consume –
For None see God and live -

                (*Poems* 1353)

This orgiastic synchronicity of poetry, love, and God gets mediated, in a small set of Dickinson's poems, by tropes such as the "Oriental Tale" and "Fabrics of the East":

Reportless Subjects, to the Quick
Continual addressed –
But foreign as the Dialect
Of Danes, unto the rest.

Reportless Measures, to the Ear
Susceptive – stimulus –
But like an Oriental Tale
To other, fabulous -

                (*Poems* 1118)

His Mind like Fabrics of the East
Displayed to the despair
Of everyone but here and there
An humble Purchaser –

For though his price was not of Gold –
More arduous there is –
That one should comprehend the worth,
Was all the price there was -

                (*Poems* 1471)

Dickinson employs "Oriental" here as one of the terms she privileged in hinting at the many phenomena that resist representation and remain beyond the scope of our minds, distant, ungraspable, in other words: radically other. Still, her references to "Eastern Fabrics" and "essences" of India highlight the very nature of the "pleasure" that India and the Far East have historically represented for the West: economic interests and matters of trade. In this way Dickinson's poems reaffirm the ambivalent – and in a double sense foundational – cultural fascination with the Orient that has been the driving force for much of American – Romantic as well as modernist – poetry while also cherishing the Orient as a trope of transport to shores beyond all economies this side of paradise.

In contrast to Dickinson's sense of the distance and proximity of the Orient, Moore's prose is said to associate China with "precision and detail, fastidiousness, brevity, concentration, wit, and wisdom" (Stamy 5), and her poems are seen as a shortcut of cultural distance by way of free-wheeling metonymic associations between the "The Plumet Basilisk" (1935) of Costa Rica and "the true Chinese lizard face," "the ambitious falling dragon, the living fire work" (20) or, in her poem "Smooth Gnarled Crape Myrtle" (1941), between a "[…] brass-green bird with grass- / green throat" and a "Chinese flower piece" (*CP* 103). Curiously enough, this idiosyncratic, often highly visual precision, rendered in a breathless, run-on syntax of fast transport results in Moore's highly opaque poems which document what Patricia C. Willis, in a comment reprinted on the cover of Zhaoming Qian's *The Modernist Response to Chinese Art* (2003), called the modernists' "baffling interest in and use of Chinese art." What, however, does this interest document?

Stamy and Qian, most notably, read Moore's engagement with Chinese culture—ranging from a fascination with mythological figures and dragons of the Far East (Stamy 57f) to the familiarity with "Confucian philosophy" (41) and Chinese art (137) to her conviction to be "born pro-Chinese" (qtd. in Qian xv)—as a "challenge posed to modernism" (Qian xvi). Stamy's book *Marianne Moore and China: Orientalism and a Writing of America* (1999) presents "Moore's poetry [… as] an extraordinarily rich site from which to analyse a tradition of American orientalism […]" and aims to show "why her borrowing of Chinese models of all kinds - from poetry to painting and philosophy - was so critical to the formation of her verse." Based on the claim that "Chinese subjects, referents, and models" are "constituent elements" of Moore's poetic practice (2), Stamy's analysis of Moore's "American orientalism" (1f) offers us no less than a complete rereading of all of the poet's aesthetic idiosyncrasies: from her syllabics (which Stamy relates to the Chinese language in which each character is a single syllable [114, 150]) to her scientific exactitude, precision, and "attention to detail" (44f, 176) to her "method of compression" (117), her favor for citations, and her "ability to defer, or dispense with, temporal reference" (69). Due to this complete overhaul of what we believed Moore's poetics was all about, Stamy's work is of particular interest here.

According to Stamy, Moore "used the Far East to express her own dissatisfaction with contemporary trends in the writing of poetry, and embraced the more ancient culture of China," thereby "resisting the American habit of looking to Europe as a singular source of cultural tradition 'at home'" (vii). Making Moore part of an Emersonian tradition with its imperative to "forget Shakespeare!" Stamy sees the poet locating "in China a cultural superiority to Europe" while taking part in "the imaginative production of the Orient" (4) as a "subversive Orientalist" (16f):[4] "All the Chinese elements in her poetry [...]," she claims, "are means of resistance" (27).[5] Thus Orientalism, considered a mode of plain cultural imperialism not too long ago, by 1999 turned into a strategy of critically engaging and transforming transatlantic modernism. In all her characteristic interplay of proximity and distance, of self and other, Moore evolves, so Stamy seems to suggest, the aesthetic mode of a genuinely American modernity.[6] Interestingly enough, though, this practice also seems to advertise a reassessment of what we had, by the end of the twentieth century, come to believe subversion is all about. Rather than challenging American ideologies, subversion, once again, takes on the meaning assigned by the Myth and Symbol School in the 1950s and returns to its status as a mark of 'true' Americanness.

Yet while either sense of subversion designates Moore's efforts at "orientalizing" American modernism a political move, Stamy considers Moore's interest in China to be of an "apparently apolitical nature" (11). Moore "endow[ed] China," she writes, "with a timeless, ethereal quality suited to the needs and preoccupations of her poetry. China represented a utopic space where turbulent exchanges with culture, class, and even gender were momentarily suspended" (11). If Stamy was right, Moore came surprisingly close to Dickinson in whose lyrics the Orient prominently figures as a realm beyond temporality and difference, even as these poems acknowledge that their very medium—language—constitutes meaning on the basis of difference and ultimately thrive on this paradox. One substantial difference between Dickinson's and Moore's Orientalisms, though, results from their distinct poetics: While Dickinson's infinities operate as much on metaphoric as on metonymic modes and, though sometimes quite down to earth, do not shy away from monumentalisms, Moore achieves her effects by "far-fetched associations" (Wand 473) that work primarily on the basis of metonymy and a "fiddle," as Moore herself famously put it in her poem "Poetry," with forms and mediated matter—other texts as much as images—that strikes us as highly insular, "private" and that may seem gendered outright "feminine." Thus instead of Moore's poetry itself it is rather (we) critics interrogating modernism and the Orient who "momentarily"—and perhaps somewhat mistakingly— (desire to) "suspend" gender matters. And as we highlight the Orient as one of modernism's privileged preoccupations that gained new prominence with the rise of postcolonial theory, the lights dim over gender critique, even though Orientalisms, of course, are all about gender as both Dickinson's and Moore's poetry unmistakingly suggest.

Still, to my mind it is neither gender matters nor a postcolonial critique nor the "genuine" nature of poetry itself that is at the core of Moore's modernist engagement with the Orient. After all, it is art and (representations of) natural phenomena[7] which constitute most of Moore's references to Oriental cultures and keep the Orient at a distance yet. Offering us representations of representations, both visual and verbal, Moore's poems have sent critics off to retrace her indiscriminate reading and viewing practices from the *Illustrated London News* to Mai-Mai Sze's *The Tao of Painting: A Study of the Ritual Disposition of Chinese Painting* (1963) which Qian has examined with much insight. While Dickinson claimed, in her letter to Thomas Wentworth Higginson on 7 June 1862, that she never "consciously touch[ed] a paint, mixed by another person-" (L. 26), Moore's poetry clearly foregrounds that we encounter Oriental cultures—a paint mixed by a person who is "other"—in highly mediated manners only. Accordingly, her lyric texts often take metaperspectives on intermediality, as does her poem "Bowls" (*CP* 59), for instance, linking writing with "ancient punctilio / in the manner of Chinese lacquer-carving, / layer after layer exposed by certainty of touch and unhurried incision" (59).

on the green
with lignum vitae balls and ivory markers,
the pins planted in wild duck formation,
and quickly dispersed –
by this survival of ancient punctilio
in the manner of Chinese lacquer-carving,
layer after layer exposed by certainty of touch and unhurried
    incision
so that only so much color shall be revealed as is necessary to the
    picture,
I learn that we are precisionists,
[…].

And as Moore's poems foreground mediation they hint at the everyday
contexts of our encounters with the Orient. Thus an ekphrastic poem
such as "Nine Nectarines and Other Porcelain"—published first in
1934 and reappearing thirty-three years later in a version which
deletes four of the originally eight stanzas and erases the part dealing
with French and British porcelain and the European tradition of China
making (cf. Bazin 63)—may, on the one hand, "refashion and adapt," as
Stamy argues, "Chinese ideas to reflect their consonances in American
thought and […] highlight what China and America share" (36-37):

Nine Nectarines and Other Porcelain

Arranged by twos as peaches are,
At intervals that all may live –
    eight and a single one, on twigs that
    grew that year before – they look like
a derivative;
    although not uncommonly
The opposite is seen –
Nine peaches on a nectarine.
        Fuzzles through slender crescent leaves
        of green or blue – or   both,
        in the Chinese style – the four

    pairs' half –moon leaf-mosaic turns
out to the sun the sprinkled blush

> of puce-American-Beauty pink
> applied to beeswax gray by the
> Unenquiring brush
> of mercantile bookbinding. [...]

Yet as "Chinese style" and "sprinkled blush of puce-American-Beauty pink" meet (or shall we say: clash?) we note dissonances, as well. Accordingly, examining the poem "firstly as a tribute to the art of the Chinese, then in terms of its sources," Victoria Bazin, on the other hand, "trace[s] the exotic back to its everyday origin" (63), highlighted by the many mundane commodity objects Moore's poetry features. Seen in this way, "Nine Nectarines and Other Porcelain" offers us the image of a Chinese plate which Moore encountered, as her poetry notebook reveals, "in a window display for the Pierce Arrow motor car" (66, see fig. below).

1930 Pierce Arrow Limousine, displayed on the company stand at the 1930 Chicago World Trade Fair and used by U.S. President Herbert Hoover during his election campaign in Boston in 1932.

The clash of "Chinese style" and "puce-American-Beauty pink" may be a subtle echo of the very experience of finding the Chinese plate next to the commercial exhibition of modern automobility. Whereas, in Bazin's view, Moore's text fails to render the graphic image (63), Moore, to my mind, makes quite a different point, reaffirming what poetry can do that visual culture can't and simultaneously adopting crucial devices of that culture such as exhibition, advertisement, and display. In fact, Moore's poem exposes every single phrase, makes every "sign," every color, number, and "look" stand out and "sell," so to speak. Like porcelain, poetry functions as a kind of "shopping window" in which to display forms and figures, framed by the turns and twists of a rather conflated syntax that guides our attention. Falling flat on "the / Unenquiring brush / of mercantile bookbinding," the text takes it for granted, though, that "bookbinding" is an art as well as a business and part of (global) commerce and trade. In this way, Moore's modernism acknowledges the conflation of aesthetics and economics in Western modernity, even as it seems to measure a substantial distance between Chinese and American cultures. In fact, the poem hints that we may be mistaken to think that "the Chinese style," appropriated and exhibited by American culture, could retain its otherness, stand aloof of a mobile economy that reaches way beyond its geopolitical borders.

Part Three: Othering or Complicating Modernism?

"Moore's poems are sometimes marginal quarrels with the books she read," writes William Logan, "Reading compensated for isolation." Reading Moore, as Qian does, "against a radically different Eastern paradigm" (xvi), critics have aimed at reducing that isolation and have relocated the poet in world literatures and cultures – a tendency that we can also observe in recent scholarship on Dickinson and that is at least as much, if not more, inspired by issues of current concern as by the agenda of the authors we eagerly reassess. "In Emerson and Buddhism, Dickinson and haiku," writes Benfey, "there is a constant oscillation, a great wave, between East and West" (88). Is that the wave we currently surf on? Where, then, does that wave, where do our revisionary moves, take us? What politics do they entail? If (an idealized) China, played a major part in Moore's "writing of America," as Stamy has it, how are we to read this America now? If, by contrast, as I argue, Moore's poems ponder a close proximity between media-specific aesthetics and economic ideologies, how am I to read my own retrospection and its particular bias? Are our readings a kind of domestication or familiarization of the unfamiliar in times of globalization? Are they a strategy of dealing with the growing economic significance of Asia and with China as a super power that allows us to amplify the political significance of literary and cultural studies as well?

It seems to me that, too often, we shy away from the implications and consequences of our revisions which call into question our (still) cherished notion that modernism "made it new." For if U.S.-American modernism(s) build on or appropriate Far Eastern traditions, they cannot be that modern after all. Instead, we may concede that modernism, preoccupied as it was with newness, otherness, and deviancy, monitored processes of normalization as well, as Simone Knewitz reminds us. This perspective allows us to see the work of Dickinson and Moore as two different moments of a wavering between awe and fascination with (radical) otherness, and a desire at domesticating and making us familiar with alterity. By orientalizing Dickinson and Moore, our current reception of their work, accordingly, tends to waver between, on the one hand, retaining modernism's otherness and, on the other, domesticating an Orient that currently moves ever closer to our homes. This is why, at the very same time, we cherish the fact that both Dickinson and Moore to a certain degree resist their Orientalization, retaining a critical bias that is, at least in part, dependent on their own gender position and the particularly contested cultural position that gender studies has carved out for poets like Dickinson and Moore.

All the while, we also risk relegating to the periphery the economic and political underpinnings of a supposedly 'revolutionary' modernist aesthetics that Dickinson's and Moore's poems do expose, if ever so subtly, underpinnings that may stand too exposed in postcolonial studies. And we also tend to forget that modernism's turn toward the Orient is both a turn away and a vicarious involvement in matters of race and ethnicity that are part of what Williams called the "American grain."[8] If, in our memory, Moore still belongs with those same modernists who lacked interest in "vogues" much closer to home in favor of the "craze for China" (Qian 38), we may want to recall that she felt the need to reassert, quoting a sermon of Reverend J. W. Darr in her poem "The Labors of Hercules,"

> that one keeps on knowing
> "that the Negro is not brutal,
> that the Jew is not greedy,
> that the Oriental is not immoral,
> that the German is not a Hun."   (CP 53)

Moore's echo of Darr is suggestive: It seems to remind us that the prominence of cultures of the Far Eastern in U.S.-American modernisms was part of a larger and complex force field in which stereotypical notions of (multiple) cultural difference are counterbalanced by both the fascination and knowledge we tend to reserve for particular cultures only. But that is another story.

Notes

1. Cf. Dickinson's poem "The Brain - is wider than the Sky - " (Fr 598), among many others, that foreground how far journeys of the mind may take us. Likewise, Cynthia Stamy speaks of Moore's "textual 'travel' as a surrogate for real journeys," "armchair journeys" (33), and "journeys of the mind" (34).

2. In turn, Dickinson's first documented Japanese reader was art historian Kakuzo Okakura who in 1898 borrowed a volume of her poems from poet and novelist Mary Fenollosa (Benfey 82).

3. See, for instance, Dickinson's poems "My Life had stood – a Loaded Gun –" (*Poems* 764), "Nature – is what we see –" (Fr 721), and "Nature and God – I neither knew" (803), among many others.

4. In fact, Emerson – as a philosopher and editor of *The Dial* more than as poet - becomes a major reference point in Stamy's view of Moore; "their concerns," she writes, "remain much the same" (14).

5. Along the way, Stamy also claims a proximity between Moore and "the Native American or 'native-born' artist" on the basis of their tendency to draw on a multitude of sources (42).

6. This mode may be proximate or kin to what Qian sees evolving as a sense of integrity in Moore's "Tedium and Integrity" ("Moore and *The Tao of Painting* 246f) as well as to the centrality of wholeness in the work Gertrude Stein.

7. Or both, as Qian has it: "Moore's interest in Chinese art is primarily an interest in Chinese animal pictures" (188).

8. Moore, after all, taught at the Carlisle Indian School for many years. See Wheeler and Gavalar, for instance.

Works Cited

Bazin, Victoria. "'Just Looking' at the Everyday: Marianne Moore's Exotic Modernism." *Modernist Cultures* 2.1 (2006): 58-69.

Benfey, Christopher. "A Route of Evanescence: Emily Dickinson and Japan." *Emily Dickinson Journal* 16.2 (2007): 81–93.

Dickinson, Emily. *The Poems of Emily Dickinson*. Ed. R. W. Franklin. Variorum Edition. 3 vols. Cambridge: Harvard UP, 1998.

___. *The Letters of Emily Dickinson*. Eds. Thomas H. Johnson and Theodora Ward, 3 vols. Cambridge: Harvard UP, 1986.

Grabher, Gudrun. *Emily Dickinson: Das transzendentale Ich*. Anglistische Forschungen 157. Heidelberg: Winter, 1981.

Haddad, Emily A. *Orientalist Poetics: The Islamic Middle East in Nineteenth-century English and French Poetry*. Aldershot: Ashgate, 2002.

Hagenbüchle, Roland. "Dickinson and literary theory." *The Emily Dickinson Handbook*. Eds. Gudrun Grabher, Roland Hagenbüchle, and Cristianne Miller. Amherst: University of Massachusetts Press, 1998. 356-84.

Kang Yanbin. "Emily Dickinson and China." Diss. Abstract. *New Voices in Translation Studies* 5 (2009). n.p.

Knewitz, Simone. "'A poet is flesh and blood as well as brain': Amy Lowell, William Carlos Williams, and the Modernist Poetics of the Material Body." Unpublished PhD dissertation. University of Bonn, 2010.

Logan, William. "The Mystery of Marianne Moore." Rev. of *Marianne Moore: The Early Poems, 1907-1924*, by Marianne Moore, edited by Robin G. Schulze. *The New Criterion* 22 (February 2004): n.p. Web. 2 February 2011.

McLuhan, Marshall. *War and Peace in the Global Village*. New York: Bantam, 1968.

Moore, Marianne. *The Complete Poems of Marianne Moore*. New York: Viking, 1981.

___. "Nine Nectarines and Other Porcelain." *Poetry* 45.2 (1934): 64-67.

___. *Poems*. New York: Egoist Press, 1921.

Pencak, William. "Emily Dickinson: Post-Colonial Feminist, Post-Modern Semiotician." *Semiotics* (1996): 13–25.

Qian, Zhaoming. "Marianne Moore and *The Tao of Painting*." *Paideuma* 32.2-3 (2002): 245-64.

___. *The Modernist Response to Chinese Art: Pound, Moore, Stevens*. Charlottesville: U of Virginia P, 2003.

Schueller, Malini Johar. *U.S. Orientalisms: Race, Nation, and Gender in Literature, 1790-1890*. Ann Arbor: U Michigan P, 1998.

___. "Orientalizing American Studies." *American Quarterly* 60.2 (June 2008): 481-89.

Sielke, Sabine. *Fashioning the Female Subject: The Intertextual Networking of Dickinson, Moore and Rich*. Ann Arbor: University of Michigan Press, 1997.

Sielke, Sabine, and Christian Klöckner, eds. *Orient and Orientalisms in American Poetry and Poetics*. Transcription 4. Frankfurt: Lang, 2009.

Stamy, Cynthia. *Marianne Moore and China: Orientalism and a Writing of America*. Oxford: Oxford UP, 1999.

Tate, Allen. "New England Culture and Emily Dickinson." *Critical Essays on Emily Dickinson*. Ed. Paul J. Ferlazzo. Boston: G. K. Hall, 1984. 81-93.

Uno, Hiroko. "Emily Dickinson's Encounter with the East: Chinese Museum in Boston." *Emily Dickinson Journal* 17.1 (2008): 43–67.

Wand, David Hsin-Fu. "The Dragón and the Kylin: The Use of Chinese Symbols and Myths in Marianne Moore's Poetry." *Literature East and West* 15.3 (1971): 470–84.

Wheeler, Leslie, and Christopher Gavaler. "Impostors and Chameleons: Marianne Moore and the Carlisle Indian School." *Paideuma: Studies in American and British Modernist Poetry* 33.2-3 (2004): 53–82.

The Flute—East/West—in Modernist Music and Poetry

Daniel Albright

Before the human race came into being, there were musical instruments of a sort: for example, sea otters, floating on the backs in the ocean, poise abalone on the chests and beat open the shell with a stone. But it is doubtful that these percussive otters mean to make noise for the sake of noise; and the first instrument created with a clear intent to make music, as far as we know, was the flute.

In June 2009 news appeared concerning a 35,000-year-old flute, found in a cave in southern Germany, made of the wing bone of a griffon vulture (Owen). A researcher who made a replica of this instrument noted that he could play on it a more-or-less in-tune version of the beginning of *The Star-Spangled Banner*, which suggests that the flute's holes were arranged to play the basic intervals of Western tonal music: the third, the fifth, and the octave. All those millennia ago, the German flautist was making music that was, in some sense, already our music.

In Asia as well, ancient flutes have been unearthed. At Jiahu, an archaeological site in China's Henan Province, Neolithic flutes have been dated at roughly 9,000 years old, though only one remains in playable condition. It has seven holes which produce "a rough scale, covering a modern octave, beginning close to the second A above middle C." Frederick Lau, an ethnomusicologist at California Polytechnic State University, says that the flutes likely had a ritualistic purpose but that he "wouldn't exclude the fact that flutes could have been used for personal entertainment." Like the much older German flute, the Jiahu flutes were made from the bones of a bird: in this case, the red-crowned crane (Fountain 1999).

If the earliest flutes were made of bone, the flute entered mythology and history as a contrivance of reeds or hollowed wood. The Greeks tended to think of wind music as quite distinct from string music:

Apollo's lyre suggested moderation, calm, the mathematical ratios of Pythagoras; wind music, on the other hand, suggested rape (as in the case of the nymph Syrinx, chased by the god Pan, her chastity saved only because she metamorphosed into reeds) or torture (as in the case of Marsyas, the satyr who challenged Apollo to a music contest, and was flayed alive after he lost). Wind music is expressive, an exercise of the mouth, like kissing itself; Athena, the goddess of wisdom, disliked the flute because it distended the cheeks and made the player ugly.

From the beginning of discourse, then, the flute has two aspects: it is nature's own voice, the voice of the wind sighing in the reeds, the voice of Pan, that is, the voice of everything—since the Greek word for *all* is *pan*. But it is also a sort of scream, the voice of sexual frustration—indeed to play a flute is almost to perform a sexual act carried out by mechanical means.

The flute's two sides—the bright and the dark—have persisted over the course of Western music. On the bright side, the flute has been the shepherd's instrument, the instrument of effortless carefree rural life. In the eighteenth century, Jean-Jacques Rousseau—a composer as well as a philosopher—deplored the artificiality of French music, its cultivation of harmonic nuance, subtle half-tints, as opposed to the simplicity and vigor of Italian music. Rousseau's preferred instrument was the flute—and late in his career, in 1775, he transcribed for solo flute the Spring concerto from Vivaldi's *The Four Seasons*, Op. 8, thereby reducing to utmost simplicity, a single melodic line, played by the most rustic of instruments, some of the most potent Italian music of his age.

There are countless illustrations of the ways in which composers use the flute to evoke pastoral. One example is the call of the nightingale in Beethoven's sixth symphony (1808), in the movement called *Scene by the Brook*; another is maybe the most famous solo in the whole flute literature which comes from the Paris version of Gluck's opera *Orphée et Eurydice* (1774), a representation of supernatural joy, blessed spirits dancing in Elysium.

But the flute was not just an instrument of nature-joy and heaven's blessing: it was also an instrument of power. In Mozart's *The Magic Flute* (1791), Tamino plays his flute at moments of crisis, both to express himself and to impose his will:

Wie stark ist nicht dein Zauberton!   [How powerful is your magic music,]
Weil , holde Flöte, durch dein Spielen [Sweet flute, for when you play]
Selbst wilde Tiere Freude fühlen.   [Even wild beasts feel joy!]

Soon the sound of the flute will attract Tamino's beloved Pamina. It almost seems to conjure her up. This cybernetic force is in no sense dark, for Tamino's flute is strictly on the side of virtue; but as the flute expanded its repertoire of possibility, it was asked to deliver more of the Pan-ic and less of the cooey and fluttery.

At the end of the nineteenth century, the flute started to display its true dark side, Pan's pantings, his sexual urgencies. Debussy wrote very little flute music, but he nevertheless managed almost single-handedly to change the semantic character of the flute. The most conspicuous example is the faun's flute at the beginning of the *Prélude à L'après-midi d'un faune* (1894). This was written as a kind of musical illustration to a symbolist poem by Mallarmé: a program note very possibly written by Debussy himself says that the music is "a succession of décors, across which there move the desires and dreams of the faun in the afternoon heat. Then, tired of chasing the nymphs and the naiads, he abandons himself to the drunkenness of sunlight, sated with dreams that have turned real, with his complete possession of universal nature" (Vallas 181). The music, then, concerns sensual glut; when Nijinsky made it into a ballet, he ended his performance by rubbing the nymph's scarf over his genitals in a scandalous but appropriate gesture, for this is music of erotic fantasy, perhaps the greatest such music ever written. That notorious flute solo at the beginning of the piece moves stepwise through the interval of an augmented fourth, the tritone, a charged interval known in the Middle Ages as the *diabolus in musica*, the devil in music. Representations of the Christian devil have always been based on images of satyrs, fauns, and other hybrid creatures, half-man, half-animal, from pre-Christian mythology. And Debussy endows his faun with a tritone, a badge of deviltry as obvious to a musician as a pair of horns would be to a painter. The music is languorous, hot, shimmery, slow; but it is instinct with sin.

Seven years later, in 1901, Debussy composed a sort of sonic environment for the recitation of twelve poems by Pierre Louÿs called

Chansons de Bilitis; the music was scored for two flutes, two harps, and celesta. In the seventh of these poems, *Le tombeau sans nom* (The tomb without a name), the reciter reads the epitaph carved on the stele, and comments, "We pour no libation. For how can you summon an unknown soul from the crowds of Hades?" The music shows that the flute's emotive possibilities include a kind of cool marmoreal grieving.

And twelve years after that, in 1913, Debussy—by now a renowned specialist in flute sex—was asked by Gabriel Mourey to write a short melodrama, *La flûte de Pan* (later published as *Syrinx*), for his play *Psyché*. In the old story, the chaste Syrinx flees from the gross importunings of Pan; her metamorphosis into a little stand of reeds leaves Pan frustrated, though so pleased by the sound of his breath over the hollow tubes that he finds a certain aesthetic consolation—as Ovid puts it in the first book of the *Metamorphoses*, in Arthur Golding's translation:

> In steade of hir he caught the Reedes newe growne upon the brooke,
> And as he sighed, with his breath the Reedes he softly shooke
> Which made a still and mourning noyse, with straungnesse of the which
> And sweetenesse of the feeble sounde the God delighted mich ...
> (Ovid, 27)

But in Mourey's play Psyché, first timorous and coy, becomes so pleased with the sound of Pan's pipes that she willingly offers him what Syrinx refused: "O Pan, the sounds of your syrinx, like a wine / Too fragrant and too sweet, have intoxicated me . . ." (qtd. in McQuinn 126).

The flute sounds as if the naiad were faint with desire, and keeps rousing herself only to faint again.

After Debussy's time, flute music evolved in still more Marsyan directions—away from heaven's beatitude, toward something coldly or hotly expressive. In the nineteenth century, orchestral flutes were made of either wood or metal; but in the twentieth century, metal was predominant. As composers started to think of flutes as shaped silver, they thought less about pastoral natural scenes and more about some inhuman purity of tone, some uninflected sine wave, as if metal itself were given a grave voice. Edgard Varèse's solo flute piece *Density 21.5* (1936) is entitled after the specific gravity of platinum, 21.5 grams per cubic centimeter—it was composed in order to inaugurate a new platinum flute. Like Debussy's *Prélude*, the Varèse piece makes much use of the tritone, but here the tritone seems to have almost no semantic content: it does not represent the devil, nor sensual delight, nor anything at all but just an interval, just as good as any other interval, with no yearning to resolve itself into a fourth or a fifth or any other consonance. We seem to have entered a domain too hermetic, too self-enclosed, to permit any notion of consonance or dissonance. The musical composition is simply a dense object made of sound, as the flute is a dense object made of metal: long sustained notes are interrupted by shrill frills, like solid planes onto which curlicues are attached: here music seems to approximate the condition of sculpture. The transverse flute is, of all musical instruments, the most expensive of breath: flautists have to breathe far more frequently than oboists or trumpeters or hornists. This very breathiness is part of its Marsyan aspect, the player's lungs are always on display, and a certain awareness of panting is always built into the listener's response to the music. But Varèse makes it possible for the player to disguise the intakes of breath, as if the piece were written for some superhuman player who never had to inhale. I have been speaking of *Density 21.5* as a coldly expressive piece, a piece expressive of metallicness itself, but maybe it would be better to speak of it not in terms of expression at all, but in terms of a new variant on the celestial aspect of the flute: maybe the composition is another Dance of the Blessed Spirits, translated into some shimmer or shiver of the inorganic.

In some later pieces, the panting quality is so far in the foreground that the listener scarcely hears music at all. For example, consider a piece by Salvatore Sciarrino, *Frammento e Adagio* for flute and orchestra (1991): Sciarrino is fond of asking flautists to do to their flutes a number of things that God and Herr Boehm never intended, such as fingering for percussive effects or blowing through the body of the flute instead of the mouthpiece. It sometimes sounds as if Sciarrino were reversing the whole evolution of the flute from reed or wood pipe to a complex contrivance of keyed metal: the flute reverts to some crude tube that a satyr might tentatively try to make a sound on, a frustrated puffing. The pan-pipes undergo a reverse metamorphosis, turn back into the nymph Syrinx, who can be wetly kissed, but not blown. In one of his most remarkable compositions, *Hermes* for solo flute (1984), Sciarrino juxtaposes the faint pure arpeggios of the modern flute with notes that are distorted, cracked, without a centered pitch, as if the half-shaped reed were trying to drown out its elegant successor. It is a sort of dialogue between two different modalities of wind: pure and impure, the blessed spirits and Marsyas.

Quite distinct from their predecessors, modernist poets, particularly William Butler Yeats and Ezra Pound, use flutes to depict a complicated interaction between the artificial and the natural; between the celestial and the sexual; between East and West. There is in fact very little of the West in Modernist flute-poetics: it is an orientalizing sort of instrument, as if every Eastern scene came decorated with a flute player providing a soft continuo for the proceedings.

Pound was a composer as well as a poet, and his opera *Le testament* was based on the sex-driven, death-driven poetry of François Villon, whose verse cuts close to the bone. Before the opening of the first song there are two bars for drum and flute: the drum taps out four sixteenth notes, which, with a final sixteenth-note rest, are gathered into a quintuplet; after five of these quintuplets, the flute plays three glissandi down the span of a fifth, from E to A. This odd figure appears at several places in the score: for example, after the *Ballade des dames du temps jadis*, where it is labeled, "Inside brothel," and we are told that the flute is a "nose flute" and the drumbeat is to be played by "small African drums." I have myself studied the flute and the recorder, and I can tell you that I grow somewhat uneasy at the thought of sticking a flute up my nose and breathing into it—it is an invasive, transgressive way of playing an instrument, a little too far into the inside of my body, more like an intubation than like a musical act. But tootling a flute shoved up your nose makes, in a certain sense, the perfect music for a brothel: and the whole scene suggests Pan playing Syrinx, a breathing that is a having-sex by different means.

In his poetry, Pound's flute music comes in two distinct genres, both exotic, both highly localized. The first genre concerns the half-western, half-eastern world of classical Greece and Hellenized Rome. In Canto XXV (1928), as in *Le testament*, the flute music has a strong erotic charge:

Lay there, the long soft grass,
            and the flute lay there by her thigh,
Sulpicia, the fauns, twig-strong,
                        gathered about her;
The fluid, over the grass
Zephyrus, passing through her …
And from the stone pits, the heavy voices,
Heavy sound:
            "Sero, sero…
"Nothing we made, we set nothing in order,
"Neither house nor the carving,
"And what we thought had been thought for too long …
"We have gathered a sieve full of water."
And from the comb of reeds, came notes and the chorus
Moving, the young fauns: Pone metum …

                        …the flute: pone metum. …
Form, forms and renewal, gods held in the air,
Forms seen, and then clearness,
Bright void, without image …

and saw the waves taking form as crystal,
    notes as facets of air,
    and the mind there, before them, moving,
    so that notes needed not move.
                        (*Cantos* 118-19)

Sulpicia was a Roman poet of the first century BCE; the Latin words *Pone metum* mean *Put aside fear*, the advice given to a young man, presumably Sulpicia's lover, when she was ill—the gods do not let lovers come to harm. Pound rather disliked Debussy, but in this great passage from Canto XXV fauns and flutes rise incessantly, as if Debussy's *Prélude à L'après-midi d'un faune* were the hidden soundtrack under the words. The sex-music of the flute resting against Sulpicia's thigh, a light, flicking, dancing sound, contrasts with the heavy voices from the stone pits, a thick useless unison—here Pound, as he does so often, contrasts something creative, life-giving, god-evoking, with some slack image of sloth, inertia, vain weight, infernal penance, such as the lotos-eaters from the Odyssey, or Madame Hyle, Mrs. Dead Matter. The great dialectic of the Cantos is light versus mud: and the flute is light turned into sound. Perhaps the most remarkable aspect of Pound's flute is not that it picks out, draws in air the outlines of the gods, but that it inscribes on the sky the notes of its own tune. A few years later Pound, in his role as music critic, heard Stravinsky play his *Capriccio*: "I had the mirage of seeing the unknown score from the aural stimulæ offered" (*Ezra Pound and Music*, 372 [1935]); and the visible flute music in Canto XXV anticipates this mirage.

In 1955, in Canto XC, Pound wrote another passage in which the flute assists theophany:

> οἱ χθόνιοι myrrh and olibanum on the altar stone
> Giving perfume,
>   and where was nothing
> now is furry assemblage
>   and in the boughs now are voices
> grey wing, black wing, black wing shot with crimson
> and the umbrella pines
>   as in Palatine,
> as in pineta. χελιδών, χειδών
> For the procession of Corpus
>   come now banners
> comes flute tone
>   οἱ χθόνιοι
> To new forest,
>   thick smoke, purple, rising
> bright flame now on the altar
>   the crystal funnel of air
> out of Erebus, the delivered,
>   Tyro, Alcmene, free now, ascending ...
>   (*Cantos* 628)

Though this passage was written long after the force of the Vorticist movement was spent, it may be the supreme moment of Vorticism. According to one of Pound's Vorticist manifestos of 1914, "The image [i.e., the poet's pigment] is not an idea. It is a radiant node or cluster; it is what I can, and must perforce, call a VORTEX, from which, and through which, and into which, ideas are constantly rushing. In decency one can only call it a VORTEX" (*Ezra Pound and Visual Arts*, 207 [1914]). Here in Canto XC, the crystal funnel is like the tip of a tornado that touches the earth, and opens up a strange subtextual space, an underwhere, from which nymphs and other figures of myth spiral up into the sky. Vorticism pertains to the bringing-to-bear of great resources of energy upon a single point: and the flute-music, and the fragrance of myrrh and olibanum, and the processing banners all lend their strength to this great effort. In Canto XXV, the flute's tones become a musical score projected visually onto the air; here the flute and the birdsongs and the sound of the lovely Greek word *chelidon* (swallow) and the perfumes and the visual emblems all commingle and summon. For Pound, the sound of the flute has an almost gluey aspect: it attracts and holds images of smell and sight into a rich pan-sensual complex. The flute tends to participate in a synesthetic matrix, in which all sense organs are engaged. Note, please, that the procession in this poem is the procession of Corpus—the procession of the body, not necessarily that of Corpus Christi, the body of Christ. The flute seems to tease goddesses into being, but there is nothing abstract, nothing extramundane, nothing too far from the body's urgencies; the most emphatic spirits present are *hoi chthonioi*, the spirits of the earth.

Now we come to the second genre of Pound's poetical flutes. The flutes of the Cantos borrow their tunes, their esemplastic force, from the flutes of Asia: specifically, from the Chinese flutes long established as instruments of loneliness and nostalgia. In *The Woman Warrior*, Maxine Hong Kingston writes of "Ts'ai Yen" (Cai Yan, ca. 177-239), a Chinese poetess kidnapped by the barbarians of central Asia. For the twelve years she lived among her captors, Cai Yan could not speak to them and instead listened to the flute music they played at night. This music "disturbed Ts'ai Yen; its sharpness and its cold made her ache [...] an icicle in the desert" (Kingston 108). After she was ransomed, Cai Yan composed poem-songs expressing the loneliness and longing for her home that she had experienced; her story has since been the inspiration of numerous poems and songs, including "Eighteen Songs of a Nomad Flute" by Liu Shang during the Tang Dynasty.

The flute's role as instrument of sorrow was well-established, therefore, by the time Li Po began to write. His poetry is fraught with flute music, both in the poems Pound translates in *Cathay* and in other poems, such as "Spring Night in Lo-yang – Hearing a Flute":

> In what house, the jade flute that sends those dark notes drifting,
> scattering on the spring wind that fills Lo-yang?
> Tonight if we should hear the willow-breaking song,
> who could help but long for the gardens of home?
>
> (Li Po 210)

The flute in China produces the "dark notes" of loneliness and melancholy; the willow-breaking song, played through the jade flute, is a song of parting. The plaintive sounds of air (breath/wind merging together) through the jade flute melds nature and humanity, transmuting both into something more, into art. Pound's translation in *Cathay* of "The River Song," in particular, is a flute-haunted poem:

> This boat is of sato-wood, and its gunwales are cut magnolia,
> Musicians with jeweled flutes and with pipes of gold
> Fill full the sides in rows, and our wine
> Is rich for a thousand cups.
> We carry singing girls, drift with the drifting water ...
>
> Kutsu's prose song
> Hangs with the sun and moon.
>
> King So's terraced palace
>   is now but barren hill,
> But I draw pen on this barge
> Causing the five peaks to tremble,
> And I have joy in these words
>   like the joy of blue islands ...
>
> And I have moped in the Emperor's garden, awaiting an order-to-
>   write!
> I looked at the dragon-pond, with its willow-colored water
> Just reflecting in the sky's tinge,
> And heard the five-score nightingales aimlessly singing.
>
> Vine strings a hundred feet long hang down from carved railings,
> And high over the willows, the fine birds sing to each other, and

listen,
Crying—"Kwan, Kuan," for the early wind, and the feel of it.
The wind bundles itself into a bluish cloud and wanders off.
Over a thousand gates, over a thousand doors are the sounds of
     spring singing,
And the Emperor is at Ko....
He goes out to Hori, to look at the wing-flapping storks,
He returns by way of Sei rock, to hear the new nightingales,
For the gardens of Jo-run are full of new nightingales,
Their sound is mixed in this flute,
Their voice is in the twelve pipes here.

(Personae, 132-33)

This is an elusive poem, partly because Pound unwittingly conflated two distinct poems by Li Po, partly because the verse movement keeps shivering away, slithering away from one theme as soon as it is touched: each of the poem's notes sets other notes vibrating. The hundred-foot vine strings seem to represent a sort of giant zither or harp, ready to respond to the poem's music, and, if we imagine them as festoons, they also seem to represent the general looping aspect, the unpredictable recurrences of things, just as nature itself is unpredictably recurrent.

The poem is an exercise in fugitive harmonies. The world seems caught up in an act of listening to itself: the slightest change in one thing creates subtle adjustments in everything else. The poet draws his pen—and as he assumes the role of artificer, the shift of his arm rocks the barge a bit, and the mountains, or their reflections in the water, seem to tremble. The act of singing, or the act of writing, changes the aspect of nature. This is as close as Pound gets to Wallace Stevens, whose famous jar tames the Tennessee wilderness, unslovens it. Kutsu's prose song becomes a physical object, pasted onto the sky, "hung with the sun and moon." While the poet awaits the Emperor's command to write, the nightingales sing aimlessly; but when the Emperor appears, the nightingales' song seems to relocate itself, get enclosed in the flute's pipes: the flute arrests the lovely birdsong, puts it in order, assimilates it into itself. Then, it was aimless; now, it is art. We do not learn whether the poet has yet received from the Emperor an explicit order-to-write, but the sense of ever-heightening artifice is strong: the improvised, delicately evanescent harmonies of the poem's beginning become ever more subject to human control, ever more tightly organized. The flute endows the nightingales' song with human meaning—it is as if mere nature-noise were enchanted by art, transformed into art.

All Asia, in Pound's imagination, is a continent in which flutes have aesthetic power, power to impose a design on external nature. Flutes play offstage in Japanese Noh drama to announce the beginning of a play. The flute's "shrill and sometimes harsh" notes seem to "come from another world [...] infinitely distant from ours" (Keene 20). Rather than the sweetness attributed to the Western flute, the Noh flute produces "an effect of disembodied sound" (69), exercising its power to establish an otherworldly, aesthetic space. In 1916 Pound published a volume of translations of Japanese Noh plays, made, like the *Cathay* translations, from the notes of Fenollosa; and Pound's Japan is much like the China of "The River Song":

> The flower of waves-reflected
> Is on his white garment;
> That pattern covers the sleeve.
> The air is alive with flute-sounds,
> With the song of various pipes
> The land is a-quiver,
> And even the wild sea at Suma
>
> Is filled with resonant quiet. (*Translations*, 235)

This is a "Chorus (*accompanying and describing the dance*)" from the Noh play *Suma Genji*; here the immortal spirit Genji dances "the blue dance of the sea waves." As the dance evokes the surges, the wave-rhythm abstracted from the waves themselves, the flutes tame the wild sea into a state of tremulous calm, just as the real waves turn into pattern-elements on the sleeve of a costume.

Still more remarkable is the aesthetic transformation in Pound's translation of the play *Shojo*: "The thin leaves of ashi, the leaves of the river-reeds, are like flute-notes. The waves are like little drums" (*Translations*, 257).

This chorus also accompanies a divine dance. Here the visual field reconstitutes itself as a set of sounds, in the way that an ideogram is a kind of picture that can be pronounced out loud. In an East-Asiatic landscape the ideograms drawn near the trees sometimes seem to branch out, to exfoliate, as if the inked characters were themselves tree-images with their own pattern of growth. But in this chorus "in praise of the wine-spirit" the leaves of the reeds are read not as words, but as music, as if they were notations for a flute score imprinted in the landscape itself.

In other Noh plays the flute's melody seems to create the space in which all things constitute themselves—an *air* not just in the sense of a tune, but also in the sense of the whole atmosphere:

A flute's voice has moved the clouds of Shushinrei. (*Tsunemasa*, in *Translations*, 266)

> Nor is this rock of earth overmuch worn by the brushing of that feather-mantle, the feathery skirt of the stars … There is a magic song from the east, the voices of many and many: and flute and sho, filling the space beyond the cloud's edge, seven-stringed; dance filling and filling. (*Hagoromo*, in *Translations*, 314)

(A sho is a bundle of seventeen tubes, somewhat like Pan-pipes, but played by breathing through a vibrating reed, not by blowing across the top of the tubes.) In these passages the flute's sound keeps occupying more and more room, until it pushes the clouds out of the way, fills the zodiac with its presence. The sun and moon and stars seem suspended in the flute's giant breath.

Most of the Noh passages I've quoted are from dance choruses that would be chanted while flutes were actually playing. The Noh theatre was more like opera than like spoken drama—the music was integral, and, just as the actors were often members of hereditary actor-clans, so there were clans of flute players: Pound quotes a note of Fenollosa's that translates an "imperial order" from AD 686: "The male singers and female flute blowers must make it their own profession, and hand it down to their descendants and make them learn" (*Translations*, 357).

The music in actual Noh performances can be rather loud and complicated, but Pound and Yeats seemed to imagine a music refined, spare, a fugitive delicacy: as Yeats said, in the introduction to his imitations (not translations) of Noh plays: "There will be no scenery, for three musicians, whose seeming sun-burned faces will I hope suggest that they have wandered from village to village in some country of our dreams, can describe place and weather, and at moments action, and accompany it all by drum and gong or flute and dulcimer" (*Essays and Introductions*, 221).

Yeats imagined these instruments sometimes as providing the accompaniment for the songs; sometimes as providing a kind of punctuation for the action; sometimes as providing a continuous underplay to pantomimed action—as, for example, in *The Cat and the Moon* (1917), where "*Blind Beggar beats Lame Beggar. The beating takes the form of a dance and is accompanied on drum and flute*" (*The Collected Works of W. B. Yeats Vol. II: The Plays*, 452).

But Yeats's use of music differed from Pound's. For one thing, Pound, a professional music critic, had a fine ear, and became a skillful self-taught composer, whereas Yeats was tone-deaf and wholly ignorant of music. And yet, as Yeats grew older, music played a larger and larger role in his dramatic art.

Yeats employed professional composers to write music for most of his Noh imitations, beginning with *At the Hawk's Well* in 1917. In that play, the musicians unfold a cloth and position it as the backdrop to the action; their songs help to interpret the narrative content of the play's events, and to cue the audience about what to feel. This provided the basic model for the role of musicians in the subsequent plays. But in the later plays the musicians started to become more and more central to the action. Yeats found that the musicians could act as surrogates for characters too unimportant to appear on stage, and as voices for supernatural creatures whose words needed to be separated from any bodily form. In *The King of the Great Clock Tower* (1934), one musician reads out the words of the Captain of the Guard, who never actually appears: he is supposed to arrest the Stroller and drag him offstage, but in fact the Stroller has to mime getting dragged offstage, or simply exit. In short, the script gives few clues about stage movements. Meanwhile, the second musician sings the songs of the Queen, who is more a sculpture than a human being: "Why sit you there / Dumb as an image made of wood or metal, / A screen between the living and the dead?" (*The Plays*, 494). After the Stroller is executed, his severed head sings a song, ventriloquized by the first musician. It is as if the action of stage takes place within the confines of the music—the spoken dialogue keeps struggling for a little space in which it can speak itself, but eternity's music keeps drowning out the speech of time.

In Yeats's last plays, the flute asserts itself with special potency. In *The Death of Cuchulain*, the Goddess of Death—"A woman that has an eye in the middle of her forehead, / A woman that is headed like a crow" (*The Plays*, 548) holds up Cuchulain's head, in the form of a black parallelogram; she puts it on the floor, and, as she dances in front of it, the audience hears "a few faint bird notes" (*The Plays*, 553), presumably played by a pipe, since among the play's musicians are a piper and a drummer. Yeats described something similar in the poem "Cuchulain Comforted," written two weeks before he died, where he remarks of the spirits of the dead, "They had changed their throats and had the throats of birds." Yeats considered the passage from death to life as a passage from realism into abstraction—parallelograms, a half-audible flute tone. Music becomes an abstraction of speech. I mention earlier of the way that flute music represented either celestial purity or the sound of the deep body—and here it seems that Yeats has conceived flute music as the speech of heaven.

But for the unchristian Yeats the afterlife is an intensely carnal place. In his late play *The Herne's Egg* (1938), Attracta, the priestess of the heron-god known as the Great Herne, plays a special flute:

> *Corney.* A flute lies there upon the rock
> Carved out of a herne's thigh.
> Go pick it up and play the tune
> My mother calls 'The Great Herne's Feather' ...
>
> *Attracta.* Strong sinew and soft flesh
> Are foliage round the shaft
> Before the arrowsmith
> Has stripped it, and I pray
> That I, all foliage gone,
> May shoot into my joy—
> [*Sound of a flute, playing 'The Great Herne's Feather'*]
>   (*The Plays*, 511, 516-17)

The flute is no longer at the margins of the stage, in the hand of a musician; it has encroached onto the stage space, become one of the play's chief props. Attracta has special access to the world beyond the grave, and her flute can summon the god; but she conceives the immanence of the Great Herne almost completely in terms of orgasm. From her point of view the Great Herne's thunderbolt descends to her in a trance at blue-black midnight; but from the point of view of the other actors she is simply gang-raped by seven soldiers. At the play's end the hero Congal dies, and Attracta hopes that she will be able to reincarnate him if one of his soldiers agrees to have sex with her; but before they have a go at it, two lustful donkeys copulate, and poor Congal will have to be reborn as an ass.

The Herne's Egg belongs to a genre almost unknown outside the work of Yeats: the apocalyptic farce. Every event of the play can be conceived either as a peculiar sort of sacred mystery, or as a lunatic sex comedy: for Yeats the shiver of the extraterrestrial was intensified by a certain smell of dung and sweat and semen. You can read the play as an exegesis of the divine, along the lines of *A Vision*, or you can read the play according to Freud, as Congal himself does:

> Women thrown into despair
> By the winter of their virginity
> Take its abominable snow,
> As boys take common snow, and make
> An image of god or bird or beast
> To feed their sensuality … (*The Plays*, 513)

The flute, with its twi-formed nature, half belonging to the calm cloudless heavenly sky, half belonging to Pan's earth and sexual revelry, was just the right instrument to negotiate this odd hermeneutic. The only really gifted composer to work with Yeats on his Noh imitation was Pound's friend George Antheil, who wrote the music for *Fighting the Waves* (1929). In that play, Cuchulain is torn between his love for Emer, his mortal wife, and his fascination with the goddess Fand. In Antheil's dance for Fand the flute is especially prominent; there is much chromaticism here, as in Debussy's *Prélude à L'après-midi d'un faune*, but here there is no languor: the seduction here feels urgent, irresistible. The goddess, with a costume that suggests "*gold or bronze or brass or silver … more an idol than a human being*" (*The Plays*, 461),

sounds something like a belly-dancer, to judge from the music.
In a poem from 1916, Yeats wrote:

> I would find by the edge of that water
> The collar-bone of a hare
> Worn thin by the lapping of water,
> And pierce it through with a gimlet and stare
> At the old bitter world where they marry in churches,
> And laugh over the untroubled water
> At all who marry in churches,
> Through the white thin bone of a hare. ("The Collar-Bone of a
>   Hare")

You can open a hole in an animal's bone and gaze at vision. In the
body's pith there is wisdom: as Yeats wrote in 1934,

> God guard me from those thoughts men think
> In the mind alone;
> He that sings a lasting song
> Thinks in a marrow-bone ... ("A Prayer for Old Age")

To think in a marrow-bone is to think with a potential flute.
Tibetan Buddhists evoke spirits with a trumpet called the kangling,
made out of a human femur. The human body is itself a little orchestra,
full of trumpets and flutes and gut strings; and the Modernists looked
to the poetry of Asia to help them learn how to play it.

Note

This essay has been enriched by three passages on Chinese and Japanese flutes
provided by Mary Bamburg, and the author is deeply grateful for her help.

Works Cited

Debussy, Claude. *Les Chansons de Bilitis*. 1901. Paris: Société des Éditions
    Jobert, 1971.

___. *Prélude à l'après-midi d'un faune*. 1895. Mineola: Dover Publications,
    1992.

Fountain, Henry. "After 9,000 Years, Oldest Playable Flute is Heard Again."
    Shakuhachi.com. 28 Sept 1999. Web. http://www.shakuhachi.com/K-
    9KChineseFlutes-Articles.html.

Keene, Donald. *Nō: The Classical Theatre of Japan*. Tokyo: Kodansha

International, 1966.

Kingston, Maxine Hong. *The Woman Warrior*. New York: Random House, 1976.

Li Po. "Spring Night in Lo-yang – Hearing a Flute." Trans. Burton Watson. *The Columbia Book of Chinese Poetry*. Ed. Burton Watson. New York: Columbia UP, 1984. 210.

McQuinn, Julie. "Exploring the Erotic in Debussy's Music." *The Cambridge Companion to Debussy*. Ed. Simon Trezise. Cambridge: Cambridge UP, 2003. 117-34.

Mozart, Wolfgang Amadeus. *The Magic Flute*. 1791. New York: Black Dog and Leventhal, 1996.

Ovid. *Metamorphoses, the Arthur Golding Translation, 1567*. Ed. John Frederick Nims. New York: Macmillan, 1965.

Owen, James. "Bone Flute is Oldest Instrument." *National Geographic News* 24 June 2009.

Pound, Ezra. *The Cantos*. 13th printing. New York: New Directions, 1995.

___. *Ezra Pound and Music*. Ed. R. Murray Schafer. New York: New Directions: 1977.

___. *Ezra Pound and the Visual Arts*. Ed. Harriet Zinnes. New York: New Directions, 1980.

___. *Le Testament*. "Paroles de Villon." 1926 and 1933. Ed. Margaret Fisher and Robert Hughes. Emeryville, CA: Second Evening Art, 2008.

___. *Personae, The Shorter Poems of Ezra Pound*. Ed. Lea Baechler and A. Walton Litz. New York: New Directions, 1990.

___. *Translations*. Intro. Hugh Kenner. New York: New Directions, 1963.

Vallas, Léon. *Claude Debussy et son temps*. Paris: Éditions Albin Michel, 1958.

Yeats, W. B. *The Collected Works of W. B. Yeats Vol. I: The Poems*. Ed. Richard J. Finneran. New York: Scribner, 1997.

___. *The Collected Works of W. B. Yeats Vol. II: The Plays*. Ed. David R. Clark and Rosalind E. Clark. New York: Scribner, 2001.

___. *Essays and Introductions*. London: Macmillan, 1961.

Proust's China

Christine Froula

Marcel Proust permeates the France of *In Search of Lost Time* with allusions to many periods and places in the Near, Middle, and Far East. The *Arabian Nights*, the Persian look of the church at Balbec, the Narrator's fascination with Ruskin's Venice with its eastern-inspired architecture and stones, and France's Jewish heritage, mapped in Swann, Bloch, and Gilberte and refracted through a contested national imaginary in the Dreyfus case: all trace France's continuities with southwest Asian history and culture. A period French orientalism surfaces in such details as Madam Cottard's comically clueless anecdote about the "salade japonaise" of Dumas fils' new play, *Francillon*, at a Verdurin dinner party; the Baron's *japoniste* fan painting; the Narrator's word paintings of landscapes and seascapes after Japanese screens and prints; and Odette's "very odd little house full of Chinese things," as one of her myriad former lovers remembers it—a very Parisian courtesan's potpourri of Oriental draperies, Turkish beads, gas-lit Japanese lanterns, silk cushions, chrysanthemums, palms in Chinese porcelain pots, fans, "fiery-tongued dragons" on a bowl or fire-screen, a silver dromedary with ruby eyes, a carved jade toad—where, in a "pink silk dressing gown," she first receives Swann for "afternoon tea" (adulterated with cream English-style), which they both feel, perhaps for different reasons, to be "something precious."[1] Not least, Luc Fraisse and Jan Hokenson observe, the overture of this work of art in search of lost time rises from "a *japoniste* cup of tea" as the Narrator likens the sudden apparition of his childhood Combray to tiny Japanese folded papers which, dropped into a porcelain bowl of water, bloom into "flowers or houses or people, solid and recognisable" (*ISLT* 1.64).[2]

It would be easy enough, Hokenson remarks, to dismiss the European Orients of the *Recherche* "as yet another modernist's

Orientalism, trite and faintly racist" (20). It would be easy, too, to see them as part of the given world in its inexhaustible contingent particularity that the Narrator brings forth, here with exquisite description, there with Daumieresque comedy, again with grim or tragic irony, so that readers can say "whether 'it really is like that,' . . . whether the words that they read within themselves are the same as those which I have written" (*ISLT* 6.508). In that case, such effects of "otherness" would be remarkable not as tokens of static essences but in their unbounded translatability as figure ("it really is *like* that") and abstraction (Bush 174-8). Further, like that cup of limeblossom tea, any detail of Proust's book may become translucent to historical depths: what appear to be solid objects may melt into the temporal flow of the conditions, things and events that produced them. Hokenson, for example, traces Proust's cup of tea to the Goncourts' late nineteenth-century milieu, when French *japonisme* was no passing fad but "the discovery of a new aesthetic continent" at a critical moment in western mimetic traditions—a "revolution in European aesthetics" of "Copernican proportions" that reaches its summa in Proust's masterly use of the Japanese aesthetic (Hokenson 17-8; Fraisse 29). As for Proust's southwest Asian themes, André Benhaïm, reading the *Recherche* from a postcolonial vantage, finds that "Proust's Orient owes little to Orientalism" but rather works to "disorient" racialized ideas of France, Frenchness, and the nation. In a new century of nationalist violence and ethnic persecution, the *Recherche* captures influences from far beyond France's borders to conjure a "vision of a past that … looks forward to the present, and beyond" (95).

Such readings illuminate the way the *Recherche* opens not only the nation's geographic borders but the very categories of the French, the European, the western to the circulating currents of historical process and a dynamic global cultural imaginary. Rather than betokening an essentialized "East," the Orients of the *Recherche* register what Ezra Pound called "the 'new' historic sense of our time" (*Guide* 30). Pound extends to Far Eastern cultures T. S. Eliot's Eurocentric description of a writer's "historical sense":

> a perception, not only of the pastness of the past, but of its presence; . . . a feeling that the whole of the literature of Europe from Homer and within it . . . the literature of his own country

has a simultaneous existence and composes a simultaneous
order. This . . . sense . . . of the timeless and of the temporal
together . . . makes a writer traditional [and] at the same time . . .
acutely conscious of his place in time, of his contemporaneity.
(4)[3]

This "'new' historic sense" of the contemporaneity of world literature
and culture, and of "tradition" as at once dynamic—sustaining within
it complex, ever-changing historical conditions and relations—open,
and "whole," its order altered by every addition, belongs to a global
cultural imaginary produced by burgeoning technologies, travel, and
trade. It is not inherited, Eliot stipulates, but attained by "great labour"
(4), and, Pound emphasizes, it is "new," if at all, only as it is constantly
made new. Artists have long labored on a more or less rapidly shrinking
globe of interpenetrating cultures, arts, and techne or know-how,
working in métiers and traditions of which any given state or product
implies the dynamic, collective, cumulative labor that produced it. In
the many "modernist" aesthetics of the early twentieth century, which
register not simple breaks and continuities but historical processes—
cross-fertilization, assimilation, creative adaptation, indigenization,
translation, and making-new, within and across locally differentiated
traditions, through centuries of uneven modernities—there scarcely
exists a purely European or western aesthetics.

Proust's China has attracted less attention than his Japan and is
sometimes sacrificed to it. His magisterial biographer Jean-Yves Tadié
writes that when Proust went looking for China at a 1911 exhibition
of Chinese paintings at the Durand-Ruel gallery, "all he found was a
hat. . . . Chinese art did not appeal to Proust and only appears in his
novel on Mme Verdurin's and Odette's screens, and on the plates in
the Goncourt parody in Le Temps retrouvé" (562). Fraisse does not
exclude Chinese art from Proust et le japonisme but emphasizes "the
dominant of the epoch" (7). Hokenson, arguing that Proust's "artist-
figures . . . rise or fall in japoniste terms," excludes Chinese art from
the novel's "counter-system of non-European aesthetics" and sees the
writer Bergotte, accused of "chinoiseries de forme," relegated with his
generation to "an arid Orientalism, quite notably not japoniste." In her
view, the likening of Vermeer's yellow wall to "a specimen of Chinese
art" signals the dying Bergotte's "superficial" Orientalism, which

reveals to him "the pointlessness and aridity of all art, including his own" (17, 34).

Yet the Orients of the *Recherche* are not one but many, and Proust's allusions operate within a poetics that Malcolm Bowie characterizes as "multifarious, iridescent, and flighty," not easily disciplined to ideological and aesthetic programs (125-33). Without seeking to reduce Proust's China to apparent homogeneity or to weigh its comparative value, I approach the allusion to Chinese art in Bergotte's death scene as a signature manifestation of an early twentieth-century artist's "new" historic sense. This scene and the meditation that encloses it align an unknown Chinese artisan with the seventeenth-century Dutch master Jan Vermeer, the novelist Bergotte, and, implicitly, the scene's author to project unique dimensions of the spatiotemporal hologram that is the *Recherche*. Taking Chinese art and Vermeer's *View of Delft* as epitomes of craft, the scene evokes the historical circulation of Chinese techne, inseparable from the global trade of a nascent European modernity, and frames a deep, world-historical awareness of craft within pre- and posthuman cosmic time. Inspired by a contemporary French critic, Proust's allusion to Chinese art registers a modernity not period-bound but borne through time and across cultures by the high craft Bergotte fears he has failed to attain.

The *Recherche* is, of course, all about time: the organic human lifetime; phenomenological, psychological, experiential time; the social, cultural, and archaeological time of history and historians; the nonlinear time of memory, voluntary and involuntary; cyclic, physical or natural time; the deep cosmological time probed by modern science; the life, in and out of time, of a work of art. All these temporal vectors traverse the famous scene—a partly autobiographical late addition to *The Captive*, volume 5 of *In Search of Lost Time*[4]—in which the novelist Bergotte expires while contemplating Vermeer's celebrated *View of Delft* (fig. 1). Vermeer's work had been brought to wide attention in the mid-nineteenth century after two centuries of relative obscurity. Thus, Christiane Hertel notes, his European reception evolved during the formative period of modern aesthetics, in which orientalisms of many kinds played crucial parts (9-139, esp. chaps. 6, 7). The invocation of Chinese art as Bergotte contemplates Vermeer's painting deepens the scene's synchronic array of the temporalities of art and artmaking—the mysterious translation of life, or lived time, into a work of art; the

Fig. 1. Johannes Vermeer, *View of Delft*, c. 1660-1661. Mauritshuis, The Hague. 98.5 x 117.5 cm. Reproduced from Gustave Vanzype, *Jan Vermeer de Delft*. Bruxelles, Paris: G. van Oest, 1908, revised 1921, 1925

historical conditions and processes of its making and reception—in different eras bounded by a vast inhuman past and future. In Bergotte's death scene, Proust's historic sense converges with his great theme of time in a meditation that registers China's profound influence on European arts and crafts during Vermeer's century, when the Dutch (United) East India Company—the *Verenigde Oostindische Compagnie* or VOC—rose to dominate global trade. To look at Vermeer's painting through Proust's historicist lens is to glimpse through Paris, Delft; through Delft, Shanghai, Jingdezhen, Hangzhou, interconnected by the trade routes that carried around the globe China's technologically advanced artifacts—not least, the treasured porcelains of which only Far Eastern artisans possessed the secret.[5]

In the last sentence of the *Recherche*, the Narrator pictures human beings as temporal giants tottering on ever higher stilts atop their increasing years, their "place in Time infinitely greater than the tiny one reserved for them in space, immeasurably prolonged" by the hours, days, years, and distant periods through which they have lived (*ISLT* 6.531-2). Bergotte's dying thoughts extend this spatial image of a life in time to the layered strata of cultural history, opening into the prior modernities of Vermeer's century of unprecedented maritime travel and trade and of a deep Chinese aesthetic culture then far in advance of relatively young, crude, upstart Europe.[6] Spanning the centuries from a China at once ancient and modern to Vermeer's early modern Delft to twentieth-century France to a posthuman future is the idea of a work of art that comes into existence by superb craft and may survive its mortal maker.

To examine the ways Proust's historic sense shapes Bergotte's death scene is to experience the *Recherche* as something like an encyclopedic hologram in which, like the glass jars plunged into the waters of the Vivonne, things become transparent to time—the now-stilled time of their making and the moving time flowing through and around them (*ISLT* 1.237). The genesis of this scene about the temporalities of art, and the various chances, choices, circumstances, and events that contributed to its making, are well known (Tadié 744-6, Fraisse 93-5). Proust's diplomat friend Paul Morand wrote that he had insisted that the Dutch organizers include the *View of Delft* in the Paris exhibition of Golden Age Masterpieces so that Marcel could see it again (*Corr.* 20:222-3, letter 114). When the exhibition opened at the Jeu de Paume in April 1921, there it was. On May 1 Proust read the first installment of Jean-Louis Vaudoyer's three-part review of the exhibition, titled "The Mysterious Vermeer," and wrote the critic an admiring letter from the workbed he seldom left.[7] When he first saw the *View of Delft* in the Hague in 1902, he wrote Vaudoyer, "I knew that I had seen the most beautiful painting in the world"; "In *Swann's Way* I couldn't keep myself from having Swann work on a study (*étude*) of Vermeer. . . . And yet I know almost nothing about Vermeer" (*Corr.* 20:226, 117). On May 14, after reading part III, Proust wrote Vaudoyer, "It is marvelous," singling out Vaudoyer's remarks on Vermeer's *The Art of Painting* (fig. 2): "This artist who turns his back so as not to be seen by posterity and who will not know what it thinks of him is an admirably poignant idea. You know that Vermeer is my favorite painter since I was twenty and among other signs of this predilection I had Swann writing a biography (*biographie*) of Vermeer in *Swann's Way* in 1912" (*Corr.* 20:263-4, letter 143; cf. "MV" III 544). (It is no accident that Swann's *étude* becomes a *biographie* at the moment when Vaudoyer evokes for the author of *Contre Sainte-Beuve* a Vermeer who paints himself with face averted, as if to know little or nothing of the artist's life—and Proust confesses he knows "nothing," while Vaudoyer observes that there is almost nothing to know—is to know all that matters.[8]) Some days later he asked Vaudoyer to accompany him to two exhibitions, "Ver Meer et Ingres" (*Corr.* 20: 289-90, letter 157, 18-24 May 1921). Vaudoyer obliged, and these Vermeer fans, artist and critic, stood together before the *View of Delft.*

Fig. 2. Johannes Vermeer, *The Art of Painting,* c. 1662-1668. 120 x 100 cm. Kunsthistorisches Museum, Vienna. Reproduced from Gustave Vanzype, *Jan Vermeer de Delft.* Bruxelles, Paris: G. van Oest, 1908, revised 1921, 1925

Proust had begun fashioning Bergotte's illness some weeks before he visited the exhibition, a year before he wrote "Fin" in his last manuscript book, and eighteen months before his own death while still revising (*Corr.* 20:166, 81, 8 April 1921; Tadié 762-5). After seeing the painting with Vaudoyer, he transmuted this experience into his character's. Bergotte, like Proust, is ill with uraemia and confined to his bed:

> But, a critic having written that in Vermeer's *View of Delft* . . . a little section of yellow wall [*un petit pan de mur jaune*] (which he could not remember) was so well painted that it was, if one looked at it by itself, like a precious Chinese work of art [*comme une précieuse œuvre d'art chinoise*], of a beauty that was sufficient in itself, Bergotte . . . went to the exhibition. . . . At last he came to the Vermeer which he remembered as more striking, more different from anything else he knew, but in which, thanks to the critic's article, he noticed for the first time some small figures in blue, that the sand was pink, and, finally, the precious substance (*la précieuse matière*) of the tiny section of yellow wall. (adapted from *ISLT* 5.244; *ARTP* 3.692)

Much ink has chased the question of which little section of yellow wall Bergotte fixes on "like a child upon a yellow butterfly that it wants to catch." Less attention has been paid to Proust's treatment of the detail that rouses Bergotte from his bed: not the rose-gold sand and figures in blue that he also notices "thanks to the critic" but the yellow wall "so well painted that it was, if one looked at it by itself, like a precious work of Chinese art." Proust's passage credits this detail to "a critic," and after Proust's death Vaudoyer recalled that Proust had been "struck by the passage about the 'little patch of yellow wall'" in his review.[9] Perhaps Vaudoyer did remark it when the two of them viewed the painting together; but in fact the yellow wall that flutters like the butterfly through the scene's text appears only in the *Recherche*, not in the review.[10] In his passage on the *View of Delft*, Vaudoyer writes that Vermeer outdoors was "as faithful as a camera," so that in black-and-white reproduction the painting might seem hardly more striking than "a very good photograph."

> But once one has contemplated the original, the memory (*souvenir*) one keeps of it transfigures any reproduction; and soon a feast of colors, light, and space sweeps through your memory (*mémoire*). You see again (*revoyez*) this stretch of rose-gold sand that takes up the first plane of the canvas, where a woman in a blue apron creates around her, by this blue, a sublime harmony; you see again the dark moored barges; and

these brick houses, painted in a material so precious (*matière si précieuse*), so massive, so full, that if you isolate a small surface of it while forgetting the subject, you believe you have ceramic (*de la céramique*) before your eyes as much as paint. ("MV" II 515)

As Vaudoyer likens Vermeer's brick houses to "precious . . . ceramic," Proust likens a plane of yellow wall to "a precious Chinese work of art." To borrow a term from poker (probably invented in China; Needham et al., 5:1, 131-2), Proust sees Vaudoyer's brick houses and raises him one yellow wall. At the same time, Proust fuses Vaudoyer's ceramic with a later passage in his review: "There is in Vermeer's craft (*métier*) a Chinese patience, an ability to hide the minutiae and work processes that one finds elsewhere only in the paintings, lacquers, and carved stones of the Far East"; by this craft Vermeer's painting makes us "think of things one can touch, like enamel and jade, lacquer and polished wood" ("MV" III 543). In a letter written about a year after their excursion, perhaps while he was at work on this scene, Proust freely echoes Vaudoyer's comparisons of Vermeer's houses to Far Eastern art objects: "I keep the luminous memory of the only morning that I saw once more, when you kindly guided my staggering steps very close to that Vermeer in which the gables of the houses 'are like precious Chinese objects'" (*Corr.* 21:292, letter 209, soon after 17 June 1922).

What to make of the absent, unspecified Chinese treasure to which Proust, inspired by Vaudoyer, compares a famous European painting? Vaudoyer not only invokes no particular Chinese artwork but compares Vermeer's painted houses to ceramic material (*de la céramique*), not even an object; and he further abstracts this "precious" substance into the superb craft metonymically signaled by a "Chinese patience" that hides the labor of production, sensed (almost literally: "things one can touch") in Far Eastern art objects. Proust follows Vaudoyer in comparing Vermeer's "gables" to "'precious Chinese objects'" (letter) and the yellow wall (absent from the review) to "a precious Chinese work of art" (*Recherche*) and in highlighting "the precious *material* of the tiny section of yellow wall" (*la précieuse matière du tout petit pan de mur jaune, ARTP* 3.692) to evoke the technical brilliance before which Bergotte stands dizzy and abashed: "'That's how I ought to have written. . . . My last books are too dry, I ought to have gone over them with a few layers of colour, made my language precious in itself, like this little section of yellow wall'" (*ISLT* 5.244).

How, then, does Chinese art become the epitome of high craft in both Vaudoyer's review and a scene depicting a French novelist gazing at a Dutch masterpiece? Vaudoyer's mention of ceramic, and his attribution of a mysterious craft exclusively to Vermeer's paintings and Chinese art (*"une patience chinoise, une faculté de cacher la minutie et le procédé de travail qu'on ne retrouve que dans les peintures, les lacques et les pierres taillées d'Extrême-Orient"*; "MV" III 543), offer clues to what I am framing as Proust's historicist's China. Associated with the rarest craft, Vaudoyer's "precious . . . ceramic" evokes what was, in Vermeer's time and indeed for more than a millennium, the hidden art of porcelain. Chinese (and later, through them, Korean and Japanese) artisans possessed sole knowledge of this art from the seventh century to the first decade of the eighteenth, when, after long effort, European

Fig. 3. Chicken Head Ewer with incised lotus-petal decoration. H. 38.7 cm. Chinese, Six Dynasties Period, 6th century. Seattle Art Museum, Eugene Fuller Memorial Collection. Photo: Paul Macapia

Fig.4. Hexagonal tea caddies. German, Meissen factory. *from left*: Böttger stoneware, unglazed, c. 1710-15. H. 14 cm. Böttger stoneware with black glaze, unfired enamel, and gilding, c. 1710-15. H. 12.7 cm. Böttger porcelain, c. 1715-20. H. 12.1 cm. Seattle Art Museum, Gift of Martha and Henry Isaacson. Photo: Susan Dirk

craftsmen succeeded in fabricating this elusive "white gold" (figs. 3, 4) (Finlay 62).[11] Indeed, one translator renders Vaudoyer's *précieuse . . . céramique* as "porcelain" (*Selected Letters* 4.381n4). Emerging during the Tang dynasty (618-906 CE) from two thousand years of ceramic and stoneware craftsmanship, porcelain fabrication required rare raw materials, sophisticated formulae, abundant fuel, and advanced high-firing technology and technique; and its makers possessed deep sculptural and decorative traditions and skills. Treasured for their hardness, translucency, impermeability, and beauty, the rare products of this mysterious art became central to Eurasian trade and cultural exchange. Porcelain traveled along the Silk Road to Southwest Asia; after Vasco da Gama discovered a sea route to India, Robert Finlay writes, it became "a truly worldwide commodity," "influencing all ceramic traditions it encountered, from Japan and Java to Egypt and England" and incorporating influences in turn: "For more than a thousand years, porcelain was both the most universally admired and the most widely imitated product in the world" as well as "a prime material vehicle for the assimilation and transmission of artistic symbols, themes, and designs across vast distances" (13, 5-6).

Porcelain reached Europe by the fifteenth century and was coveted by royals, potentates, and humanist scholars as a precious substance "not to be believed," "more exquisite than crystal," for their collections of rare and marvelous things (Hochstrasser 122-24). In the first decade of the seventeenth century, Dutch traders captured two Portuguese ships laden with tens of thousands of porcelains and auctioned them in Amsterdam, launching this modern commodity on the European market (fig. 5).[12] Throughout Vermeer's lifetime, Chinese porcelains were commissioned by Dutch traders for Holland and Europe, and they

Fig. 5. Dish, Jingdezhen Kraak hard paste porcelain with underglaze blue dragon decoration. Chinese, Ming dynasty (1368-1644), c. 1610-1619. Diam. 51.5 cm. Seattle Art Museum, bequest of Joan Louise Applegate Dice. Photo: Paul Macapia

appear in many Dutch Golden Age paintings, such as Vermeer's *Young Woman Reading a Letter at an Open Window* (1657). Vaudoyer's likening of Vermeer's painted surfaces to precious ceramic gestures toward the artist's familiarity with the Chinese porcelain that first circulated in Holland in the seventeenth century: not low-fired pottery but that rare substance produced by an art that was, to Europeans of Vermeer's time, ancient and secret as well as new—its early name (Portuguese *porcellana*, Dutch *porselein*, English *porcelain*) augmented in English by another that identifies it with the faraway place of its fabrication.[13] Two centuries later, Oscar Wilde could still find it "harder and harder every day to live up to my blue china," nor perhaps is it easier now, to judge by the prices Chinese porcelains have fetched in recent auctions.[14]

Proust wrote into Bergotte's death scene not just Vaudoyer's review but the "critic" ("a critic having written"), and it appears that Vaudoyer used "*précieuse . . . de la céramique*" advisedly in associating Vermeer's technical brilliance with "Chinese patience" and the supreme techne of Far Eastern art. Because Vaudoyer's expertise and sensibility color this scene and its making, it is useful to recall that he came from a "dynasty" of eminent Parisian architects whose works, including prestigious state projects, extend over nearly a century (Bergdoll). Jean-Louis declined his vocational patrimony, but "if he was a poet and a novelist," writes Daphné Doublet, "he was, above all, an historian of art" who possessed "a perfect knowledge of aesthetic and technical problems; a knowledge almost inborn, 'in his blood'" (Bergdoll, Préface 6). Vaudoyer put his historical knowledge of aesthetics and techne to versatile use. Besides writing poetry, novels, art criticism, and the libretto for Diaghilev's 1911 ballet *Le spectre de la rose*, he was associated with the Museum of the Decorative Arts in Paris, served as a curator for the Carnavalet Museum of the history of Paris, where the furnishings of Proust's cork-lined room were later enshrined, and administered the Comédie Française during the German occupation.

Vaudoyer's extensive historical knowledge of art, materials and techniques, and aesthetics would surely have extended to porcelain. In 1921 the Cernuschi Asian Art and Guimet museums were in their third decade.[15] In 1894 and 1911 Ernest Grandidier (1833-1912) donated to the Louvre his "magnificent collection" of six thousand Chinese ceramics, "one of the most complete in Europe"

(Desroches); and in 1894 he published a monograph with sections on porcelain's origins and history and on the materials and techniques of its fabrication. Grandidier—whose early grasp of the importance of Chinese porcelains leads the Guimet's current porcelain curator to describe him as an explorer and inventor as well as a connoisseur and collector—recounts the transport of Chinese porcelains to the Arabian peninsula and Egypt from the ninth century on; Marco Polo's reports of porcelain in 1295; the longstanding Levantine and Oriental trade of Venice, Florence, Barcelona and France; the porcelain gifts received by Charles VII of France and Lorenzo de Medici in the fifteenth century; the importation of Chinese porcelain by the Portuguese in the sixteenth century; and the seventeenth-century VOC trade that disseminated Chinese porcelains in European countries (Grandidier 1-28, 231-2). Nor could a French expert in the decorative arts have been unaware of European rulers' race to emulate porcelain, won in 1709 by Augustus the Strong, King of Poland and Elector of Saxony; the subsequent rise of a vigorous European porcelain industry; and the chinamania ignited by Louis XIV, "imitator of the kings of Asia," who commissioned the Trianon de Porcelaine and filled Versailles with priceless porcelains, including fourteen hundred Kangxi pieces presented by Siamese ambassadors (Finlay 211-12).

Vaudoyer, in short, would have possessed at least a general awareness of the facts Timothy Brook marshals to detail the influence of the Dutch China trade on Vermeer's paintings.[16] The Dutch Golden Age was launched when the Dutch commandeered two Portuguese ships full of Chinese porcelains in 1602 and 1604, sold the cargo on the European market (whereas the Portuguese had traded porcelain mainly in the Far and Middle East), founded the VOC, and controlled the European China trade for the next century through its four Chambers—one located in Delft, its long red warehouse roof visible in the *View of Delft* (14-15). In seventeenth-century Europe, porcelain remained a miraculous substance with the prestige of gold and silver, a scarce luxury, a sign of wealth and status (though the Chinese reserved their finest wares and considered their export porcelain second-rate). As Julie Emerson notes, the Chinese blue-and-white porcelains depicted in many Dutch Golden Age paintings evolved through the early Ming dynasty's Persia trade, as China's porcelain technology converged with Persian-mined cobalt ore and Persia's soft-paste ceramic traditions to produce Chinese-fabricated porcelain vessels, larger than those customary in China to accommodate Persian communal dining customs, featuring Persian-influenced designs (fig. 6) (Emerson et al. chaps. 5, 8, 9).[17]

Fig. 6. Dish, Jingdezhen porcelain with underglaze cobalt blue decoration. Chinese, Yuan dynasty, 14th century. Diam. 47.6 cm. Seattle Art Museum. Purchased in memory of Elizabeth M. Fuller with funds from the Elizabeth M. Fuller Memorial Fund and the Edwin W. and Catherine M. Davis Foundation, St. Paul, Minnesota. Photo: Paul Macapia

The VOC imported millions of Chinese blue-and-white pieces over the next decades, bringing vast wealth and luxury goods (such as the oriental carpet, pearls, and gold of Vermeer's paintings) to Holland and Europe (Volker 227); these porcelains inspired the low-fired tin-glazed Delft Blue ware that local potters began making after the emperor Wan Li's death in 1619 disrupted the China trade (fig. 7) (Caiger-Smith 129). If, as seems likely, Vaudoyer was aware that the Chinese porcelains of Vermeer's time were precious (some worth their weight in gold) and inimitable—the art of fabricating them being then mysterious and secret—his "precious ceramic" evokes a historical world in which a profound, technically advanced aesthetic tradition entered Delft through the China trade and inspired its potters and painters in both high craft and iconographic detail[18]—not least Vermeer, who, with house painters, decorators, glass engravers, stained-glass workers, glaziers, potters, embroiderers, carpet weavers, sculptors, engravers, booksellers, printers, art dealers, and other artists, formed the Delft artisans' Guild of St. Luke (Montias, *Vermeer*).

Fig. 7. Delft Blue Ware. 18th century. Ernest Cognacq Museum, Saint Martin de Ré,
Ile de Ré, France. Photo: Ernest Cognacq Museum

Proust already knew something about Chinese art when
Vaudoyer's esteem for Far Eastern techne in the context of Vermeer
sparked his imagination. In *Within a Budding Grove,* the Narrator
sells a fine Chinese porcelain vase, with the intent to lavish flowers
on Gilberte, and receives from a dealer not the thousand francs he
expects but ten thousand. Later, he sees in memory his great-aunt
Léonie's "magnificent" collection of old porcelain, to which this vase
once belonged, shining like "a multi-colored inset" in grey, rustic
Combray just as Indian buttercups and Persian lilacs glow before
its train station, stained glass windows in its somber St. Hilaire, and
magic lantern images in his darkened room in aunt Léonie's house
(*ISLT* 2.272, cf. 2.661, 6.7; *ARTP* 2.258, 1465). Still, Vaudoyer may
have furthered the evolution of such superficial and indirect aesthetic
appreciation on the Narrator's part, mediated by desire, money, and
memory, into the historically grounded references of the later books.
Hertel notes that Vaudoyer's Orient developed over time from one of
sensual fantasy to one historically superior in aesthetic tradition and
technique. In 1911 Vaudoyer characterized Fragonard's orientalism as

"the enjoyment of sensuality and freedom"; in 1921 his focus is craft: "The notion that whatever smallest detail one singles out in a Vermeer painting, one might 'imagine oneself before a glass case enclosing the most precious and most singular knick-knack [*bibelot*].' The theme of the precious, glazed and polished Far Eastern art object functions here as the real analogue of Vermeer's techniques and colors" (105-6). Situating Vaudoyer's orientalist rhetoric among various European orientalisms that played a part in Vermeer's painting and reception, Hertel finds an early moment in this historicist turn in a 1913 monograph by the American luminist painter Philip Hale, who sees past Thoré's iconography ("a Turkish rug . . . a Japanese blue bowl . . . hair in Chinese style"') to Vermeer's cosmopolitan clientele, who "had adventured in the India trade," "tasted every form of aesthetic enjoyment," "could go to war over a few precious tulips," and were "great collectors of rich wares from China and from Japan" (Hertel 99, citing Hale).

Not unlike Vaudoyer's Orient, Proust's China evolves from Odette's sensualist décor in the house where Swann talks about his work on Vermeer, and from the Narrator's painterly memories of glowing porcelains in dim Combray, to the historical allusions of Bergotte's death scene and later moments in *The Captive* and *Time Regained*—for example, the Baron de Charlus's wartime anecdote about Augustus II, the great collector of Far Eastern porcelain under whose mandate the first European porcelain was made and the Meissen factory established at Dresden (*ISLT* 6.151). Soon after Bergotte's death scene, the Baron asks the Narrator whether he is working as they enter the Verdurins' hall one evening. No, he replies, but at the moment he is very interested in "old dinner services of silver and porcelain" (*ISLT* 5.299, *ARTP* 3.731). The Baron—who shares a connoisseur's and collector's interest in Far Eastern porcelain with his historical model the illustrious Comte Robert de Montesquiou-Ferenzac—assures him that none more beautiful than the Verdurins' exist and offers to have them show him their treasures, inconvenient though that might be on the evening of their party.[19] The Narrator declines—"I begged him to do nothing of the sort"—and a deleted passage just here marks the divergence of the Narrator's newly acquired discrimination from the Baron's:

I didn't dare tell him that what could interest me was not the mediocre services of the richest bourgeois silver but at the least that of Mme du Barry. I was much too preoccupied—and had I not been, when I was in society I was much too distracted and agitated to fix my attention on more or less pretty objects. This could be captured only by the call of some reality addressing itself to my imagination, for example, some beautiful view of this Venice of which I had thought so much. (*ARTP* 3.1747, my translation)

Time Regained displays the fruits of what it proves to have been Proust's as well as the Narrator's researches into old porcelain and silver à la Mme du Barry in the pastiche of the Goncourt journals, which the Narrator reads while visiting Gilberte at Tansonville. Together with the Narrator's musings on it, the "journal" elaborates on the canceled passage. In a description of the same dinner party, those "more or less pretty objects" call the enraptured diarist to a reality unheeded by the Narrator[20]:

an extraordinary cavalcade of plates which are nothing less than masterpieces of the porcelainist's art, whose artistic chatter, during an exquisite meal, the amateur's titillated attention hears most contentedly—Yung-Tsching plates with nasturtium-coloured borders and purple-blue irises, leafless and tumid, and those supremely decorative flights of kingfishers and cranes trailing across a dawn sky . . . Saxe [Meissen] plates, daintier and of more graceful workmanship, with drowsy, bloodless roses fading into violet, with ragged-edged tulips the color of wine-lees, with the rococo elegance of a pink or a forget-me-not—Sèvres plates meshed with the close guilloche of their white fluting, whorled in gold, or knotted with a golden ribbon that stands in gallant relief upon the creamy smoothness of the paste—finally a whole service of silver plate arabesqued with those myrtles of Luciennes that were not unknown to the du Barry. . . .[and] a marvelous Tching-Hon platter streaked with the purple rays of a sun setting on a sea whereon sails a droll flotilla of crayfish, their spiky stippling rendered with such extraordinary skill that they seem to have been moulded from living shells, with a border made of a little Chinese boy who plays on his rod and line a fish whose silver and azure belly makes it a wonder of iridescent colour. (adapted from *ISLT* 6.30-1, cf. *ARTP* 4.289-90)[21]

Writing about a Verdurin party like those the Narrator has described, the "Goncourt" diarist may seem to join his hosts and other invitees as unwitting guests of Proustian satire.[22] No doubt Proust is having fun, yet matters are not so simple. As that gifted mimic explained, he sought by "voluntary pastiche" to purge himself of "involuntary pastiche"; to sign the Goncourt name to the signature Goncourt prose exuded by his inner Goncourt, the better to write as "Proust"—or the distinctive *"je"* of the writer/narrator—outside quotation marks (*Corr.* 18:380, letter 213, August 1919; Proust, *Chroniques*, cited by Milly 37).[23] As the ghostwritten "Goncourt" diarist appreciates, the Verdurins' porcelains are technically dazzling, precious, and rare[24] while the silver adorned with Luciennes myrtles might have brought Madam du Barry a madeleine-like blast from the past (*ARTP* 4.1193n2; Davy 68-80 esp. 73; Saint-André; Tallandier). Like the Sansovino well-head that now ("regrettably") receives the guests' cigar ashes, these enduring treasures, mute yet eloquent, highlight the shifting conditions and values of their original and new surroundings, as when the diarist remarks to his host what an exquisite pleasure it must be for him to consume a choice repast from "a collection such as no prince today possesses in his show cases" and records Mme Verdurin's melancholy interjection that her eccentric spouse would be happier drinking cider on a Normandy farm (*ISLT* 6.31-2).

Though the Narrator does not count his interest in old porcelain as "work" (*ISLT* 5.299), Proust seems to have done a little swotting up of Chinese porcelain and the Dutch-French-China trade, possibly after his 1921 exchange with Vaudoyer. Tadié dates the Goncourt pastiche from 1917-8 (665); but, as neither of two extant sketches of the pastiche in the Pléiade edition fully describes the Verdurins' porcelains, a later date may be possible for these passages.[25] The first sketch dwells on the now fire-blackened pearls purchased from Mme de La Fayette's descendant and refers to Sèvres figurines. The second sketch breaks off and resumes as the diarist spies the sign of the "Little Dunkirk" shop, a Parisian relic of seventeenth and eighteenth century Dunkirk, where Far Eastern treasures raided from Dutch ships were "cheapened" and sold, as attested by rare old engraved invoices of Louis XV "with a headpiece representing a billowy sea laden with vessels" (*ISLT* 6.28-9). It then introduces the "porcelain masterpieces" passage, where the Yung-Tsching plates first appear (resembling an export *famille rose* plate that Proust might have seen in the Grandidier collection then in the Louvre, its nasturtium-colored border encircling a blue iris if not yet "leafless" at least bearing a caterpillar[26]), followed by the Meissen and Sèvres. The second sketch then breaks again (just before the butter in the sauce for the brill), leaving a lacuna eventually filled by the "especially esoteric" "Tching-Hon" (tchi-hong, chi-hung, jihong) platter, its glaze recherché enough to emulate the Goncourts' terms of art and indeed to have gone missing in two English translations.[27] As for those spiny, stippled crayfish encircled by a little boy fishing, they may derive from descriptions of the exceedingly rare Xuande chi-hung wares in the *Tao Shuo*: "white porcelain decorated with red fishes," examples of which are said to be "few and far between" inside China and hardly known in the west.[28] Notwithstanding Proust's passion for precise detail and his eminent collector-friends, it seems doubtful, given the extreme rarity of authentic Tching-Hon porcelains, that this platter with its exuberant iconography corresponds to an actual object. Perhaps, laying color upon color like Bergotte's Vermeer, the Proust in the diarist's inkpot is an improvisatory porcelain painter as well as a voluntary pasticheur, projecting from his research trompe l'oeil crayfish in this most exotic and mysterious of glazes.

As Jean Milly points out, the *Recherche*, almost fully achieved by this point, opposes its vast mass to the diarist's arty antiquarianism; and, though the Narrator has yet to write the book that contains him, both the pastiche and his reflections on reading it advance him toward its conception. In their note on the text of *Le Temps Retrouvé*, Pierre-Louis Rey and Brian Rogers suggest that the pastiche (which some find more Goncourtlike than the Goncourts, the faked original of their parody) evokes a novel different from the one we are reading, one that Proust "perhaps dreamt of writing," of which this fragment presents itself to his hero (*ARTP* 4.1174)—one in some ways enough like his own to require this casting-off. The ghostwriting Proust is obviously the source of the diarist's historical minutiae, a fact that the genre of the pastiche avows before it disavows. Is it a case of "dual personality"

(*ISLT* 6.36f), as we are led to suspect when, tongue in cheek, it mirrors the redoubled and thrown authorial voice that constitutes it in Dr Cottard's patient, who, "while he behaves most respectably in the first life, has more than once been arrested for thefts committed in the second, in which he is . . . an abominable scoundrel" (*ISLT* 6.37; Link-Heer)?

It is not simply that the diarist is a material boy and "Proust" is not. Who after all dreams up these porcelains whose chatter pleases the connoisseur's ear better than the guests', this Tching-Hon platter no prince can boast? It is more a matter of what is to be gained by "hiding the minutiae and work processes," the quality Vaudoyer found in Far Eastern art and Vermeer. Though the diarist, faithful to "the exterior," captures in unfiltered detail the company's Venice-in-Paris setting, exquisite repast on precious plates, and conversation, much of what he brings home from the party—Madam Verdurin as the unacknowledged genius behind Elstir/Whistler's still lifes and portraits; whether Napoleon's books now in the Duc de Guermantes's library are tobacco- or liquorice-stained—amounts to trivial pursuits (*ARTP* 4.750). This "manifest naïvety" rouses the Narrator's anti-Sainte-Beuve "objections to literature," yet it also makes him feel, first, that he cannot see; then, that he can in his way, as singular as the Goncourts'. The diarist's account makes the Narrator long to see again everything he records, everything he might have seen himself had he not been so "blind" as to find the guests "commonplace," "insipid," full of "vulgarities": "Goncourt knew how to listen, just as he knew how to see; I did not" (*ISLT* 6.38-9, 43). On the other hand, it's not that he sees nothing: though "the apparent, copiable charm of things and people escaped me . . . I was like a surgeon . . . . If I went to a dinner-party I did not see the guests: when I thought I was looking at them, I was X-raying them," seeking like a "geometer" the "essences" situated "behind actual appearances" (adapted from *ISLT* 6.39-40, *ARTP* 4.296-7).

In mid-June 1922 Proust wrote Vaudoyer that he was studying the black-and-white reproductions in Gustave Vanzype's *Jan Vermeer de Delft*, which Vaudoyer's review had cited so that it intercedes between the painting and his readers in an oddly Proustian way. Vaudoyer, we remember, describes not the *View of Delft* then hanging in Paris for his readers to behold but the way "one's memory (*souvenir*)" of it, once one has seen the original, "transfigures any reproduction" by "a feast of colors, light, and space that sweeps through your memory (*mémoire*)," making you "see again" (*revoyer*) the rose-gold sand, blue apron, dark barges, and brick houses that look like (absent) precious ceramic. Not the painting but a photograph; not a photograph but a memory; not an object but a substance; not that substance but a simile; not your actual eyes but your mind's eye: the painting is, and is like, a material object, a made thing, a "world" that both exists and persists in immaterial memory, in the absence of the object. The bedridden artist (Proust, Bergotte) exerts himself to see it "again" because his memory fails to perform the chromo-photographic feat Vaudoyer describes: he goes to the exhibition so that he can "see it again" in memory as vividly as Vaudoyer says "you" do—as if what he is after is not the painting as object but an impression or memory that he can really "see" only in the absence of the thing that inspired it.

In perusing Vanzype's reproductions, Proust was tracking "identical incidental details in different paintings" (*Corr.* 21:292, letter 209, shortly after 17 June 1922) to develop Bergotte's death scene. Late in *The Captive* the Narrator describes "the Vermeers" to Albertine (who earlier takes them to be living people) as "fragments of an identical world . . . it's always . . . the same table, the same carpet, the same woman, the same novel and unique beauty, an enigma . . . if one doesn't try to relate it all through subject matter but to isolate that distinctive impression produced by the colour" (*ISLT* 5.508). For the Narrator, these always identical details betoken the "world" that the artist illuminates beyond the frame, whether of one painting or all: both that singular way of seeing and that historical, quasi-documentary world in which the identical table in this and that painting once corresponded to a material object. In this light, the exquisitely painted yellow wall comes into focus not as the fetish it can easily seem but as exemplary of the luminous details of a never completed whole—never completed not only because the artist's death (Vermeer's, Bergotte's, Proust's) interrupts it but because those "fragments of an identical world," that "distinctive impression produced by the colour," can only suggest it.[29] Techne, the craft ("style for the writer . . . colour for the painter," *ISLT* 6.299) that imbues a detail with "a beauty sufficient in itself," overrides formal completeness and perfection (cf. Staten 422). In light of this sufficiency of the well-crafted detail or fragment, the *Recherche* appears not more "the meaningful whole which is the *work*" than "that hole-filled meaning which is the *text*" (Weber 919): an enigmatic whole, a hologram impossible without holes, the dark spaces that set off Vermeer's signature yellow, an absent Chinese artwork, a figurative yellow butterfly.[30]

The counterpoetics articulated through the Narrator's reading of the "diary" extends from the genetic origins of the *Recherche* in *Contre Sainte-Beuve* (1908-1909) to the very late scene of Bergotte's death (inserted in *The Captive*'s third typescript), which conjures a deep but finite history of artists who labor in obscurity, with "Chinese patience," to net the yellow butterfly in clay, fire, paint, ink, words. As we noted, after Proust reads Vaudoyer on *The Art of Painting*, Swann's study of Vermeer becomes retroactively a biography—or more properly an anti-biography, a practical corollary of his anti-Sainte-Beuve poetics. Bergotte's death in a museum, where works of art cross from private commission, creation, and enjoyment into public space and history, signals the precarious fate of a work of art once it leaves—or survives —its maker. (The *View of Delft* was the first Vermeer to enter a public collection, in 1822; Nash 6, 11). In contemplating not a reproduction in a private space but the actual, unique painting at an actual public exhibition, Bergotte not only contributes to the painting's reception almost as if he were not a fiction but highlights the different modes of "presence" of Proust, the fictional Bergotte, and "Vermeer" at the exhibition and in its historical record and cultural memory. In the museum where the literary lion Bergotte ponders the momentous question of an artist's life after death, the "mysterious" Vermeer remains almost as obscure as the unknown Chinese artisan to whose precious, lasting handiwork a critic compares his yellow wall.

Bergotte's death scene stages from various angles the artist's imponderable translation of organic life into a work of art that captures its maker's flowing life in material form and carries it on in time. Like the reluctantly dying Bergotte, the Narrator meditates on the arduous submission to craft by which the artisan, epitomized in Vermeer, transforms the materials of a given métier into a made thing whose fineness, strength and beauty endow its power to endure, whether for days and years or for decades, centuries, millennia. As the *View of Delft* confronts Bergotte with the demands craft makes on a brief human life, he voices resistance to life's finitude, its shocking vulnerability to time and death: "'I shouldn't like to be the headline news of this exhibition for the evening papers,'" he thinks just before he pitches off the settee (*ISLT* 5.245). In his dying apprehension of his own work's mediocrity beside the eternal freshness of Vermeer's, Bergotte glimpses another temporality, that of a made thing that may survive its maker as Vermeer's paintings and Chinese porcelains, lacquers, carved stones so spectacularly outlast theirs.

If Bergotte is not "Dead for ever," the Narrator remarks, that is not because the "soul" survives death but because, as an artist unaccountably obeying "unknown laws," he will prove to have succeeded in transmuting organic life into enduring art[31]:

> All that we can say is that everything is arranged in this life as though we entered it carrying a burden of obligations contracted in a former life; there is no reason inherent in the conditions of life on this earth that can make . . . an atheist artist consider himself obliged to begin over again a score of times a piece of work the admiration aroused by which will matter little to his worm-eaten body, like the patch of yellow wall painted with so much skill and refinement by an artist destined to be for ever unknown and barely identified under the name Vermeer. (*ISLT* 5.245-6)

The yellow wall that catches the light centuries after the hand that made it has been eaten by worms is not just a material thing but a precious substance, like earth fired into porcelain. It is "Vermeer," a trace of the painter's actual life, his labor in time and the event of its making: painting as participle (Arasse, *Le Détail* esp. 158-60). Proust, facing death with his book unfinished, composes a triangulated mirror scene: an artist who, though personally obscure and ostensibly "dead," remains as alive as the unknown Chinese artisan, more alive than the dying writer gazing at a still-living painting; an invisible third, he likewise pours his living, writing, and dying into a work of life-become-art, laying color on color in a race with mortal time while defending his precise detail to a reviewer who preferred Saint-Simon's "more 'summary'" method (fig. 8) (*Letters* 445-46, 17 June 1921).

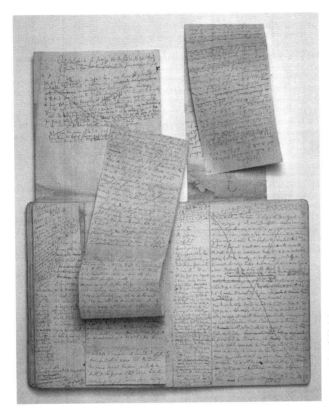

Fig. 8. Paperoles from the workshop of Marcel Proust. Bibliothèque nationale de France, Paris

Proust's invocation of an absent, precious Chinese artwork is more precise than it may at first appear, for its historical character resonates in the rich material surround of Vermeer's paintings and as an emanation of China's long history of supreme techne. Bergotte's anxious glimpse of the enduring life of Vermeer's art occasions a longer view in a final invocation of the painter, added in the margin of the manuscript of *Time Regained*: "Thanks to art, instead of seeing one world . . . we have . . . as many worlds as there are original artists, worlds which, centuries after the extinction of the fire from which their light first emanated, whether it is called Rembrandt or Vermeer, send us still each one its special radiance" (*ISLT* 6.299, *ARTP* 4.474 & 1267). Like the Chinese porcelains in dim Combray, these luminous worlds radiate in cosmic time, even conceivably outlasting the human species on which their legibility depends.[32] In another very late addition in this book's fifteen-year compositional history (Winton 1:115n1, 316-17; Tadié 770-777), Proust extends the Chinese and Vermeerean temporalities of Bergotte's death scene into still vaster cosmic time, imagining the aging Bergotte

> growing steadily colder, a tiny planet offering a prophetic image of the greater, when gradually heat will withdraw from the earth, then life itself. Then his resurrection will have come to an end, for, however far forward into future generations the works of men may shine, there must none the less be men. . . . if we suppose Bergotte's fame to have lasted until then, suddenly it will be extinguished for all time. (*ISLT* 5.240, *ARTP* 3.689, 1738-9)

This posthuman time contains, like Chinese boxes, the scene's scaled temporalities: China's deep artisanal time, Vermeer's early modern time, Bergotte's hoped-for life-in-art, figured by his open pages like angel wings keeping vigil in lighted shopwindows; the many temporalities of the *Recherche*, from its maker's lived and remembered life transmuted into a book and held in the dimensionless spacetime of the mind's eye to narrative, historicist, and physical or natural time. Framing Bergotte's doubtful reckoning of his life's work and its possible future within a cosmic time that precedes human origins and supersedes the human future in the apocalypse rendered imaginable by scientific modernity, the scene's play of epochs and temporalities participates in the twentieth century's "new" historic sense and the turbulent history of global modernities that at once challenges, eludes, and complicates heuristic period boundaries, as it animates the making, the it, the new, and the day in a Chinese emperor's (r. 1675-1646 BCE) modernist motto: MAKE IT NEW . . . Day by day make it new.[33]

Notes

1. Proust, *In Search of Lost Time,* hereafter cited as *ISLT,* 1.363, 597, 310-13. See Schwartz 105-7, Fraisse, and Fuss 165-7, 244n.

2. Fraisse, 13-4, 25n31, cites Proust's letter asking "do you know the little Japanese (or Chinese? which?) game that consists in putting little papers into water, which then unfold, becoming people, etc. Can you inquire of your Japanese acquaintants what it's called, but above all if it is sometimes done with tea, if it is done in either

cold or hot water, and if the most complex versions of it can have houses, trees, people, and such" (*Correspondance*, hereafter *Corr.*; 10.321 & n12; cf. Hokenson 33, Joyce 628, Woolf 83). The antiquarian Swann would have known that tea, like coffee and chocolate, was introduced to Europe's elites in the seventeenth century; the harbor scenes painted on many porcelain services mark this exotic origin. Odette emulates French aristocrats' emulation of Far Eastern luxury.

3. "Tradition and the Individual Talent," published just after the Great War, specifies "tradition" as European; *The Waste Land* (1922) with its Sanskrit echoes enlarges its expanse, in parallel with Pound's long engagement with Japanese and Chinese art, thought, and literature.

4. See *À la recherche du temps perdu*, hereafter *ARTP*, 4.687f, 1737-40. Winton notes that "the account of Bergotte's death . . . [is] not in the MS" of *La Prisonnière/ The Captive* (1:44-45, 321) and that the passage on Bergotte's cooling life ("*Il allait ainsi se refroidissant . . .Alors la résurrection aura pris fin*") may have been added very late: "more apocalyptic than any is that part of the long insertion on Bergotte's death which likens his illness to the ultimate extinction of Earth; these lines may have come at an even later stage than the bulk of the addition" (1:115n1, 316-17).

5. Brook points out geographical features common to seventeenth-century Delft, which the Dutch built below sea level and whose name derives from Dutch *delven* (digging), and Shanghai, "which could be translated On the Ocean" and is a shortened form of "Shanghaibang, Upper Ocean Sluice"; both are built on bogland that was once undersea and depend on sluices for drainage. Both were walled cities "crisscrossed with canals and bridges," with direct sea access; both anchored artisanal networks within an agricultural economy; both had upper-class cultures of art patronage and consumption; and in Shanghai was born Vermeer's near-contemporary Dong Qichang (1555-1636), "the greatest painter and calligrapher of his age," who "laid the foundations of modern Chinese art" (2, 5-6) and whose style influenced later Ming (1368–1644) porcelain. Jingdezhen, Jiangzi Province, was long the world capital of porcelain, having produced high-fired wares since the Tang dynasty (618-906 CE), a breakthrough prepared by a two-thousand-year development of firing technique. Jingdezhen supplied the porcelain exported to Europe in the seventeenth century.

6. Diamond notes that until 1450 science and technology flowed into Europe mainly from the eastern Mediterranean, Fertile Crescent, and China, which was "technologically much more innovative and advanced than Europe, even more so than medieval Islam," having already invented "canal lock gates, cast iron,

deep drilling, efficient animal harnesses, gunpowder, kites, magnetic compasses, movable type, paper, porcelain, printing . . ., sternpost rudders, and wheelbarrows. . . . [T]echnology was less advanced in western Europe than in any other 'civilized' area of the Old World until the late Middle Ages" (253, cf. 409f).

7. Arasse translates Vaudoyer's review, a "crucial document in [Vermeer's] critical fortunes" (*Vermeer: Faith* 87-97). Proust "already admired" Vaudoyer's "appreciation of Vermeer" in 1910 (Tadié 145, 893n159; *Corr.* 10:163).

8. Swann's project is called an *étude* (*ARTP* 1.195, 236, 347-8), an *essai* (1.293), and one of his *travaux* (1.460); it is never a *biographie*, and when Odette essays a biographical approach, Swann replies that nothing is known about Vermeer (1.237). *Contre Sainte-Beuve*, the signal point of departure for the *Recherche*, was written in 1908-1909 and published posthumously in 1954.

9. Tadié quotes Vaudoyer's letter to Jacques Rivière of 9 January 1923, which recalls his visit to the exhibition with Proust (745-6 & 924n78). That Proust mentions only this detail ("the gables of the houses 'are like precious Chinese objects'") in his letter to Vaudoyer of mid-June 1922 suggests that Vaudoyer may have expanded on the Chinese connection in their conversation (*Corr.* 21:292, letter 209).

10. Variants of the phrase *petit pan de mur jaune* occur eight times in the paragraph recounting Bergotte's death. See also the section on the phrase at Essential Vermeer.

11. Chinese ceramic tradition does not distinguish high-fired stoneware from porcelain, both fired at temperatures above 1350° C; it classes both as high-fired *ci*, in contrast to low-fired *tao* (Emerson et alia 15). According to Needham, Kerr, and Wood, the earliest known ceramics (ca. 24,000 BCE) were found at the Dolni Vestonice site near Brno (5:12, 119, 379n1). Pottery some 17,500-18,300 years old has been found in southern China (Boaretto et al.). Finlay notes that "Koreans made porcelain from the ninth century and Japanese from the early seventeenth; yet this was done under Chinese tutelage, wholly dependent on more than two millennia of Chinese craft expertise and technology" (9). The first European porcelain was fabricated by Ehrenfried Walther von Tschirnhaus and erstwhile alchemist Johann Friedrich Böttger for Augustus II of Poland and Saxony (Emerson et al., chap. 2, "Europe's First Porcelain," esp. 28).

12. The Dutch referred to Chinese export wares as "kraak" porcelain after the Portuguese carracks (from Spanish and Portuguese *carraca*, ship) from which they were seized.

13. The clay for Jingdezhen porcelain was mined from nearby Mount Gaoling southwest of Hangzhou, from which "kaolin" derives. With ample sources of kaolin and fine-grained porcelain stone, Jingdezhen remained the global capital of porcelain production from ancient times until the eighteenth century and is still a world center. The *OED* notes early usage of *china*: 1579 *Drake's Voy.* in Hakluyt (1600) III. 736 Fine China-dishes of white earth . . . 1598 FLORIO, *Porcellana*.. whereof they make China dishes, called Porcellan dishes. 1603 SHAKES. *Meas. for M.* II. i. 97 They are not China-dishes, but very good dishes. 1646 SIR T. BROWNE *Pseud. Ep.* II. v. §7 We are not thoroughly resolved concerning Porcellane or China dishes, that according to common belief they are made of Earth.

14. A very rare double-walled Qing dynasty Qianlong (1736-95) porcelain vase, a technical tour de force, was auctioned in England for £51,600,000 in November 2010—then a record for Chinese art and the eleventh highest price paid for an artwork at auction www.cbsnews.com/stories/2010/11/12/world/ main7046950.shtml 1 December 2010. In July 2005 a Yuan dynasty (1271-1368, Mongol emperor Kublai Khan) Gui Gu Zi blue and white porcelain jar brought £15.688 million at auction in London; http://www.china-99.com/Chinese_ technology/2010/0521/3491.html 13 January 2010.

15. Emile Guimet first exhibited his Asian art collection in Lyon in 1879 and opened the Paris museum in 1889 (www.guimet.fr/History-of-the-museum 7 December 2010). Henri Cernuschi's Asian arts museum opened in 1898; some 2500 of its 10,000 objects are ceramics (Engel et al. 8; Béguin et al. 11). Vasselot and Ballot's bibliography lists 34 monographs on Asian art and ceramics published from 1856 to 1921 in Shanghai, Paris, London, Berlin, Leipzig, New York, and Chicago.

16. Brook shows how the oriental rugs, porcelain bowl, pearls, coins, and other objects depicted in Vermeer's paintings map Dutch Golden Age trade by the distances they have traveled. Vaudoyer mentions the "famous geographical map" depicted in several of Vermeer's paintings ("MV" III 544). See also Liedke; and Alpers, chap. 4 & epilogue.

17. Cobalt has been detected in Egyptian sculpture and Persian jewelry of the third millennium BCE, in Pompeii (destroyed CE 79), and in Tang (618–907) and Ming (1368–1644) dynasty China, though no Tang influence has been found in Ming blue-and-white.

18. The Chinese export blue-and-white dish in Vermeer's *Young Woman Reading a Letter* is a *klapmutz* (Brook 77). As for precious ceramic "substance," Smith

notes the special archaeological and historical value of ceramics, since pottery is easily broken, and potshards are not usually transported far from the site of their destruction, nor can they be melted down and recast: "The material itself was virtually indestructible and could not be reused. Different places made pottery in their own ways, and styles and decorative fashions changed over time. Also, various types of clay contained elements from different places, all of which give archaeologists a good idea of when and where a piece originated" (8). Ongoing excavations of Song kiln sites in China "confirm that many similar wares originated from widely distributed kilns and that many large kiln complexes produced more than one type of ware"(*Deft Hands Discerning Eyes* 1).

19. In the records of Montesquiou's collection, "Chinese objects are represented by Tang and Yuan enameled ceramics, large round porcelain vases, cloisonnés, enameled Ming porcelains, Kangxi *familles verte* and *rose* vases, and seventeenth-century porcelains" (Bertrand 1:131, citing Bibliothêque nationale MS Nafr. 15289). Schwartz notes, "As one might expect of a friend of Montesquiou, Proust's books often give evidence of a real interest in Far Eastern things" (106 & n1).

20. On the Goncourts as representatives of "the artistic conception of reality," see Milly 26, 43-45.

21. This translation substitutes "crayfish" (*langoustes*) for the translators' "lobsters"; restores Proust's period transliteration of *Yung-Tsching* (Yongzheng, 1723-1735) for Yung-cheng (*ISLT*); and restores *Tching-Hon*, which *ISLT* omits and for which *Finding Time Again* repeats "Yung-Chêng" (18).

22. On the mutual influence of Chinese and European design traditions in eighteenth-century porcelain, see Emerson et al., esp. chaps. 12-16; and Finlay, esp. 277-82, 300-5. Finlay notes that western chinoiserie designs reduced "Chinese visual culture to stereotyped constituents, thereby rendering it picturesque and accessible rather than potent and enigmatic," while Chinese potters mirrored Western fantasies of China on export porcelain; this "immense simplification" produced "new decorative patterns with international currency. The world grew closer together through mutual misunderstanding" (301).

23. In a note to himself about the placement of some material before the first sketch, Proust identifies with the Narrator: "Perhaps right before Goncourt when I (*je*) open the volume to say" [or: to read? *lire* for *dire*?] (*ARTP* 4.750).

24. On Yongzhen period *famille rose* porcelain with its "new painterly effects," see Emerson et al. 127-32 and 245 fig. 1. In 2010 a Yongzhen red imperial vase was

appraised at \$30,000-50,000 (www.pbs.org/wgbh/roadshow/archive/201003A46. html 17 January 2011). The diarist's Tching Hon platter recalls the platter of seafood that reminds the Narrator of "a ceramic dish of Bernard Palissy" (*ISLT* 3.152).

25. See *ARTP* 4.750-61; cf. 1.clxi-clxii, 4.1168f, 1176-7 on Cahiers 55 and 74. Tadié notes that Proust did considerable work on *The Captive* and *Time Regained* during his last eighteen months. On 8 April 1921, a few weeks before reading Vaudoyer's review, he announced *The Captive* "all ready"; but he revised it heavily into 1922 (after mentioning its ending in October 1921) and hired a typist for it in February 1922. That May he chose its title, *La Prisonnière*. In early November he pronounced it "ready but needs to be reread"; at his death on November 18, he "had reached page 136 of the third typescript," into which he had inserted the scene of Bergotte's death, revised from notes in Cahier 62. "The length of *La Prisonnière* and of Albertine shows how much Proust wrote in 1922" (743, 756-7 & passim).

26. *Plat à décor floral*, Chine, Jiangxi, Jingdezhen, Qing, Yongzheng ou Qianlong c. 1725-1740, Porcelaine Famille rose, 22.5 cm, G43 www.guimet-grandidier.fr/ html/4/index/index.htm 21 January 2011.

27. Tching-Hon: "a matter not of an emperor but of an especially esoteric ceramic, 'sacrificial red,' called Tchi-Hong" (*ARTP*4.1194n6). Bushell's translation of the *T'ao Shuo* describes "*Sacrificial Red (Chi hung)* cups . . . glazed with red precious stones from the West reduced to powder" and other "cups decorated with a cinnabar-red glaze. . . . If the glaze was laid on very thickly, it rose in tubercles like the skin of an orange" (71). The "deep red (chi hung) glaze" was made from "a silicate of copper, the base of the sang de boeuf, 'peach-bloom,' and other monochrome glazes so highly appreciated by collectors"; *chi* originally meant "'sacrificial' and referred to the colour of the wine-vessels" used by the Emperor Xuande "'for sacrificing upon the Altar of Heaven'" (5); besides *chi hung*, the Kangxi palette included an iron sulfate red, deep and light blues, celadon, crimson, green, gold, silver, and black (5-6). Jacquemart and Le Blant describe *Tsi-hong-k'i* glaze after Entrecolles and Julien and cite "no. 206" in the Louvre (128n2). Grandidier uses "*Ki-hong*" (65). Pierson notes that the "copper red glaze is still something of a mystery" and "extremely difficult to control" (22).

28. Brinkley follows Bushell in describing the Ming dynasty's "grand, dazzling reds that subsequently became so priceless in the eyes of Chinese virtuosi. Among the porcelains of the *Hsuan-tê* [Xuande] era (1426-1435) the *Tao-lu* says that

vases of *rouge vif* were classed as 'precious,' and that they were glossy, solid, and durable. The same book quotes this passage from another work: 'In the *Hsuan-tê* period there were manufactured at the Imperial workshop cups of the red called *Chi-hung*, having handles shaped like fishes. To produce this red the potters mixed with the glaze the powder of a precious red stone which came from the Occident. On emerging from the kiln the fish blazed out from the body. The glaze was lustrous and thick.' . . . *Chi-hung* signifies the clear red of the sky after rain. . . . H'siang, in his Illustrated Catalogue, speaks of the same red as 'the colour of liquid dawn' (*Liu-h'ia-hung*), a term finely descriptive of its clear, pure brilliancy. . . . the description quoted by the *Tao-lu* is somewhat confusing, being applicable equally to white porcelain decorated with red fishes, or to red porcelain having fish-shaped handle. . . . both kinds were manufactured with marked success by the *Hsuan-tê* experts" (1:280). Further: "these early *Ming* specimens are now known only by written descriptions and by H'siang's illustrations," which cannot convey the color; "reproduced on paper," these reds "lose the brilliancy and lustre to which so much of their beauty is due. The enormous values quoted by H'siang for the *Chi-hung* pieces illustrated in his catalogue prove that the successful production of such ware had virtually ceased before the era of which he wrote (second half of sixteenth century)" (1:283). "Outside China there are virtually no *Ming Chi-hung* monochromes in existence, and in China they are few and far between. The connoisseur must be content to know them vicariously, and to accept as true indications of their beauty the expressive names deservedly given them by their Chinese admirers, ruby red, the rosy blush of liquid dawn, and the crimson glow of the sky after rain and storm" (1:286). According to one website, only ten of more than 10,000 objects in the Jingdezhen Ceramics Museum are *Chi-hung/ Jihong* porcelains, and there are fewer than 100 in museums worldwide www. chinaculture.org/library/2008-01/22/content_82221_4.htm 24 January 2011.

29. Notwithstanding his work's posthumous dependence on his editors (prefigured in the editing of composer Vinteuil's papers by his daughter's friend), Proust was at pains to hide the minutiae of his own work process, ordering some notebooks and letters destroyed and hesitating to sell his manuscripts and proofs lest they end up in a public library: "It isn't very agreeable to think that anyone (if anyone still cares about my books) will be able to study my manuscripts, compare them with the definitive text, and infer suppositions which will always be incorrect about my manner of working and the evolution of my thought, etc. All that rather bothers me. . ." (*Corr.* 21:243, mid-July 1922, to Sidney Schiff, in Tadié 753, cf. 762).

30. Proust's yellow may also evoke the glacial loess—*huangtu*, yellow earth, the

material of Chinese ceramics from the bronze age forward—which colors the Yellow River, the Yellow Sea, the Forbidden City rooftiles (Finlay, 87f).

31. Bergotte's model Anatole France won the Nobel Prize for Literature in 1921 and would survive Proust by almost two years; that summer, Paris bookshops displayed *Le Côté de Guermantes* and *Sodome et Gomorrhe* and Proust weathered their mixed reception by reviewers and friends. See *ISLT* 4.244-46 and *ARTP* 1.cv-cvi "Introduction générale."

32. The Southern Song Dynasty (1127–1279) Official Kiln Museum in Hangzhou, built on the site of the ancient Jiaotanxia Official Kiln, incorporates all but indestructible excavated porcelain shards in its outdoor pavings.

33. "Tching prayed on the mountain and / wrote MAKE IT NEW / on his bath tub / Day by day make it new" (Pound, Canto LIII/264-65).

Works Cited

Alpers, Svetlana. *The Art of Describing: Dutch Art in the Seventeenth Century.* Chicago: U of Chicago P, 1983.

Arasse, Daniel. *Le Détail, pour une histoire rapprochée de la peinture.* Paris: Flammarion, 1992.

___. *Vermeer: Faith in Painting.* Trans. Terry Grabar. Princeton: Princeton UP, 1994.

Béguin, Gilles et al. *Arts de l'Asie au musée Cernuschi.* Paris: Paris-Musées, 2000.

Benhaïm, André. "From Baalbek to Baghdad and Beyond: Marcel Proust's Foreign Memories of France." *Journal of European Studies* 35 (2005): 87-110.

Bergdoll, Barry. *Les Vaudoyer: Une dynastie d'architectes.* Paris: Editions de la Réunion des musées nationaux, 1991.

Bertrand, Antoine. *Les Curiosités Esthétiques de Robert de Montesquiou.* 2 vols. Geneva: Droz, 1996.

Blanc, Charles. *Vermeer de Delft, Nouv. Edition revue et augmentée.* Bruxelles-Paris: Van Oest, 1921.

Boaretto, Elisabetta, et al. "Radiocarbon dating of charcoal and bone collagen associated with early pottery at Yuchanyan Cave, Hunan Province, China." *Proceedings of the National Academy of Sciences of the United States of*

America. www.pnas.org/content/early/2009/06/01/0900539106.abstract. July 1, 2010.

Bowie, Malcolm. "Reading Proust between the Lines." In *The Strange M. Proust.* Ed. André Benhaïm. London: Modern Humanities Research and Maney Publishing, 2009. 125-33.

Brinkley, Frank. *China, its History, Arts and Literature.* 4 vols. Boston and Tokyo: J. B. Millet, 1902.

Brook, Timothy. *Vermeer's Hat: The Seventeenth Century and the Dawn of the Global World.* London: Bloomsbury P, 2008.

Bush, Christopher. "The Other of the Other? Cultural Studies, Theory, and the Location of the Modernist Signifier." *Comparative Literature Studies* 42.2 (2005): 162-80.

Bushell, Stephen W., trans. *T'ao Shuo, Description of Chinese Chinese Pottery and Porcelain.* Oxford: Clarendon, 1910.

Caiger-Smith, Alan. *Tin-Glaze Pottery in Europe and the Islamic World: The Tradition of 1000 Years in Maiolica, Faience and Delftware.* London: Faber and Faber, 1973.

Costuras, Nicola. "A Study of the Materials and Techniques of Johannes Vermeer." *Vermeer Studies.* Ed. Ivan Gaskell and Michiel Jonker. Washington, D. C.: National Gallery of Art, 1998.

Davy, E. M. "A King's Favorite." *Belgravia: A London Magazine* 71 (Jan.-Apr. 1890): 68-80.

Deft Hands Discerning Eyes: Chinese and Korean Ceramics from the Harry B. and Bessie K. Braude Memorial Collection. Chicago: Art Institute of Chicago, 2008.

Desroches, Jean-Paul. "The Collection: Introduction." http://www.guimet-grandidier.fr 18 January 2011.

Diamond, Jared. *Guns, Germs, and Steel: The Fates of Human Societies.* New York: W. W. Norton, 1997/2005.

Eliot, T. S. "Tradition and the Individual Talent." *Selected Essays.* 1919. New York: HBJ, 1950.

Emerson, Julie, Jennifer Chen, and Mimi Gardner Gates. *Porcelain Stories: From China to Europe.* Seattle and London: Seattle Art Museum and U of Washington P, 2000.

Engel, Nicolas, et al. "Chefs-d'oeuvre de l'Extrême-Orient au musée

Cernuschi." *Le musée Cernuschi: Guide pratique.* Paris: Société Française de Promotion Artistique, 2005.

Essential Vermeer. www.essentialvermeer.com/proust/proust.html 3 July 2010.

Finlay, Robert. *The Pilgrim Art: Cultures of Porcelain in World History.* Berkeley: U of California P, 2010.

Fraisse, Luc. *Proust et le Japonisme.* Strasbourg: Presses Universitaires de Strasbourg, 1997.

Fuss, Diana. *The Sense of an Interior: Four Writers and the Rooms that Shaped Them.* New York: Routledge, 2004.

Grandidier, Ernest. *La céramique chinoise: porcelaine orientale: date de sa découverte, explication des sujets de décor, les usages divers, classification.* Paris: Firmin-Didot, 1894.

Hale, Philip Leslie. *Jan Vermeer of Delft.* Boston: Small, Maynard, 1913.

Hertel, Christiane. *Vermeer: Reception and Interpretation.* Cambridge: Cambridge UP, 1996.

Hochstrasser, Julie Berger. *Still Life and Trade in the Dutch Golden Age.* New Haven: Yale UP, 2007.

Hokenson, Jan. "Proust's *japonisme*: Contrastive Aesthetics." *Modern Language Studies* 29:1 (Spring 1999).

Jacquemart, Albert, and Edmond Le Blant. *Histoire artistique, industrielle et commerciale de la porcelaine.* Paris: Techener, 1862.

Joyce, James. *Ulysses.* 1922. New York: Modern Library, 1992.

Liedke, Walter. *Vermeer: The Complete Paintings.* Belgium: Ludion and Walter Liedke, and New York: Harry N. Abrams, Inc., 2008.

Link-Heer, Ursula. "Multiple Personalities and Pastiches: Proust *père et fils.*" *SubStance* 88 (1999): 17-28.

Milly, Jean. *Les Pastiches de Proust.* Paris: Armand Colin, 1970.

Montias, John Michael. *Artists and Artisans in Delft: A Socio-Economic Study of the Seventeenth Century.* Princeton: Princeton UP, 1982.

___. *Vermeer and His Milieu: A Web of Social History.* Princeton: Princeton UP, 1989.

Nash, John. *Vermeer.* London: Scala/Rijksmuseum Foundation, 1991.

Needham, Joseph, and Tsien Tsuen-Hsuin. *Science and Civilization in China:*

Volume 5, Chemistry and Chemical Technology, Part I Paper and Printing. Cambridge UP, 1985.

Needham, Joseph, Rose Kerr, and Nigel Wood. *Science and Civilisation in China: Volume 5 Chemistry and Chemical Technology Part XII Ceramic Technology.* Cambridge: Cambridge UP, 2004.

Pierson, Stacey. *Earth, Fire and Water: Chinese Ceramic Technology.* London: Percival David Foundation of Chinese Art, 1996.

Pound, Ezra. *Guide to Kulchur.* 1938. New York: New Directions, 1970.

___. *The Cantos.* New York: New Directions, 1995.

Proust, Marcel. *À la recherche du temps perdu.* Ed. Jean-Yves Tadié et al. 4 vols. Paris: Gallimard/ Bibliothèque de la Pléiade, 1988.

___. *Chroniques.* Paris: Éditions de la Nouvelle revue francaise, 1927.

___. *Correspondance. Texte établi, presénté et annoté.* Ed. Philip Kolb. 21 vols. Paris: Plon, 1970-93.

___. *In Search of Lost Time.* 6 vols. Vols. 1-5 trans. C. K. Scott Moncrieff and Terence Kilmartin. Vol. 6 trans. Andreas Major and Kilmartin. Revised by D. J. Enright. New York: Modern Library, 1993.

___. *In Search of Lost Time, vol 5: The Prisoner.* Trans. Carol Clark. London: Penguin, 2002.

___. *In Search of Lost Time, vol 6: Finding Time Again.* Trans. Ian Patterson. New York: Penguin, 2002.

___. *Letters of Marcel Proust.* Trans. and ed. Mina Curtiss. New York: Random House, 1949.

___. *Selected Letters.* Vol. 4, 1918-1922. Ed. Philip Kolb. Trans. Joanna Kilmartin. London: Harpercollins, 2000.

Saint-André, Claude. *A King's favourite, Madame du Barry, and her times from hitherto unpublished documents . . . with a introduction by Pierre de Nolhac and 17 illustrations.* New York : McBride, Nast, 1915.

Schwartz, William Leonard. *The Imaginative Interpretation of the Far East in Modern French Literature 1800-1925.* Paris: Librairie Ancienne Honoré Champion, 1927.

Smith, Richard L. *Premodern Trade in World History.* New York: Routledge, 2009.

Staten, Henry. "Art as Techne, or The Intentional Fallacy and the Unfinished

Project of Formalism." *A Companion to the Philosophy of Literature*. Ed. Garry L. Hagberg and Walter Jost. Chichester: Wiley-Blackwell, 2010.

Tadié, Jean-Yves. *Marcel Proust: A Life*. 1996. Trans. Euan Cameron. New York: Penguin, 2000.

Tallandier, Jules. *Historia*. Paris, 1909.

Thoré, Théophile (William Bürger). *Musées de la Hollande: Amsterdam et la Haye*, vol.1. 1858.

Vanzype, Gustave. *Vermeer de Delft, Nouv. Edition revue et augmentée*. Bruxelles, Paris:Van Oest, 1908, rev. 1921, 1925.

Vasselot, J. J. Marquet de, and M.-J. Ballot. *La Céramique Chinoise*. 2 vols. Paris: Louvre, 1922. Also published as *Chinese Ceramics*. 2 vols. Paris: Albert Morance, 1922.

Vaudoyer, Jean-Louis. "Le mystérieux Vermeer." *L'Opinion, journal de la semaine*, Part I: April 30 (487-9), Part II: May 7 (514-6), Part III: May 14 (542-4), 1921.

Volker, T. *Porcelain and the Dutch East India Company, based on the Daghregisters of Batavia Castle, those of Hirado and Deshima, and other contemporary papers, 1602-1682*. Leiden: E. J. Brill, 1954.

Weber, Samuel M. "The Madrepore." *Modern Language Notes* 87 (Dec. 1971): 919.

Winton, Alison. *Proust's Additions: The Making of 'À la recherche du temps perdu'*. 2 vols. Cambridge: Cambridge UP, 1977.

Woolf, Virginia. *Jacob's Room*. New York: HBJ, 1922.

Chu Shi and *Ru Shi*: Robert Frost in Taoist Perspective

Qiping Yin

Quite a number of scholars have dealt with the affinity between Robert Frost (1874-1963) and Taoism. Cheng Aimin, for instance, maintained that Frost "had been influenced, directly or indirectly, by the philosophical thinking of Lao Tzu and Zhuang Tzu" (Cheng 80). Few, with the exception of Hong Qi, however, have taken an in-depth look at the similarities between the themes of Frost and such philosophical ideas as proposed by either Laozi (Lao Tzu) or Zhuangzi. In an article on the resemblance between the themes of Frost's poems and Zhuangzi's philosophical vision, Hong Qi argues that their commonality lies in "a quest for a thorough freedom," namely, freeing oneself from the bonds of nature, society and the self (Hong 164-166). While there is validity in Hong Qi's views, her interpretation seems a bit too reductive in the sense that too much emphasis is given to the tendency, in both Frost's and Taoist philosophy, to *Chu Shi* (to renounce the world) to the neglect of the fact that this tendency is subtly balanced by a willingness to *Ru Shi* (to accept the world). Taking my lead from Barry Ahearn, who has argued for the subtly original modernist strategy in Frost's sonnets, I wish to probe into Frost's poetic philosophy in terms of a Taoist equilibrium between strategic retreat from and ultimate engagement in world affairs. In other words, I will examine the way in which Frost bears affinities to Taoism in the aspect of *Ru Shi* as well as that of *Chu Shi* in a manner that links his work to other modernists.

The notions of *Chu Shi* and *Ru Shi* are originated from the key concept of Taoism, namely, the Tao. According to Laozi, the Tao is a universal, irresistible and all-inclusive law which determines the motion of all the substances in the universe, and this belief is expressed in Chapter Fifty-One of *Tao Te Ching*, in which Laozi describes the

Tao as the mother of everything, or the origin of all the things in the universe, for "Tao gave them birth (道生之)", and "The 'power' of Tao reared them, shaped them according to their kinds, perfected them, giving to each its strength (道畜之，物形成，势成之)" (Lao Tzu 109). Therefore, among "the ten thousand things there is not one that does not worship Tao and do homage to its 'power' (是以万物莫不尊道而贵德)" (Lao Tzu 109). Chapter Twenty-Five makes an attempt to categorize the nameless Tao or "Way": "There was something formless yet complete, that existed before heaven and earth . . . Its true name we do not know; 'Way' is the by-name that we give it. Were I forced to say to what class of things it belongs I should call it Great" (有物混成，先天地生。吾不知其名，字之曰"道"，强为之名曰"大") (Lao Tzu 53). Interestingly, Robert Frost's poetic philosophy reveals a similar preoccupation with the nameless "Way" which falls into the category of "by-names," as the analysis below shall demonstrate.

One stumbling block to a comparative study of Frost and Taoism is the difficulty of tracing the genealogy of influences. No solid evidence seems to have been produced which can point to any direct impact of the ancient Chinese philosophy on Frost. Is, then, an approach to Frost from a Taoist perspective legitimate?

The legitimacy of such an approach is two-fold. First, Frost lived in an era when ancient Chinese philosophy had long been one of the shaping forces of Western literature, and plenty of evidence supports the influence of Taoist thinking on a number of major Western writers who in turn influenced Frost one way or another. It is now universally acknowledged that the Transcendentalists left their imprint on Frost, who once praised Emerson's "Uriel" as the "best western poem yet" (Parini 99). As Chang Yaoxing has pointed out, "Frost did write very much in the Wordsworthian tradition, and there is a good deal of Emerson in him" (Chang 268). Huang Zongying has also affirmed this conclusion by suggesting that "Emerson's doctrine lies behind Frost's continuous and instinctive sense of correspondences between his 'outer' and 'inner' weather" (Huang 149). Frost himself has acknowledged his debt to Emerson. In one of his essays, after naming Emerson as one of his "four greatest Americans" (the other three being George Washington, Thomas Jefferson and Abraham Lincoln), he makes it clear that he has never been able to get over Emerson's influence: "Some of my first thinking about my own language was certainly Emersonian…I am not submissive enough to want to be a follower, but he had me there. I never got over that" (Frost 860-861). And traces of Oriental culture are visible in the works of Emerson, who "copied aphorisms from Confucius in his *Journals*, mentioned Confucius in his translation of selected sayings of Confucius (such as from *The Analects*) in *The Dial*" (Toming 90).

Furthermore, Emerson's lifetime witnessed the West's interest in and passion towards Taoism. The first English translation of *Tao Te Ching* appeared in 1868, followed by the publication of almost a hundred versions of its kind in the West (Zhao 315). Such an important cultural trend, for such a sensitive and erudite scholar as Emerson, could not have gone unheeded. Frost's similarity with Taoism, therefore, emanates indirectly from the influence of Transcendentalism which is synthesized from several cultural sources, Taoist philosophy not the least among them.

Second, Frost's poems abound in details that are redolent of those in Taoist works such as *Tao Te Ching*. Of all the striking similarities, two images are worthy of particular attention, namely, the images of "road/way" and "water." Just as these two images form part and parcel of Taoist philosophy, so do they occupy a predominant position in Frost's poetry. The surprisingly similar ramifications centering around the images above in both Frost's poems and Taoist works compel close examination and legitimize a meticulous comparative study.

"West-Running Brook," with its central image of brook at once as water and road, offers itself as a good point of entry into this investigation. The brook, being both a metaphor and a synecdoche, is nothing short of a key to the true understanding of Frost, who preferred to call himself a "synecdochist" and once gave the following definition of poetry: "Poetry is simply made of metaphor . . . Every poem is a new metaphor inside or it is nothing" (Frost 786). For him, metaphor is "the height of poetry, the height of all thinking, the height of all poetic thinking, that attempts to say matter in terms of spirit and spirit in terms of matter" (Cox and Lathem 41). All this is reminiscent of a saying in ancient Chinese philosophy, namely, "to set up an image to make the most of the significance" (立象以尽意 ").[1] This being no mere coincidence, we are once more justified in embarking on a journey down the meandering brook under Frost's pen.

1. *Chu Shi*: Frost as a "Terrifying" Poet

"West-Running Brook," like many other poems, confirms Lionel Trilling's well-known claim that Frost's universe is "a terrifying one" and that Frost himself is "a terrifying poet" (Trilling 445). The "terrifying" tone begins with the title itself and the opening scene: The brook that Fred and his bride are contemplating runs west, contrary to the direction of "all the other country brooks" flowing "east to the ocean" (Frost 236). Throughout the poem a sense of fear and helplessness can be detected, and a seemingly sinister aspect looms large, particularly in the following passage:

> It is from that in water we were from
> Long, long before we were from any creature.
> Here we, in our impatience of the steps,
> Get back to the beginning of beginnings,
> The stream of everything that runs away.
> Some say existence like a Pirouot
> And Pirouette, forever in one place,
> Stands still and dances, but it runs away,
> It seriously, sadly, runs away
> To fill the abyss' void with emptiness.
> It flows beside us in this water brook,
> But it flows over us. It flows between us
> To separate us for a panic moment.
> It flows between us, over us, and *with* us.
> And it is time, strength, tone, light, life, and love—
> And even substance lapsing unsubstantial;
> The universal cataract of death
> That spends to nothingness—and unresisted,
> Save by some strange resistance in itself,
> ...   (237-38: ll. 45-63)

Here the destructive power of water could not be more obvious, between "The universal cataract of death/That spends to nothingness—and unresisted" and "existence" that "seriously, sadly, runs away/ To fill the abyss' void with emptiness."

In terms of the characters within the poem, the brook/water

provides the platform on which Fred and his bride can communicate with each other. A brook is really a road on which human beings can travel. In this poem, the brook implies a new road of life for a newly married couple and symbolizes a quest that would presumably result in their marital relationship growing to maturity and harmony. Unfortunately, however, their communication fails. What should be a moment of mutual understanding is revealed as the physical conjunction of two people whose thoughts are running on different tracks. The wife's thoughts are characterized by wishful thinking:

> As you and I are married to each other,
> We'll both be married to the brook. We'll build
> Our bridge across it, and the bridge shall be
> Our arm thrown over it asleep beside it.
> Look, look, it's waving to us with a wave
> To let us know it hears me,
>
> (236: ll. 16-21)

But Fred, the husband, sees just the opposite:

> 'That wave's been standing off this jut of shore
> Ever since rivers, I was going to say,
> Were made in heaven. It wasn't waved to us.'
>
> (237: ll. 32-34)

While his bride holds on to her views, Fred continues to stick to his and becomes ironic, even cynical:

> 'Oh, if you take it off to lady-land,
> As't were the country of the Amazons
> We men must see you to the confines of
> And leave you there, ourselves forbid to enter, —
> It is your brook! I have no more to say.'
>
> (237: ll. 37-41)

The failure of communication is obviously a sign of alienation, at least for Fred, made poignant by the foregrounded image of brook, suggesting both the unruliness of water and the perils of travel on a road. In a word, there is something "terrifying" here indeed.

As a matter of fact, the "terrifying" image for Frost appears time and again in many of his poems. The opening part of "Mending Wall" is another typical example:

Something there is that doesn't love a wall,
That sends the frozen-ground-swell under it,
And spills the upper boulders in the sun;
And makes gaps even two can pass abreast.

                                                    (39: ll. 1-4)

Undoubtedly this "something" refers to the fearful and formidable natural force which defies mankind's violation of its fixed rules to such an extent that it forthrightly overthrows the very icon of this intrusion in this poem, the wall, by "spilling" its stones to form a gap so big that "two can pass abreast."

A careful look at this "something" reveals its similarity with, among other creeds, the Tao in ancient Chinese philosophy since both represent the indomitable power of the natural law which governs the whole universe. Han Feizi (ca. 280–233 BC) explains the Tao as "the origin and the fundamental essence of the universe" ("道者，万物之所然也，万物之所稽也。……道者，万物之所以成也"),[2] which is as objective as the existing "something" in Frost's poetry. Literally speaking, the Chinese character "道" （Tao） reminds us first and foremost of the image of road, as defined in *The Related Associations* or *Shuo Wen Jie Zi* （《说文解字》）: "Tao, the road one takes" （"道，所行道也"） (Su 72). What surprises us is that one of the predominant images in Frost's poetry is the "road," and this "road" is as "irretrievable" and "irresistible" as the law in Taoism. In "Stopping by Woods on a Snowy Evening," Frost talks about the destined "road" we must take even if we want to make a "death-wish" choice and to abandon the obligation of our lives. Similarly, "The Road Not Taken" embodies an everlasting sigh about the "irretrievability" of the "road": "I doubted if I should ever come back" (Frost 103).

The fearfulness of the "road" also lies in its namelessness, shapelessness and formlessness, as suggested by something that "makes gaps even two can pass abreast" in "Mending Wall," and by a more "terrifying" something that causes "even substance lapsing unsubstantial" in "West-Running Brook." It is exactly this namelessness that many readers of Frost fail to identify. Even Trilling's thought-provoking description of Frost as "terrifying" often renders the reader hopelessly conscious of the indescribable terror of his nature. Here a Taoist perspective may help shed light on the significance of this nameless "road" or Tao. Tao, in Laozi's words, is characterized by

"shapeless shapes" and "forms without form (无状之状，无物之象),"
and is overwhelmingly everywhere but beyond senses of smelling,
seeing and touching (Lao Tzu 29). In his *Tao Te Ching*, Laozi begins
with the following famous lines: "The Way that can be told of is not
an Unvarying Way. The names that can be named are not unvarying
names (道可道，非常道；名可名，非常名)" (Lao Tzu 3). In other
words, the Eternal Way and the Eternal Name simply defy naming, just
as the defiant brook under Frost's pen runs west rather than east. The
west-running brook carries along all the things in this universe, either
sensible or insensible. So it is "time, strength, tone, light, life and love-
/ And even substance lapsing unsubstantial" (Frost 238: ll. 59-60). It
contains "death," changes itself into the "unresisted" nothingness, and
combines not only man and women but also humankind and nature. In
short, it "flows between us, over us, and with us" (Frost 58) as an all-
inclusive law which shares characteristics with the Tao. As previously
mentioned, the Tao is a universal, irresistible and all-inclusive law
which determines the motion of all the substances in the universe, and
this all-inclusiveness steeps, in its transcendental splendor, heaven and
earth alike. Rather than succumbing to human efforts to categorize it
into a clear shape and definite name, the Tao has an irresistible power
to shape and form everything humanly imaginable—a power which
is "terrifying" in a way. This "terrifying" aspect forges a link between
Taoism and the poetic philosophy of Frost. Just as Laozi can only give
a by-name to his Tao, so Frost finds himself wrestling and grappling
with a nameless west-running brook. No matter how we name Frost's
"brook"—"road" or "universal cataract of death"—these labels are
bound to be by-names.

The call for eternal naming naturally gives rise to the yearning to
transcend time and space. That is why critics such as Hong Qi have
found Frost an escapist. It is true that the escapist vision is there. In
the lines quoted above, we find Frost indicating a wish to "[g]et back
to the beginning of beginnings" (237: 48) and contemplating "the
stream of everything that runs away" (237: l. 52). Here is undoubtedly
a longing for *Chu Shi*, a desire to renounce the world and to transcend
mundane affairs. Another example can be found in these lines: "Some
say existence like a Pirouot/ and Pirouette, forever in one place,/ Stands
still and dances, but it runs away,/ It seriously, sadly, runs away"(237:

50-52). As two ideal characters in a French pantomime, Pirouot and Pirouette stand for the beautified fixed existence of life which defies any progress. All this is reminiscent of "Wu-wei" (无为), a key notion of Taoism, which means "non-action" or quietism, very much in line with the philosophy of *Chu Shi*.

But does *Chu Shi* constitute the only aspect in which Frost bears affinities to Taoism?

2. *Ru Shi*: Frost as a Positive Poet

In Frost's poetic philosophy, *Chu Shi* is offset by *Ru Shi*. In other words, the poet's desire to renounce the world is offset by his desire to accept the world. The image of water, with its drift and counter drift, is like a pervading thread running throughout Frost's career. It appears in his earliest poems and in his last one. In "The Pasture," which is among the first three poems he published, water appears in the form of "spring": "I am going out to clean the pasture spring" (Frost 3: l.1). Then the image of water runs through his poetry just like the "confident" west-running brook, and finally it returns in his last poem "Directive," which contains another philosophical statement: "Here are your waters and watering place, /Drink and be whole again beyond confusion"(342: ll.61-62). The very act of "drinking" implies an attitude of acceptance.

Similarly, as a countercurrent in "West-Running Brook," although "the brook does run west" (Frost 236: l. 3), therein symbolic of the drift to nothingness, there exists also a drift toward renewal—Fred in the poem has observed "contraries" and urges his bride to "see how the brook/In that white wave runs counter to itself" (ll. 43-44). The poem in fact abounds with contraries and contrasts. Sadly running away as it is towards the end, the brook is, at the same time, going back to the beginning. There is unmistakably a "throwing backward":

It has this throwing backward on itself
So that the fall of most of it is always
Raising a little, sending up a little.
Our life runs down in sending up the clock.
The brook runs down in sending up our life.
The sun runs down in sending up the brook.

And there is something sending up the sun.
It is this backward motion toward the source,
Against the stream, that most we see ourselves in,
The tribute of the current to the source.
It is from this in nature we are from.
It is most us.'   (Frost 238: 66-77)

For all the "death," "nothingness," "void" and "emptiness" discussed above, the brook carries with it a confident belief that "being downstream" is equivalent to "being upstream," since the whole process runs in endless circles. In this sense, the west-running brook is an integral part of all those brooks flowing east. To "fall" is actually to "rise," while to head for the west is the same as heading for the east.

All the contraries are, therefore, solved and harmonized with the west-running brook's flowing "by contraries." What is more, Frost regards the west-running brook's "backward motion toward the source" as a "tribute" of the current to the source of the water, which explicitly shows his admiring attitude towards "going back," and it cannot but remind us of Laozi's appraisal of "returning" (反). In Chapter Forty of *Tao Te Ching*, Laozi clearly says that "In Tao the only motion is returning（反者道之动）" (Lao Tzu 87). And Tao being "Great," as analyzed in the previous section, it "also means passing on/ And passing on means going Far Away/And going far away means returning (大曰逝， 逝曰远， 远曰反)" (Lao Tzu 53). In a way, the west-running brook could be regarded as a symbol of this returning Tao, or a unifying principle, which combines all the oppositions into a unity with its endless circulation. Apparently, both the Tao and the philosophical west-running brook stem from an objective observation regarding the law of the universe. And this objectivity might lead to the "affinity" in a certain way.

As we have already observed, all the contraries in "West-Running Brook" revolve around the central image of water, which has one particularly significant property: the propensity to run down. But it runs down only to send up, as indicated in the line "The brook runs down in sending up our life" (Frost 238: 70). For all its perils and destructive power, which are likely to breed a desire for *Chu Shi*, the water in question is nonetheless a sign of restoration and resuscitation reaffirming the need for *Ru Shi*. A striking similarity can be found in

Tao Te Ching, where water also flows down (and keeps "staying in the lowly place") but in the meantime symbolizes "the highest good":

> The highest good is like water
> Water benefits all things generously without striving with them.
> Staying in the lowly place that men disdain, it is close to the Tao.
> It knows to keep to the ground in choosing the dwelling.
> It knows to hide in the hidden deep in cultivating the mind.
> It knows to be gentle and kind in dealing with others.
> It knows to keep its words in speaking.
> It knows to maintain order in governing.
> It knows to be efficient in handling business.
> It knows to choose the right moment in making a move.
> Since it does not strive with others,
> It is free from blame.   (qtd. in Zhou and Liang, 59-60)

Laozi's philosophy is often misunderstood as purely characterized by *Chu Shi*. In the quotation above, however, we can clearly see a paradoxical eagerness to act, to govern, to handle business and to achieve the highest good. That is to say, Taoism does not object to *Ru Shi* at all; rather, it prefers to "choose the right moment in making a move" and "does not strive with others."

Similarly, Frost's poetic philosophy is apt to be misinterpreted as focusing on an escapist vision, which we have already seen emphasized by such critics as Hong Qi. It is true that Frost does indicate from time to time a wish for standing off and being far from the madding crowd, just as the wave of the west-running brook has been "standing off this jut of shore" (Frost 237: l. 23). Even a wish for death can be spotted every now and then. The reasons are not hard to come by. Frost lived in a post-industrial period which witnessed the unchecked spreading of materialism and the spiritual emptiness caused by the war. It is quite natural that such a social reality would spur him to turn from it and to seek some way to "be whole again beyond confusion" (Frost 342, "Directive"). Many lines exemplify his weariness of life, such as "I am overtired / Of the great harvest I myself desired" in "After Apple-Picking" (70: l. 28-29); in "Birches," his wish to be "a swinger of birches" again because he is "weary of consideration" and because "life is too much like a pathless wood" (Frost 118: ll. 43-45); or his momentary impulse to stay forever in the woods that "are lovely, dark and deep," as strongly expressed in "Stopping by Woods on a Snowy Evening" (Frost 207:10). All this wish for escape, however, is counterbalanced by a strong sense of mission for one's own world, which is equally, if not more emphatically, prevalent in Frost's poems. As we have seen in "West-Running Brook," even in the very nature of the drift to "the abyss' void with emptiness" (237: l. 54), there exists a counter drift toward fullness and "something sending up the sun" (238: 72). Frost's dialectical thoughts on "emptiness" ring a bell again, for we are once more reminded of Laozi who has, in his *Tao Te Ching*, given the following remarks: "What is most full seems empty（大盈若冲）" (Lao Tzu 97).

The counter drift is not confined merely to "West-Running Brook" but asserts itself repeatedly in Frost's poetry in a variety of forms. In his essay on Frost's sonnets, Ahearn rightly points out that Frost "wants to maintain humanity's exceptional status" and " prefers to believe in an essential, crucial distinction between humankind and the rest of nature, a distinction he wishes to retrieve" (Ahearn 45). The wish to retrieve the distinction between humankind and the rest of nature is undoubtedly a wish for *Ru Shi*, which dovetails with the above-mentioned image of "the counter drift." Similar instances abound. In "Stopping by Woods on a Snowy Evening," for instance, the poet finally refuses the call of the "lovely" woods and determines to accomplish his journey, although it means "miles" of arduous journeying (15-16). He has "promises to keep" (14), and those promises have nothing to do with *Chu Shi* and everything to do with *Ru Shi*. In "The Road Not Taken," the poet eventually comes to terms with the fate resulting from his previous choice of "the one less traveled by," although he knows "that has made all the difference" (15-16). And in "Birches," Frost makes it clear that his wish to be away from the "earth" will last only "awhile," and then he would like to "come back to it" again since "Earth's the right place for love: /I don't know where it's likely to go better" (118: ll. 49-54). He even indicates a fear that fate might misunderstand him:

> May no fate willfully misunderstand me
> And half grant what I wish and snatch me away
> Not to return…
>   (118: ll. 51-53)

So the poet here does want to return, i.e. to *Ru Shi* in Taoist terms. It would be wrong, then, to look upon Frost merely as an escapist. "Birches" is one of the poems which most vividly and adequately displays the philosophical attitude of Frost towards the reality of earthly life, and that attitude is most aptly embedded in the final image of "a swinger of birches":

> I'd like to go by climbing a birch tree,
> And climb black branches up a snow-white trunk
> *Toward* heaven, till the tree could bear no more,
> But dipped its top and set me down again.
> That would be good both going and coming back.
> One could do worse than be a swinger of birches.
>   (118: ll. 55-60)

For all his fantasy about "climbing" toward heaven, toward *Chu Shi* in a sense, the poet never fails to see the restricted ability of the birch tree which, having struck roots deeply in the earth, will eventually send him down to the earth again. *Ru Shi*, or accepting the world, is therefore Frost's ultimate choice or, in his own opinion, "man's sacred duty."[3] In the swinging of birches, we can see a curve—or rather two curves similar to the waves in "West-Running Brook": a drift and a counter drift.

In Frost's prose, too, we can see the counter drift repeatedly asserting itself. Take "A Monument to After-Thought Unveiled," for instance, in which Frost reveals his views on what he calls "aggressive life": "Aggressive life is two-fold: theory, practice; thought, action: and concretely, poetry, statesmanship; philosophy, socialism—infinitely" (Frost 636). In its context, we learn that Frost is actually talking about the elements that go into the making of a leader: "Not in the strife of action is a leader made, nor in the face of crisis, but when all is over, when the mind is swift with keen regret, in the long after-thought. The after-thought of one action is the forethought of the next" (Frost 636-637). Here a clear balance is struck between the drift of thought and the counter drift of action. Whereas Frost emphasizes after-thought, rather than action, as the shaping and constituting element of leadership, he does not lose sight of the necessity of action, for the after-thought is important only in the sense that it will be the forethought of another action. A similar example can be found in "The Poetry of Amy Lowell":

> The most exciting movement in nature is not progress, advance,
> but expansion and contraction, the opening and shutting of the
> eye, the hand, the heart, the mind. We throw our arms wide
> with a gesture of religion to the universe; we close them around
> a person. We explore and adventure for a while and then we
> draw in to consolidate our gains.   (Frost 712)

Once more we see a subtle balance here, between a drift in the forms
of "contraction" and "shutting," on the one hand, and a counter drift
in the forms of "expansion" and "opening," on the other hand. What
is particularly worthy of our attention in the above statement is Frost's
emphasis on the need to "draw in," counterbalanced by the ultimate
aim to "consolidate our gains," which belies those interpretations of
him as a mere escapist.

Far from being merely escapist, Frost placed great emphasis on
"doing" and the need to be aware of "much good in the world":

> There is something we can always be doing without reference to
> how good or how bad the age is. There is at least so much good
> in the world that it admits of form and the making of form. And
> not only admits of it, but calls for it. . . .
> When in doubt there is always form for us to go on with.
>   (Frost 740)

Go on he would, and in this world. He carried on not only with form,
but also with such causes of justice as the fight to abolish slavery and
child labor. A typical example can be found in his praise of Sarah
Cleghorn's anti-slavery poems:

> One of her best poems was about a Negress who personally
> conducted troop on troop of runaway slaves northward. Many
> lightly argue that since we have tolerated wage slavery and
> child labor, we might as well have tolerated Negro slavery. She
> reasons the other way round: that since we have abolished
> Negro slavery we are bound in logic to abolish all other slavery.
> She is the complete abolitionist. She has it in for race prejudice
> and many another ignobleness besides.   (Frost 751)

Here the admiration Frost held for Sarah Cleghorn and the proactive
position he took manifest themselves unmistakably. More interestingly,

he even makes no secret of his envy for those involved in politics:

> I have envied with admiration the lives of fine senators like Flanders and Aiken from the state I vote in, but since there was no hope of my being elected like them by backers behind I can content myself with being selected from in front and a way may be found for my taking some small part in what I like to call politics.   (Frost 845)

This sentiment indicates Frost's propensity for *Ru Shi*, or an inclination which can be likened to "the counter drift" in "West-Running Brook." Frost may have been seized with countless impulses to renounce the world, but he has voiced his concern for and faith in humankind on numerous occasions as well. Just as Robert Bernard Hass writes, "Frost, near the end of his life, remains confident that human beings will endure" (Hass 180). It is this faith in human endurance, in other words, that constitutes a beautiful counter drift in Frost's prose as well as his poetry.

With the publication of "Directive," the west-running brook of Frost's poetic career completes a full cycle and ultimately arrives at a place of acceptance rather than a place of refusal. His sincere acceptance of earthly reality is fully consistent with the Taoist philosophy of *Ru Shi*, which means, in Chuang Tzu's words, to "bear the doomed fate with equanimity" (安之若命) and to "be content with what you have" (安时处顺).[4] Just as the Taoist "water" (the highest good) always presupposes "having tranquility in the hustle and bustle" (结庐在人境，而无车马喧),[5] so is Frost's west-running brook eternally returning to its origin.

Conclusion

Thanks to the west-running brook, we have come to see a closer link between the poetic philosophy of Frost and the ancient Chinese philosophy of Taoism. A cross-reading of Frost and Taoist works confirms Radcliffe Squires' view that "West-Running Brook" is "the summit of Frost's poetry" (Squires 104). A summit it is, for it contributes to bridging the gap between the philosophical thoughts of the East and the West. Although they are remote from each other in time and space, Frost's poetic philosophy and Taoism bear striking affinities that call for a meticulous comparative study of more of his poetry as well.

Reading Frost from a Taoist perspective, as shown by our analysis above, is conducive to exploring the undercurrents of and counter-drifts in his poetry, which will lead to an understanding of Frost not as a mere escapist nor as a merely "terrifying" poet but as a sage with a more balanced philosophical attitude toward life. True, the poetic lines of Frost often betray an impulse to renounce the world, but that impulse is always offset by a willingness to accept and even embrace the world. The west-running brook may head for *Chu Shi*, but it will eventually end up in *Ru Shi*.

Notes

1. The phrase "立象以尽意" comes from Chapter Thirteen of 《易传・系辞上》. For further consultation, see *Yi Zhuan*（《易传全译》）translated and edited by Liu Dajun and Lin Zhongjun (Chengdu: Bushu Bookstore, 2005).

2. This definition comes from Han Feizi's analysis of Lao Tzu's philosophy in his book, *Han Feizi*（《韩非子》）. For further consultation, see also *Han Feizi*（《韩非子译著》）translated by Liu Qianxian (Harbin: People's Press of Heilongjiang, 2002).

3. This idea comes from Radcliffe Squires' introduction to *The Major Themes of Robert Frost*, which says: "His [Frost's] life has spanned the violent and war-torn years of the 20th century, yet his poetry is dominated by a belief in man's sacred duty to endure" (Squires, front cover).

4. Both of the ideas come from *Chuang Tzu*（《庄子》）. "安之若命" comes from 《庄子・人间世》, and "安时处顺" comes from《庄子・养生主》. For further consultation, see *Chuang Tzu*（《庄子今注今译》）translated by Cheng Guying and edited by Wang Yungwu (Taibei: The Commercial Press of Taiwan, 1983).

5. This saying is adapted form Wang Rongpei's translation of the fifth poem of Tao Yuanming's poetry series, "Drinking Wine." The original poetic line is "结庐在人境，而无车马喧，" and translated by Wang Rongpei as "My house is built amid the world of men/ Yet with no sound and fury do I keen." For further consultation, see Wang Rongpei's *The Complete Poetic Works of Tao Yuanming*（《英译陶诗》）(Beijing: Foreign Language Teaching and Research Press, 1999).

Works Cited

Ahearn, Barry. "Frost's Sonnets, In and Out of Bounds." Viorca Patea and Paul Scott Derrick, eds. *Modernism Revisited: Transgressing Boundaries and Strategies of Renewal in American Poetry*. Amsterdam: Rodopi, 2007. 35-52.

Cheng Aimin. "The Consanguineous Cultivation of a Fictitious Land of Peace—A Comparative Study of Tao Yuanming's and Frost's Poems on Nature." *Journal of PLA University of Foreign Languages*, Vol II, 1996. 75-81.

［程爱民："同是世外桃源里的耕耘——论陶渊明与弗罗斯特的自然诗"，《解放军外语学院学报》1996（2）：75-81。］

Chang Yaoxin. *A Survey of American Literature*. Tianjin: Nankai UP, 2002.

［常耀信：《美国文学简史》。天津：南开大学出版社，2002年。］

Cox, Hude, and Lathem.E.C. "Introduction." Hude Cox and Lathem.E.C., eds. *Selected Prose of Robert Frost*. New York: Macmillan, 1968.3-50.

Frost, Robert. *Collected Poems, Prose and Plays*. Eds. Richard Poirier and Mark Richardson. New York: Library of America, 1995.

Hass, Robert Bernard. *Going by Contraries: Robert Frost's Conflict with Science*. Charlottesville: UP of Virginia, 2002.

Hong Qi. "An Extrication Transcending Time and Space—The Theme of Frost in Chuang Tzu's Perspective." *Theory Horizon* 4 (2004): 164-166.

［洪琪："超越时空的解脱—以庄子的视角看弗罗斯特诗歌的主题，"《理论界》4（2004）：164-166。］

Huang Zongying. *A Road Less Traveled By—On the Deceptive Simplicity in the Poetry of Robert Frost*. Beijing: Peking UP, 2000.

［黄宗英：《一条行人稀少的路：弗罗斯特诗歌艺术管窥》。北京：北京大学出版社，2000年。］

Lao Tzu. *Tao Te Ching*. Trans. Arthur Waley. Beijing: Foreign Language Teaching and Research Press & Cumberland House, 1997.

Parini, Jay, and Brett C. Miller. *The Columbia History of American Poetry*. Beijing: Foreign Langage Teaching and Research Press & Columbia UP, 2005.

Su Baorong. *Shuo Wen Jie Zi*. Xian: People's Publishing House of Shanxi, 2003.

［苏宝荣：《〈说文解字〉今译》。西安：陕西人民出版社，2003年。］

Squires, Radcliffe. *The Major Themes of Robert Frost*. Ann Arbor: University of Michigan Press, 1963.

Trilling, Lionel. "A Speech on Robert Frost: A Cultural Episode." *Partisan Review* 26 (summer), 1959. 445-452.

Toming, Liu. *A History of American Literature*. Nanjing: Yilin Press, 2002.

Zhou Yi, and Liang Yihua. *Chinese Culture*. Nanning: Guangxi Education Press, 1993.

Zhao Yiheng. *The Goddess of Poetry Traveling Faraway: How the Modern American Poetry Has Undergone a Metamorphosis in China*. Shanghai: Shanghai Translation Publishing House, 2003.

［赵毅衡：《诗神远游—中国如何改变了美国现代诗》。上海：上海译文出版社，2003年。］

The Modernist Page: Joyce and the Graphic Design of Chinese Writing

Ira B. Nadel

And there is an Irishman called James Joyce. His name in international literary circles is probably similar to Lenin's in international politics because he is both worshipped and attacked like him.

I

This passage is from the first commentary ever made by a Chinese reader of Joyce, poet Xu Zhimo studying in England in 1921-22. It appeared in a preface to his own poems translated by the late Jin Di, the first Chinese translator of *Ulysses* (qtd. in Tsoi 3). The comparison to Lenin may be unorthodox but it does mark the early Sino response to *Ulysses* which made its way to China in 1923. That year Joyce himself wrote to Harriet Shaw Weaver that ten copies had been sent to Beijing.[1]

But I am less interested in China's reception of Joyce than Joyce's reception of China. We know a great deal of China's impact on Yeats and certainly Pound, and even of the importance of the Orient for the Bloomsbury Group. We know little about Joyce's response. But Joyce, whose appreciation of oriental art and writing was less overt than Yeats, Pound, or the Bloomsbury Group, nonetheless found in its visual characteristics elements that greatly contributed to his idea of text and the graphic presentation of the modernist page.[2]

How might Joyce have known of China?

Joyce's Chinese education—with an emphasis on obedience, authority and scholasticism—began with the Irish Jesuits. Their emphasis on master and student and focus on uniform performance stressing a plan or system of teaching and study paralleled that of the ancient Chinese. Both the Jesuits and Chinese had a mandatory program of study, often with a set of required texts. The orderly five stages of "prelection" as identified in the *Ratio Studiorum,* the Jesuit guide to education, follows a pattern of reading, translation, explication, analysis of poetic or rhetorical structure and *erudition* which insured the common treatment of texts (Sullivan 72-4). Joyce absorbed these exercises at Clongowes Wood and Belvedere College. The study practice of *emulatio,* a kind of friendly academic rivalry often expressed in competition among students, and *repetitio,* repetition or rote study, were also Jesuit techniques found in Chinese teaching.

The Jesuits, like Chinese educators, also opposed "originality" or independence of mind believed to emulate free thought or rationalism. On pedagogic as well as theological terms, this was discouraged. Focus was on the study of concrete particulars and the moral and ethical development of students. Collectively, accuracy and thoroughness replaced speculation or imagination through the practice of "prelection." Joyce excelled at the Jesuit educational system until his young maturity when he turned away from Catholicism, although not from the training of the Jesuits.

Education in ancient China stressed knowledge of key texts approached via study guides. The commentaries of Zhu Xi (Chu Hsi, 1130-1200) to *The Great Learning,* preceded by his work *Elementary Learning* (1187)—an anthology of selections from the Confucian Classics—were studied in detail in the Song dynasty. Zhu's selection of *The Four Books* ("The Great Learning," "Doctrine of the Mean," "The Analects" and the "Mencius") formed the basic primer of Chinese education. Zhu's philosophy emphasized logic, consistency, and the conscientious observance of classical authority, especially that of Confucius and his follower Mencius.

"The Learning of the Way" became another revered text, necessary for success on the Imperial Examinations which were essential to enter the civil service. These exams, which began in 581 AD and lasted until 1905, were crucial for advancement and in certain cases lasted days. No less than the emperor examined finalists. The exams followed a pattern beginning with the ability to compose poetry and knowledge of the Classics. For candidates at the local level this was the first hurdle. At departmental and palace examinations, more weight was given to the ability to write prose expositions and responses to policy. Exegesis, along with expository writing, was fundamental for success at the palace examinations. After 1070, the highest level of examination consisted of only one session featuring a policy response question often posed by the emperor or one of his court advisors (de Weerdet 53-60). The exam practice and goals were similar to that of Jesuit study (mastery of material and concentrated thought); the Jesuits, in fact, prepared a *ratio* for China in 1624, a set of pedagogical rules to structure their nascent colleges throughout the country (Brockey 255-63).

Rigorous education, constant exams, and competition define education in both ancient China and Irish Jesuit schools. Originally designed for the sons of aristocrats prior to the time of Confucius, education of the Chinese literati, those responsible for production, use and care of books and documents essential for the government, was well-defined. Topics included ancient literature, poetry, music, law, state annals, ancient records and official documents. After extensive training following their success, students were expected to serve as government bureaucrats. For Joyce, it was the Church; for the Chinese, it was the state.

The Irish Jesuits also introduced Joyce to a direct knowledge of China. He took geography all four years at Belvedere College (1894 – 1898) and it likely included discussion of the Jesuit's early explorations of China. This began with Matteo Ricci who founded the first successful Jesuit mission in China in 1583. The popularity of Ricci's diaries, published in Rome in 1615, resulted in multiple editions in Latin, French, German, Spanish and Italian for the next thirty-three years. What Ricci emphasized in a chapter on Chinese education was the universally recognized meaning of Chinese characters, although there were major differences in pronunciation. But writing with its visual meaning, rather than speech, was privileged, as Juan de Mendoza summarized in 1585 when he wrote that the Chinese "write by figures" (in Porter 35).

Joyce's Jesuitical education and introduction to China made him sympathetic and perhaps curious of Chinese script and its decipherability. As Fenollosa wrote, "The Chinese have been . . . experimenters in the making of great principles," expressed in the question, "How can the Chinese [written] line imply, *as form*, the very element that distinguishes poetry from prose"(Fenollosa 42, 44)? Fenollosa understood and developed the idea that "relations are more real and more important than the things which they relate" (54). Joyce may have early on accepted Fenollosa's emphasis on image and sound creating a "thought-picture" (Fenollosa 45). Indeed, the *verbal idea of action*," as Fenollosa phrased it, connects Joyce to Chinese script (Fenollosa 45).

Travelogues were another possible China resource for Joyce. Frederick Thompson's *In the Track of the Sun: Diary of a Globe Trotter* (1893) is alluded to by Bloom in the "Calypso" episode (*U* 4. 99).[3] Among the titles in the catalogue of Bloom's books in "Ithaca" is *Voyages in China* by "Viator," a title (in red ink) likely made up by Joyce (*U* 17. 1339). In his Trieste library, Joyce owned not only a travelogue but Fenollosa and Pound's *"Noh or Accomplishment: A Study of the Classical Stage of Japan* (1917).[4]

Irish Orientalists also introduced Joyce to China, the most prominent to promote Irish/Oriental connections the eighteenth century historian/linguist Charles Vallancey who argued for linkage between the Phoenicians and the Irish. Joyce cites him in his 1907 Trieste lecture, "Ireland, Island of Saints and Sages," suggesting that Gaelic was Oriental in origin. Standish O'Grady's influential *History of Ireland* (1878) was another source of such relations earlier explored by Thomas Moore in his verse tale *Lalla Rookh* (1817). In his 1902 essay, "James Clarence Mangan," Joyce celebrated the Irish Orientalist poet who expressed "the light of imaginative beauty . . . . East and West meet in that personality; images interweave there like soft, luminous scarves" (Joyce, "Mangan" 57). These and other examples confirm Joseph Lennon's statement that there was a "long tradition of Oriental representation in Irish culture" (Lennon 123).

The later stereotypes of the Orient in Joyce's work, whether in *Dubliners* or *Ulysses,* attest to his inheritance of broadly based popular views. In "A Little Cloud" (1906), Chandler thinks of Gallaher's "rich Jewesses" with their "dark Oriental eyes" later expanded in *Giacomo Joyce* (1914). The facile visions of Bloom as to the exotic Orient as a place of escape underlie Joyce's perception of a possible affiliation between Ireland and earlier, sophisticated but foreign civilizations like China.

For Bloom (and no doubt Joyce), the East is a world of secrets, fertility, unbounded sexuality and generative if often hidden energies. It is not only curiosity that stops Bloom in front of the Belfast and Oriental Tea Company in Westland Row at the opening of "Lotus-Eaters" but dreams of his own transformation into the luxuriant world of the East (*U* 5. 17-20). His journey on to the post office allows him to conjure a fabulous image of the Orient as "the garden of the world" (*U* 5.30). Such a world expands in "Circe" when Zoe fondles Bloom (*U* 15.1324-1330) creating a kind of exotic space to indulge in sensual delights. Joyce summarizes its captivating power when he writes in that episode that "it burns, the orient, a sky of sapphire, cleft by the bronze flight of eagles" (*U* 15.1327-8). It is no surprise that at his "Turkish Bath," Bloom fantasizes the "fleshpots of Egypt" (*U* 5.548). To no one's surprise, Molly, lying in her bed at end of the novel, will come to embody not only "the Oriental prize of Dublin" but Oriental sexuality (Kershner 274).

II

Another source of Joyce's Chinese education was popular culture. Dublin's pantomimes and their presentation of stylized Orientals, as well as advertisements for a range of events and products, supplemented Irish Orientalism for Joyce. The official catalogue for the Araby bazaar of 1894, used by Joyce in "Araby," for example, refers to the event on its front page as a "Grand Oriental Fete." The back cover lists its representation of "an Oriental City" displaying "Eastern Magic," tableaux, theatricals and "Bicycle Polo" (Ehrlich 312). The central feature of the Araby fair was the representation of an Oriental City, a theatrical microcosm in the tradition of nineteenth century panoramas. Egypt and the Arab world was the central but not exclusive attraction of the week long fair advertised on some 1200 "Araby in Dublin" posters in railway stations throughout Ireland, England and Scotland. These large commercial posters had exotic script which read "Araby in Dublin, Grand Oriental Fete." It showed an Arab riding a camel and was similar to the poster Bloom encounters for the Mirus bazaar in Ulysses (Cheng 88; *U* 8.1162).

Pantomimes such as "Turko the Turk," cited four times in *Ulysses*, were popular late nineteenth century theatrical entertainments promoting stereotypical views of the East.

Indeed, throughout the century the Orient had fascinated the British public as British theater made dramatic space exotic. Stage design, lighting and costumes emphasized Oriental images. Preceded by early nineteenth century panoramas, dioramas and even cosmoramas and other optical entertainments, the idea of the Orient took shape as spectacle and entertainment framed by the romantic and mystical. The theatre and entrepreneurs capitalized on this attraction and Joyce himself appeared as a mandarin in an 1891 Clongowes Wood production of "Aladdin and the Wonderful Scamp" (Sullivan 235).

Oriental pantomimes consistently exploited these early ideas of the East promoting impressions of Oriental mysteriousness, mysticism and magnificence of the indolent East. Dialogue and music, supplemented by extravagant costumes and scenic splendor, overtook the stage. Entertainment reigned, Emma Clery telling Stephen in *Stephen Hero* that she had been to the pantomime three times (SH 64). *Sinbad the Sailor* and *Turko the Terrible* were two of the more popular Irish pantomimes that appear in *Ulysses*—as well as the detail that Bloom himself once contracted to write a topical song for a pantomime to be produced at the Gaiety Theatre (17.431). Importantly, the pantomime in Ireland entertained all classes and educational levels.[5]

The mass appeal of the Orient suggested magic, a touch of melancholy and constant mystery which Joyce capitalized on. Promotion of the Orient through popular culture was key and in *Finnegans Wake* II. i, Joyce includes a playbill for a likely Oriental pantomime (FW 219.3-222.20). This appears in the section entitled the "Mime of Mick, Nick and the Maggies," referring, of course, to pantomime. Footnoting Irish awareness of the myth of the East was a new translation of *One Thousand and One Nights* (1904: Robert Louis Stevenson's *New Arabian Nights*). Three years earlier, John Payne's translation, *Oriental Tales: The Book of the Thousand Nights and One Night*, a verse and prose translation in 15 volumes, edited by Leonard C. Montesquieu Smithers, had already become available.

Another source of Joyce's orientalism was Trieste. As John McCourt has emphasized, Joyce's sense of Jewishness partially embodied "Orientalness." His experiences with the Jewish community of Trieste reinforced this attitude expressed in *Giacomo Joyce* and *Ulysses*

(McCourt 41). Joyce's knowledge of the Orient derived in part from aspects of the Orient encountered in the city, meeting people who had been born in, or descended from, "Oriental" countries. Their dress, homes and customs maintained such links. Trieste was a crossroads of the East and Western Europe. The vogue for *chinoiserie* in England and Europe at this time (ca. 1890-1935) was also strong. This was visible in such public forms as the Chinese Pagoda in Kew Gardens, the Brighton Pavilion and even Liberty's department story in London. Privately, Chinese art via ceramics, paintings, calligraphic scrolls and *objets d'art* had been circulating in British and Irish homes since the eighteenth century. This was the appropriation of a foreign aesthetic transformed into something glamorized and domesticated, reflecting a consumerist culture. Since the mid- seventeenth century, imports of Chinese porcelains, lacquerware, furniture, silks and wall hangings rose steadily. Exotic design motifs began to appear in living rooms, bedrooms and even kitchens, perhaps most notably in the blue and white willow patterns of Wedgwood and Spode-Staffordshire. Chinese taste became immensely popular and Chinese costumes and ornaments drew crowds to theatres (Porter 134ff). The sitting room and the garden were suddenly sites of orientalism. As Patricia Laurence has noted in *Lily Briscoe's Chinese Eyes*, the "visual and aesthetic principles embodied in arts and wares kept China in the eye of the British, preparing for the ethos of modernism" (Laurence 327).

There was equal fascination with *chinoiserie* in France, and Nora Joyce, after the Joyces moved to Paris in 1920, sought to keep up with the new fashion encouraged by her daughter-in-law, Helen Kastor Fleischman. She began to frequent Paris couturiers (once the Joyces received increased "grants" from Harriet Shaw Weaver), selecting items in the Chinese style. In a well-known 1924 photo of the Joyce family, all formally dressed, Nora wears a black and white Chinese print of embossed velvet, possibly from the Lucien Lelong collection. Nora's shoes display a Byzantine-style diamante buckle. Lucia wears a similar outfit (Maddox 300-01).

By the early twentieth century, art critics were frequently commenting on the public's continuing absorption with the Orient. In March 1910 Roger Fry published "Oriental Art," a discussion of

Oriental aesthetics in painting. In 1911, he published *Chinese Porcelain and Hand Statues.* By 1925 another monograph by Fry in the *Burlington Magazine* entitled "Chinese Art" soon expanded to become *Chinese Art, An Introductory Handbook* by Fry, Laurence Binyon and others (1925).

By 1933-34, Fry devoted the Slade Lectures at Cambridge to Chinese art and in 1935-36 the International Chinese Art Exhibition took place to great acclaim at Burlington House in London. Travelers to China during this time included G.L. Dickinson, Cambridge political philosopher, who visited in 1910-11 and 1913-14; I.A. Richards, literary critic, who made five trips to China, his first in 1927; Beatrice and Sidney Webb (Fabian socialists); Harold Acton (British writer and dilettante); and Julian Bell (nephew of Virginia Woolf) who taught English in China from 1935 to 1937. It would be difficult for Joyce to overlook the presence of the Orient in Europe, whether in Trieste, Zurich or Paris, let alone in England (Laurence 15, 16).

The most insistent personal voice of the Orient was American: Ezra Pound. He published *Cathay* in 1915 and *Noh or Accomplishment* and *Certain Noble Plays of Japan* both in 1916. Pound had also been revising and publishing Fenollosa's *The Chinese Written Character as a Medium for Poetry* in four installments in the *Little Review* before its appearance in book form in 1920. Joyce referred to Fenollosa as early as 1916 when Pound alerted him to his editing. *The Chinese Written Character* was a work which demonstrated the manifest, phenomenal presence of images in words, while performing the signifying operations of language as both an object and act. Fenollosa showed how the visual form of language produces linguistic meaning at the same time it is an object in itself. Joyce listened, as did Arthur Waley, whose *One Hundred and Seventy Chinese Poems* appeared in 1918.

D.B. Murphy, the red bearded sailor in "Eumaeus," neatly summarizes the allure of the Orient for Joyce when he describes to Bloom and Stephen the unusual pills a "Chinese" had: when placed in water, they opened "and every pill was something different. One was a ship, another was a house, another was a flower" (*U* 16. 570-3). Such variety and exoticism express the representation of the Orient in Joyce's texts, expressed by Murphy's body which has possessed the East: on his chest he has "an image tattooed in blue Chinese ink intended to represent an anchor" (*U* 16.668-9). But superseding this use of the Orient as a topos is a more immediate, material presence for Joyce: Chinese script and Chinese printing.

III

That Joyce actually knew Chinese is not in dispute. He did not, although in both *Ulysses* and *Finnegans Wake*, he refers often to the Chinese language and China. In the *Wake*, for example, the narrator includes what he calls Chinese pidgin which Bloom also speaks in "Circe." In a 1925 notebook, Joyce made the first of several references to Confucius ("Confucius he Beyond Blind" [*James Joyce Archive* 30:210]), while late in the *Wake*, the speaker conflates Confucius and Euclid: "Hell's Confucium and the Elements" (FW 485.35)! Earlier, the novel transfers features of the Chinese landscape from the Yellow River and the Imperial City to Ireland. At another point, Joyce equates China's capital with Ireland's, rendering Erin in an orthography evocative of Chinese pidgin (FW 541.34).

The representation of Chinese script in early accounts of China from missionaries, travelers, and traders intensified Europe's fascination with the Far East. Language projectors and reformers of the seventeenth century soon argued that the script was "a paragon of linguistic rationality" and expression of "representational legitimacy," which as a model remained a common thread in the varied cultural discourses making up the European encounter with the Orient (Porter 6, 7).

There was, however, a European compulsion to read Chinese script as a pure form of signification and to systematize its notation. This, according to David Porter, was "ideographic fantasy" based on a European desire to see a "transcendent order" in the writing which became the basis of an assessment of Chinese religion and social policy based on hierarchy. But cross-cultural legibility is more complex and the longing for linguistic stability in this alien culture drove early students of the language to presume a purity that was not there. Yet the changelessness of Chinese script showed the West with its Babel of languages that through its antiquity and consistency, rationality and order persisted. Chinese reflected a stable culture over centuries. In this reading, the Chinese language became part of the historical construct of China in the Western imagination which Joyce absorbed.

Chinese script represented a systematized, non-alphabetic writing system that did not depict an arbitrary sequence of sounds as in an alphabet-based language. It seemed intrinsically logical and visually related to the ideas it represented. The script was independent of the spoken language implying a semantic universality. For language reformers from Bacon to Leibniz this was crucial: language was consistent over time unlike the nature of the multi languages of Europe. This would appeal to Joyce, especially during the composition of *Finnegans Wake*. The image of the written word takes on a validity arising from its history and originary nature (Porter 19).

This last point grounds my discussion of the graphic influence of Chinese script on Joyce's writing in the philosophic and philological need to reform the corrupted languages of Europe. Chinese writing visually embodied the order and universality missing in Western forms of verbal communication. The indecipherable Chinese script was evidence of linguistic legitimacy over centuries, the Chinese writing system a remedy for ambiguity. And writing it well mattered: in the early Chinese dynasties, candidates for the civil service would be dismissed from their exams if they wrote their characters inaccurately (Porter 47).

IV

But how did typography and visual forms originating in Chinese script establish a modernist text for Joyce? How did the Chinese ideogram and its presentation influence Joyce's treatment of the printed page? The sources are varied and incorporated by Joyce in various ways as section III outlined but the visible language of modernism (the subtitle of Jerome McGann's 1993 study, *Black Riders*), how a modern page physically "reads," has emerged in the last two decades as an important dimension of modernist study.[6] The physical aspect of the page possesses heuristic value displaying conceptual as well as linguistic meaning. Capitalization, italics and even paragraphing are signs of graphic *and* semantic meaning. The form of a modernist page is as much its meaning as what it says expressed by Joyce's punning phrase, "too dimensional" (FW 154.26).

For Joyce, visuality defines textual subjectivity. "Ithaca" concludes with a black dot to symbolize not only a grammatical mark, a period, but a darkened globe, a world come to rest. In Joyce's universe punctuation marks have visual meaning, typographically expressing completeness (*U* 17. 2332). It is the thing itself, a semiotic expression linking modernist form with content. A text and its production establish a kind of conceptual authority both on and off the page, transforming the page itself into a modernist object parallel to the textual practices of Chinese writing.

Treating written expression as a material object (the visual rendering of language producing linguistic meaning) demonstrates printing as performance, which Joyce understood. "Circe" with its presentation as dramatic dialogue, Molly's soliloquy as blocks of text or the columnar shape of Book II, Chapter 2, of the *Wake* highlight the performative nature of print for Joyce. But for Joyce, the visual potential of the page originates in the Orient. Indirectly or directly, Joyce learned from, and borrowed from, Chinese in the formation of his material. One quick example: classical Chinese was free of punctuation and spacing before 1917. Joyce, unwittingly perhaps, parallels this in his own linguistic experiments, notably in Molly's soliloquy at the end of *Ulysses* with its circumscribed punctuation. His creation of his magnificent, all-encompassing words such as the Citizen's "national gymnasium museum sanatorium andsuspensoriumsordinaryprivatdocentgeneralhistoryspecial professordoctor Kriegfried Ueberallgemein" or the thunder word from the *Wake* further links his visible language with Chinese through the construction of onomatopoeic words that have graphic resonance (*U* 12. 567-8; Laurence 134).

The ideogrammic method (brought to Joyce by Pound) is a key source of Joyce's sense of oriental visual style. Joyce understood that Chinese characters possessed an extra temporality, the ideogram a sketch of a process transforming image and idea (Kenner, *Pound* 160). This concept of the image in script appealed to Joyce who sought confirmation in Chinese script that characters registered things.

Christopher Bush's recent study *Ideographic Modernism*, an attempt to re-inscribe China in "the text of literary modernity" (xiv), aids in understanding the importance of Chinese writing for Joyce. Bush seeks to restore China's historical and interpretive significance for literary modernism. Through his focus on the ideograph as the intersection of the critique of orientalism, grammatology and media theory, Bush seeks to reconstitute the specific historical relationship between China and the West. He begins with Kafka's 1917 parable "An Imperial Message" and uses it as a launching pad to explore the West's difficulties in recognizing China's reality (xxvii-viii). He argues that China acquires its textual function not by its figural presence (which is itself a sign of modernity's repression of China's historical reality) but by its use only as citation. Allegorical or figural readings of China are forms of its non-recognition. But Joyce, through his adoption of the graphic elements of Chinese writing, runs counter to Bush's argument. Or rather, he, Joyce, fully buys into the idea of the ideograph (a Western term and invention Bush claims) and the notion that "'China' is in many ways an 'ideograph' writ large" (Bush 7). But to understand Joyce's creation of China, it is necessary to turn to Chinese printing history conscious that Chinese writing acts as a synecdoche of "cultural forms and social institutions" (Bush 6).

Printing in China has, of course, an ancient history. Unlike the West and its use of moveable type, printing in early China was dominated by xylography, printing by making impressions on paper from a carved wooden block, although movable type printing had been invented as early as the eleventh century. Nonetheless, xylography remained the preferred method because of the nature of the Chinese language, which meant reproducing several thousand characters. This made the use of moveable type fonts too expensive for most printers (Brokaw 8; MacDermott in Brokaw 81). Those books that used moveable type— expensive to cast and then reset—were sponsored by the government who could shoulder the cost.

In the West, movable type and its technology meant rapid printing of multiple copies of a single text. The cost of resetting type for each page for a new run encouraged long print runs. A printer had, furthermore, to calculate the cost of storage and risk of slow sales as an offset to printing more copies than he needed or could sell. The economics were different with woodblock printing, the initial cost only that of the initial carving. And block carvers did not even have to be literate, while the printer could make as many or as few copies as needed. To "reprint" simply meant printing off the old blocks; there was no cost to reset type and no heavy investment in labor. Xylography also allowed for a greater decentralization in the organization and structure of the printing industry. Block carvers could easily travel even if the woodblocks themselves were too bulky to transport. They could offer themselves to those wanting to publish an individual text or set of texts. With a modest investment, anyone could become a publisher if he could afford a carver, had access to the appropriate hardwood (pear, jujube camphor, etc.), paper and printer's ink. The *literatus* was in business printing as many or as few works as he could afford. Again, the carvers did not require the technical skill of type makers, typesetters, compositors, supervising printers or those who produced matrices for printing in Europe (typesetters needed to know the letters of the alphabet but did not need to be literate).

There was also a huge surplus of scribal labor in China reducing the cost of printing. And it was fast. In the sixteenth century, Matteo Ricci commented on how fast Chinese carvers cut blocks, remarking that "no more time is consumed in making one of them than would be required by one of our printers in setting up a form of type and making the necessary corrections" (in Chow 69). This is somewhat exaggerated but the comparison is apt. At that time, a compositor in Rome or Frankfurt might take a day to complete one to three forms, while a skillful printer in China could turn out as many as 1500 copies from a single block in one day (Chow 69, 70).

The process itself was simple: the characters were inked onto blocks. The carver only had to carve out the wood around the character shape. Importantly, this process, which lasted through the 19th century, provided a visuality and individuality to the text the printing press did not (Ruskin on the Gothic stone carvers in *The Stones of Venice* makes a similar point). I stress this method and its differences from Western typesetting to emphasize the simple art of carving which provided the visual quality to the Chinese written character representing the spatial form of lettering. And the most valuable Chinese books for collectors were those that reproduced, through elegant calligraphy, the appearance of a manuscript.[7]

There is a parallel, here, to Joyce who creates what I venture to call "Oriental time" in his texts. This is time suspended and defined by space, a variant of what Joseph Frank in 1945 called "Spatial Form."

Or what in Chinese painting would be the aesthetic where subject and object are one and where technique is not hidden (as Woolf presents Lily Briscoe painting in *To the Lighthouse*). For Joyce, this is when the written word constructs a textual space that is not separate from its expression. The word is written in the picture space of the page becoming, or defining, the page space. "Oriental time" is the merging of space and sequence into a single moment of apprehension for the writer and reader. It is the singular plane of Chinese art reflecting multiple perspectives and the collapse of outside and inside, one folding into the other, consciousness and perception uniting. "Wandering Rocks" in *Ulysses* may be an extended example of this process. Chinese writing is the source of Joyce's "spatial power" and textual practice, the phrase actually used by Marshall McLuhan in "Joyce: Trivial and Quadrivial" (McLuhan 31; Laurence 356).

Joyce, like the Chinese, understood that books are a spatial phenomenon and not subject to chronological pressure (Kenner, *Stoic* 74). Time is what the reader brings to the text, the book itself possessing its own spatial measurement or geometry which, of course, possesses no deadline. A word inhabits "typographic space" without a sense of time or urgency differing from, say, a note of music. Indeed, a page of music is entirely about time and tempo; a page of printed text is about space. The paradox, however, is that print fixes voices in time, its own limitation, locking in a sound. The format of a book like *Ulysses* unifies its discontinuities. Juxtaposition persists because of the page which can be revisited time and time again by the reader.

Ulysses, then, is a book organized in space rather than time, Joyce always reminding us of this fact through his play with the spatial organization of printed marks, inserting headlines, advertising signs or account books. Ironically, the spatially arranged "Circe" episode, a drunken phantasmagoria, is, nonetheless, expressed in rigid typographic form with discrete speeches, capitalized speakers and italicized narration. Here, everything, even if not understood, is visible at a glance. As Mrs. Breen says to Bloom, "You were the lion of the night with your seriocomic recitation and you looked the part" (*U* 15.447-8). For Joyce, looking the part through type matters.

The spatial dimension of Joyce finds earlier expression in Chinese script, especially the practice of writing from top-to-bottom in columns and read from right to left. Bamboo, wood and silk were the traditional and earliest materials used for books and documents in China requiring a top to bottom style: the narrow width of bamboo and wood mandated it. Wooden tablets, precursors to books as we know them, were no more than narrow strips often strung together by leather or hemp (imagine a number of jointly tied wooden flutes). Length varied with use, although there were standard sizes for bamboo tablets for literature. The longer lengths were used for more important texts, the shorter for commentaries and records (Tsien 116).

The reason for the vertical writing of Chinese texts, resulting in more efficient reading, may also be related to the predominantly downward strokes of the brush. In this instance, writing in this fashion is the product of the materials and tools for making letters and texts. The grain of bamboo and wood, and the narrow writing strips, allowed for only a single line of characters on the surface. Holding a tablet with the left hand, it was easier to write with the right in a downward sequence. Vertical reading is also faster than horizontal (Tsien 204).

Joyce displays this preference for Oriental verticality at several points in *Ulysses*, notably the opening of "Sirens" with 57 statements of song in columnar form, supposedly the tuning up of an orchestra. In the "Ithaca" section of *Ulysses*, the narrator, in answering the question concerning Bloom's comment on the possibilities "unexploited of the modern art of advertisement," emphasizes the "verticality of maximum visibility" (*U* 17.582) because such presentations create interest and attention for the public. Throughout this section, Joyce calls attention to verticality: Bloom's breakfast plates are vertically stacked, (*U* 17.298); he considers a vertical shaft of 5000 feet sunk to the center of the earth; a vertical piano sits in his living room; and a vertical "fume redolent of aromatic oriental incense" emanates from a cone he lights (*U* 17.1303). Here, space and culture unite, the vertical and Oriental becoming one – or creating in Joyce's language the "verbivocovisual" (FW 341.18).

Connections between the vertical and expressive in the *Wake* are even more dramatic. Pages 260-308, dealing with the comments of the twins Shem and Shaun, visually express the Chinese practice of vertical writing with marginal commentary, a common Chinese practice. As noted earlier, Book II, Chapter 2, of the *Wake* displays a similarly narrow column of text surrounded by commentary. But even this in Joyce's hands is unstable since the voices and positions—right or left to the main text—change midway. The voices switch sides as if to emphasize the uncertainty of statement and text. Modernity's uncertainty replaces the Orient's clarity at least in written form.[8]

Reading a finished, printed text in China was also curiously proto-Joycean. During the late Imperial period, commentaries of Zhu Xi on the Four Books formed a basic handbook of examination study. But students learned from an early age that to read a text was also to be interrupted by commentaries often on the same page which encouraged an engagement with the text, a dialogue that Joyce would elaborate not only through the self-conscious remarks of Bloom but through the visually marked textual interruptions and interrogations in the margins and footnotes of the *Wake*, notably Book II, Chapter 2, based on a school notebook with marginalia and footnotes. Doodles and a Euclidean drawing round out the text (Brokaw/ Chow 15; Joyce, *Letters* I. 406). This method of textual disruption was also applied to fiction and drama of the late Ming period.

For Joyce, the idea of a commentary addresses the reading practices of the novel. In confronting the discontinuous surface of the novel at whatever pace the reader likes, a reader still searches for continuity, of joining spaces. Echoes which occur throughout the novel offset the varied if not contradictory narrative styles physically present in the text. A line from "Circe" for example, "Potato Preservative against Plague and Pestilence, pray for us" (*U* 15. 1952) echoes "potatoes and marge, marge and potatoes" found in "Lestrygonians" (*U* 8.42) and "Potato I have" from "Calypso" (*U* 4.73). The reader may note cross references to the allusions, forming his/her own mental commentary, and thereby enacts the unity of the novel, which is spatial not sequential. A book makes it possible to review, examine and relocate such references via numbered pages. Offsetting the broken or fragmented narrative are the recurrent references to singular items throughout the text.

What Joyce offers is what he labels "Cathay cyrcles" (FW 119.23) in a passage dealing with the sigla of the *Wake*, adding a reference to Hong Kong. Here, he may be referring to an actual Chinese source, an unidentified Chinese student he asked to send him some "letterwords," as he told Harriet Shaw Weaver (2 March 1927, *Letters* I. 250). The last symbol sent to Joyce "means 'mountain' and is called 'Chin,'" he explains to Weaver, "the common people's way of pronouncing Hin or Fin," and he adopts the term for his own shorthand: "I am working away at the suite of W [Chin]," he tells her (*Letters* I. 250). The symbol Chin, he soon explains again, is a block letter meaning "H.C.E. interred in the landscape," adding that "Chin" "seems to be rolling round the globe over all kinds of toes" (*Letters* I. 254).

Finally, if briefly, is the inscription of the text and body. The issue of inscription and Shem writing on his body in *Wake* (185.35-6) has been frequently discussed but it should be noted that it has an origin in Chinese practice: book copying was a sign of reverence and a way of earning merit. Copying sutras—sometimes with one's own blood—was a means of manifesting devotion to Buddha and gaining religious merit. Copying a text was a way of possessing it, absorbing it through an act of personal reproduction. Printing emerged in China in close connection with Buddhist piety, in which practices of recitation, stamping, and hand copying both encouraged the development of wood block technology and continued to co-exist alongside it, although in ways increasingly influenced by printing. Shem, the "pixillated doodler" (*FW* 421.33), self-inscribes himself as text.

The look, presentation, design, typography and even size of the modernist page become its own object with a meaning parallel to, or possibly in conflict with, the significance of the words. As Beckett said of Joyce and the *Wake*, "his writing is not *about* something; *it is that something itself*" (Beckett 14). The materiality of Chinese script transformed itself into the modernist page.

This discussion began with a commentary from one of the earliest Chinese readers of Joyce. I end with another Chinese observer, less sympathetic, perhaps, to Joyce and his enterprise. *Ulysses* comes in for particular attack. The critic is Zhou Libo:

> *Ulysses* is a notoriously obscene novel, as well as a notoriously abstruse book . . . . the one person who first appreciated it and promoted it was a very wealthy aesthete. Few other people have been interested in this book, where the reader, cutting through a boundless forest of words, would find nothing but worthless trifles and erratic images. Who but a person with an excess of fat would need such a book? (1935; in Tsoi 4)

Who indeed?

Notes

1. That same year Joyce also wrote to Weaver that at a dinner with John Quinn in Paris, a friend of his told Joyce that there is a "club in the far east where Chinese ladies . . . meet twice a week to discuss my mistresspiece. Needless to say the said club is in -- shavole Shanghai!" (23 October 1923. *Lett.* I: 206). A Japanese translation of *Ulysses* appeared in two volumes in Tokyo in 1931 and 1934.

2. As early as 1908, Roger Fry cited Chinese painting as possessing both expressive and representational qualities; two years later, he noted how Oriental paintings form "a part of the surface which they decorate, and suggest visions to the imagination, rather than impose them upon the senses"(Fry 88).

3. Reference to *Ulysses* is to episode number and line number in the Gabler edition used for this paper. "Calypso," for example, is the 4th episode of the novel; *U* 4.99 means *Ulysses,* episode four, line 99. References to *Finnigans Wake* are to page number and line number. For example, *FW* 341.18 means *Finnegans Wake* page 341, line 18.

4. Useful discussions of Joyce and the Orient include Lynne A. Bongiovanni, "'Turbaned Faces Going By:' James Joyce and Irish Orientalism," *Ariel* (Oct. 2007) 25-49; Brandon Kershner, "Ulysses and the Orient," *James Joyce Quarterly* 35 (1998) 273-96; and Carol Shloss, "Joyce in the Context of Irish Orientalism," *James Joyce Quarterly* 35 (1998) 264-71.

5. On the pantomime in Ireland see Cheryl Herr, *Joyce's Anatomy of Culture* (Urban: U of Illinois P, 1986) 104-118. Pages 116-7 refer to advertising pantomimes and pp. 125-30 highlight *Dick Whittington* as a central pantomime for "Circe." It was produced at the Theatre Royal in Dublin on 26 January 1904.

6. Jerome McGann's *the Textual Condition* (1991) and George Bornstein's *Material Modernism* (2001) are two examples. Work by Johanna Drucker such as *Figuring the Word* (1998) and *Graphic Design Theory, Readings from the Field,* ed. Helen Armstrong (2009) are also helpful.

7. According to Joseph McDermott, it took approximately eight centuries from the end of the seventh to the start of the sixteenth before imprints dominated manuscripts in the collections and book markets of the culturally developed regions of the country. McDermott, "The Ascendance of the Imprint in China," *Printing and Book Culture in Late Imperial China,* ed. Cynthia J. Brokaw and Kai-wing Chow (Berkeley: U of California P, 2005) 78.

8. Many of the Chinese terms used today relating to the format and page layout of

books derive from the early use of bamboo and wood. Even after the introduction of paper in the second century A.D., bamboo and wood still survived for some three centuries, partly because the materials were as indigenous to China as papyrus was to Egypt (Tsien 96-7). Silk was used for illustrations appended to books of bamboo tables, as well as maps because the surface was wider than the wooden board. Silk (the term appears 44 times in *Ulysses*) was also used for inscriptions of worship or sacrifice and used primarily by royal houses to transmit the sayings of sage/ kings. Silk was also used for permanent records of exceptional honors, notably for statesmen and military heroes. But silk proved to be expensive and bamboo bulky for writing; hence, the introduction of something less costly, light and cheap: paper. Tsuen-Hsuin Tsien, *Written on Bamboo & Silk, The Beginnings of Chinese Books & Inscriptions*, 2nd. Ed. Chicago: U of Chicago P, 2004, *passim*. On the popularity of paper, see Tsien 150-52.

Works Cited

Beckett, Samuel. "Dante . . . Bruno . Vico . . . Joyce," *Our Exagmination Round his Factification* . . . . 1929. New York: New Directions, 1962. 3-22.

Brockey, Liam Matthew. *Journey to the East, The Jesuit Mission to China, 1579-1724*. Cambridge, MA: Harvard UP, 2007.

Brokaw, Cynthia J. and Kai-wing Chow, eds. *Printing and Book Culture in Late Imperial China*. Berkeley, U of California P, 2005.

Bush, Christopher. *Ideographic Modernism, China, Writing, Media*. New York: Oxford UP, 2010.

Cheng, Vincent J. *Joyce, race and empire*. Cambridge: Cambridge UP, 1995.

Chow, Kai-Wing. *Publishing, Culture, and Power in Early Modern China*. Stanford: Stanford UP, 2004.

De Weerdt, Hilde. *Competition over Content, Negotiating Standards for the Civil Service Examination in Imperial China (1127-1279)*. Cambridge, MA: Harvard UP, 2007.

Ehrlick, Heyward. "'Araby' in Context: The 'Splendid Bazaar,' Irish Orientalism and James Clarence Mangan," *James Joyce Quarterly* 35: 2/3 (1998): 309-331.

Fenollosa, Ernest and Ezra Pound. *The Chinese Written Character as a Medium for Poetry: A Critical Edition*. Ed. Haun Saussy, Jonathan Stalling, and Lucas Klein. New York: Fordham UP, 2008.

Fry, Roger. "The Grafton Gallery – I." *A Roger Fry Reader*. Ed. Christopher Reed. Chicago: U of Chicago P, 1996. 86-89.

Joyce, James. *Finnegans Wake*. New York: Viking, 1982.

___. "James Clarence Mangan," *Occasional, Critical, and Political Writing*. Ed.Kevin Barry. Oxford: Oxford World's Classics, 2000. 53-60.

___. *James Joyce Archive*. Ed. Michael Groden, et al. New York: Garland, 1977-79.

___. *Letters*, vol. I. Ed. Stuart Gilbert. Reissued with corrections, 1966. 1957. New York: Viking Press, 1966.

___. *Ulysses*. Ed. Hans Walter Gabler. New York: Vintage Books, 1986.

Kenner, Hugh. *The Pound Era*. Berkeley: U of California P, 1971.

___. *The Stoic Comedians, Flaubert, Joyce and Beckett*. Boston: Beacon, 1962.

Kershner, Brandon. "*Ulysses* and the Orient," *James Joyce Quarterly* (35: 2/3) 1998. 273-96.

Laurence, Patricia. *Lily Briscoe's Chinese Eyes, Bloomsbury, Modernism and China*. Columbia, SC: U of South Carolina P, 2003.

Lennon, Joseph. *Irish Orientalism, A Literary and Intellectual History*. Syracuse: Syracuse UP, 2004.

McLuhan, Marshall. "Trivial and Quadrivial" (1953). *The Interior Landscape: The Literary Criticism of Marshall McLuhan 1943-1962*. Ed. Eugene McNamara. Toronto: McGraw Hill, 1969.

McCourt, John. *The Years of Bloom, James Joyce in Trieste, 1914-1920*. Dublin: Lilliput Press, 2000.

Maddox, Brenda. *Nora, A Biography of Nora Joyce*. London: Hamish Hamilton, 1988.

Porter, David. *Ideographia, the Chinese Cipher in Early Modern Europe*. Stanford: Stanford UP, 2001.

Sullivan, Kevin. *Joyce Among the Jesuits*. New York: Columbia UP, 1958.

Tsoi, Pablo Sze-pang, "Joyce and China: A Mode of Intertextuality, The Legitimacy of Reading and Translating Joyce," Working Paper, Lam Institute for East-West Studies, Hong Kong Baptist University, 2007.

Tsien, Tsuen-Hsuin. *Written on Bamboo & Silk, The Beginnings of Chinese Books & Inscriptions*. 2nd ed. Chicago: U of Chicago P, 2004.

Ziter, Edward. *The Orient on the Victorian Stage*. Cambridge: Cambridge UP, 2003.

Virginia Woolf's Truth and *Zhenhuan* in Chinese Poetics

Fen Gao

What is literary truth? In Western poetics, there are two kinds of general assumptions, mimetic truth and idealist truth. The former insists that literature is most truthful when it represents things in themselves outside the human mind. The latter holds that literature affords access to Ideals or Forms themselves, which may either be the principles of reality inherent in nature and the mind, or the transcendental forms, or the symbolic forms.[1] As a contrast, in Chinese poetics, literary truth has long been regarded as *Zhenhuan*, namely the unification between the truth of life (*Zhen*) and the illusion of art (*Huan*).

Could we transcend binary opposed views of truth—that of things in themselves and that of Divine or spiritual mind in us, and get to something integral? What is the primordial essence of truth? These are the questions Virginia Woolf explores all her life. From 1919 to 1929, she perceived truth in the tradition of Western literature, questioned and debated with Arnold Bennett, displayed a vision of truth through Lily Briscoe's Chinese eyes, then summarized five modes of truth from Western novels, and finally elaborated on her view of truth in "Phases of Fiction" and *A Room of One's Own*.

Virginia Woolf, however, has long been regarded as a pursuer of subjective truth. For instance, she is criticized by Georg Lukacs as "an extreme example" of the modernist writers who identify subjective experience with reality.[2] Since the 1980s, critics have begun to disclose "synthesis" and the nature of "transcendence" in Woolf's truth, and interpreted it as "the interfusion of three realms: reality, the external world of things and the internal world of our thought" (Barzilai 21) or as "a yearning for transcendence of the world of time and death on the part of a particular character, or a suggestion in the narrative structure of an abstract 'gap' in actual life that cannot be directly referred to in language, but is certainly a potential experience of human being" (Hussey 96). With these enlightening revelations as the base, we can explore not only Woolf's critique of traditional truth, her summary of literary modes, and her insight into truth, but also how her perception is similar to *Zhenhuan* in Chinese poetics.

A Critique of Binary Opposition

Woolf expresses in "Reading," a 1919 article, her awareness that literary truth varies with human cognition of the world and self. She perceives in the early forms of fiction, a truth of magnificent conception of the Knight and the world, which remains forever "an unassailable statement of man and the world" (178). She discovers that, when the light of human spirit changes from the slight shape of the grasshopper and beetle into the great and beautiful shape of the moth with huge and glowing underwings, an exploration of the truth of self begins. As Sir Thomas Browne puts it, "The world that I regard is myself; it is the microcosm of my own frame that I cast mine eye on: for the other I use it but like my globe, and turn it round sometimes for my recreation" (173). While in modern society, Woolf believes we need a new truth of art: "We want something that has been shaped and clarified, cut to catch the light, hard as gem or rock with the seal of human experience in it, and yet sheltering as in a clear gem the flame which burns now so high and now sinks so low in our own heart" (170). Generally, Woolf's initial understanding of literary truth is that: human cognitions of the world, self, and consciousness are represented respectively in literary trends; literary truth is a likeness to its object.

But such an impression is not powerful enough to make her a firm believer of the traditional view of truth; rather her confusion is more precisely expressed in "Monday or Tuesday" (1921). Here Woolf's inquiry appears in the form of a heron, flying beneath the sky. It can perceive via senses all things in the world, witness all human activities, and recollect all words rising, blossoming and penetrating. But what is the truth?

Woolf clarifies the relationship between truth and facts, truth and spirit, by analyzing materialists and spiritualists in "Modern Fiction" (1925) and "Mr. Bennett and Mrs. Brown" (1925). She criticizes the materialists, represented typically by Arnold Bennett, for they focus on facts only, regardless of the deeper reality underlying the appearances: "they write of unimportant things; that they spend immense skill and immense industry making the trivial and the transitory appear the true and the enduring" ("Modern Fiction" 159). She also points out the problem of the spiritualists, represented typically by James Joyce, who tend to express the innermost flame of spirit only, disregarding whatever seems to them adventitious, which not only prevents the reader from imagining, but also centers themselves in self ("Modern Fiction" 162). To Woolf, the truth of art is neither that of facts nor that of spirit, but that of life itself. As she puts it, what literature can do is to "get closer to life itself," for "without life nothing else is worthwhile" ("Modern Fiction" 163) and the character is just "the spirit we live by, life itself" ("Character in Fiction" 436). To be more specific, life itself may be presented in fiction as a unity of facts and reality, as found in English fiction, or as a unity of spirit and its extrinsic facts, as found in Russian fiction. Her comment on Thomas Hardy's view of truth justifies her own position. After reading Hardy's statement, "The exact truth as to material fact ceases to be of importance in art, I want to see the deeper reality underlying the scenic, the expression of what are sometimes called abstract imaginings," she questions his idea in this way: "But it was a question how far abstract imagination could be expressed in a novel. Would not realities fatally conflict with that observation of manners and customs which Hardy, so simply and so modestly, had accepted as the staple of the novelist's trade?" ("Half of Thomas Hardy" 68). Such a comment clarifies not only her attention to the unification of facts and reality, but her position of transcending the thing itself, whether it refers to appearance or reality.

Eventually, Woolf develops even more forcefully her understanding of truth, when she expresses in *To the Lighthouse* (1927) that the unification of reality and spirit is the truth of art. In the novel, the protagonist Lily Briscoe devotes herself to depicting life itself, with the Ramsays as the proper stuff of her painting, but she is troubled by the dark passage from the visual things to artistic work. She tries to perceive life, through her Chinese eyes, between Mr. Ramsay, who devotes himself to the reality of things only and is incapable of untruth, and Mrs. Ramsay, whose instinct is to turn infallibly to the human race, to build her nest in the human heart, and to bring unity to all separate things and people. The confrontation of their stances expresses itself unconsciously in Lily Briscoe's painting in the way that she cannot connect the mass on the right with that on the left without breaking the unity of the whole. Indeed, she cannot get a solution until ten years later, after the Great War, when the link which usually binds things together has been cut and everything is floating aimlessly, when she realizes the importance of the connection between the two sides of masses. She understands that "nothing [is] simply one thing" (273), in the same ways that the lighthouse with its silvery and misty-looking tower and the lighthouse with its white-washed-rock tower can both be true. Life is a wholeness, comprised of globed compacted things, and the truth of art is to "achieve that razor edge of balance between two opposite forces, Mr. Ramsay and her picture" (283), the former referring to external reality, "to feel simply that's a chair, that's a table," the latter referring to human perception, "it is a miracle, it's an ecstasy" (296). And the balance of reality and ecstasy can only be achieved when we are in a state of unreality, "between things, beyond things" (281). It is a distant stance with which her Chinese eyes benefit her and which helps her draw a line in the center, allowing her finally to have a vision of the unity of reality and spirit.

Woolf therefore completes her perceptive process from understanding truth as a binary agreement with the thing or with the spirit to seeing truth as the unification of reality and spirit in this way. Woolf's insight into truth is similar to the concept of *Zhenhuan* in Chinese poetics, in which *Zhen* (the true) and *Huan* (the illusive) are a pair of dialectical aesthetic terms. Indeed, their unity has long been considered to be the criterion of art in Chinese poetics.

The Chinese character *Zhen* (眞), composed of four parts, "匕" (change),"目"(eye), "一"(hiding), "八"(vehicle), originally refers to "the immortal transfiguring to ascend to Heaven,"[3] which indicates "the primordial," "the natural," "the inherent," "the real," and "the sincere." And the original meaning of the Chinese character *Huan* (幻) is "the illusory and the changing." In Chinese poetics, the two terms *Zhen* and *Huan* are not regarded as contradictory but as supplemental and complementary. On the one hand, things and emotions presented in literature are real, and on the other hand, a work of art is imaginary and illusive to uncover the primordial, the natural and the sincere. As a result, artistic creativity is by nature a unity of *Zhen* and *Huan*. The unity finds its initial and everlasting expression in the works of Laozi (Lao Tzu) and Zhuangzi. When interpreting "Tao," Laozi says that it is a thing impalpable and incommensurable, in which there are images and entities. It is shadowy and dim, yet within it there is the real. The real is true and can be justified.[4] While answering the question what *Zhen* is, Zhuangzi says, "*Zhen* refers to the highest state of sincerity. Without sincerity, no one could be moved....*Zhen* is valuable for it is the primordial intrinsic and the spirit extrinsic.... *Li* (礼) is formulated by human beings, while *Zhen* is natural and can never be changed."[5] Both Laozi and Zhuangzi perceive that *Zhen* is primordial to the world and human beings, as it embodies both the image of things and the primordial significance beyond them, and their views formulate the essential thought of Chinese poetics.

Woolf may or may not have read any works by Laozi or Zhuangzi, but it is not surprising that they reach similar insights originating in human intuition.

A Sum of Five Modes of Truth

In addition to developing her definition of truth as a unity of reality and spirit, Woolf further summarizes five modes of truth through a synchronic comparative review of Western novels in both *A Room of One's Own* (1929) and "Phases of Fiction" (1929).

Her question about literary truth is as follows:

> Which was the truth and which was illusion . . . . What was the truth about these houses, for example, dim and festive now with their red windows in the dusk, but raw and red and squalid, with their sweets and their boot-laces, at nine o'clock in the morning? And the willows and the river and the gardens that run down to the river, vague now with the mist stealing over them, but gold and red in the sunlight—which was the truth, which was the illusion about them?
>
> (*A Room of One's Own* 15-16)

This question recalls Lily Briscoe's perception in *To the Lighthouse*: the lighthouse with its silvery and misty-looking tower and the lighthouse with its white-washed-rock tower can both be true; the most important thing is to reach a balance between them. It is obvious that her aesthetic discussion in *A Room of One's Own* and "Phases of Fiction" is a continuation of the exploration of the idea of truth in *To the Lighthouse*.

Woolf's five modes of literary truth are as follows.

First, fact-recording is only part of truth: "It is part of truth—the sting and edge of it. . . It walks beside the fact and apes it, like a shadow which is only a little more humped and angular than the object which casts it" ("Phases of Fiction" 102). The truth-tellers, like Trollope, W. E. Norris, and Maupassant, represent all concrete things and all that is visualized, its brightness and its credibility, but facts are all there is. To Woolf, literary truth is not literal truth; there must be hidden truth beneath the surface, like some Providence or morality as suggested by Daniel Defoe.

Second, for Woolf the truth of imagination should be based on facts. Woolf believes that "what one must do to bring her to life was to think poetically and prosaically at one and the same moment, thus keeping in touch with fact—that she is Mrs. Martin, aged thirty-six, dressed in blue, wearing a black hat and brown shoes; but not losing sight of fiction either—that she is a vessel in which all sorts of spirits and forces are coursing and flashing perpetually" (*A Room of One's Own* 46). Literary imagination for want of facts may turn out to be ridiculous. The woman in literary works is a typical case: "Imaginatively she is of the highest importance; practically she is completely insignificant," like "a worm winged like an eagle; the spirit of life and beauty in a kitchen chopping up suet" (*A Room of One's Own* 45-46). Robert Louis Stevenson's and Mrs. Radcliffe's romantic novels are other cases, which are emotional and imaginative, but their absurdity is evident by obliterating facts ("Phases of Fiction" 103-110).

Third, the truth of emotion involves integrity, presented as a shape of many different judgments and feelings, flowing from an incandescent mind. Woolf believes that a literary work is a whole structure of infinite complexity, which is "made up of so many different judgments, of so many different kinds of emotion," and what holds them together is "something that one calls integrity." And this "integrity" itself conveys the truth of literature: "What one means by integrity, in the case of the novelist, is the conviction that he gives one that this is the truth"

(*A Room of One's Own* 75). Integrity can only be achieved by the artist with an incandescent state of mind, for "in order to achieve the prodigious effort of freeing whole and entire the work that is in him," an artist "must be incandescent, like Shakespeare's mind...There must be no obstacle in it, no foreign matter unconsumed"(*A Room of One's Own* 58). Among English "character-mongers and comedians," Woolf appreciates Jane Austen most, whose detachment from the work, aloofness, completeness and architectural sense of form bring "a quality which is not in the story but above it, not in the things themselves but in their arrangement," expressing "a significance" beyond the story itself ("Phases of Fiction" 117).

Fourth, the truth of psychology is to illuminate the consciousness from its roots to the surface. Woolf appreciates Proust highly, for his work unifies the thinker and the poet: "on the heel of some fanatically precise observation, we come upon a flight of imagery... as if the mind, having carried its powers as far as possible in analysis, suddenly rose in the air and from a station high up gave us a different view of the same object in terms of metaphor" ("Phases of Fiction" 125). A psychological view of the world, therefore, is put on display. Dostoevsky is another perfect "psychologist," according to Woolf, who devotes himself "to reveal[ing] the soul's difficulties and confusions" through contradictions and contrasts ("Phases of Fiction" 127).

Finally, the fifth truth, the truth of mind, is a poetic, satirical and distant viewing of the soul as a whole. The satirists, such as Sterne and Peacock, do not explore the depths of the soul by analyzing people's sensations, confusions, and contradictions; instead, they focus on a distant and poetic viewing of the oddities, whims, fancies, and sensibilities of the mind, which makes possible a grasp of the human soul wholly. "In the satirist," Woolf concludes, "we get not a sense of wildness and the soul's adventures, but that the mind is free and therefore sees through and dispenses with much that is taken seriously by writers of another calibre" ("Phases of Fiction" 132-133).

Woolf's summary of the five modes expresses her firm belief that literature is a form of art which gives "a full and truthful record of the life of a real person" ("Phases of Fiction" 141). To Woolf, life is like a globe, integral and complete: "So the days pass and I ask myself sometimes whether one is not hypnotized, as a child by a silver globe, by life; and whether this is living. It's very quick, bright, exciting. But superficial perhaps. I should like to take the globe in my hands and feel it quietly, round, smooth, heavy, and so hold it, day after day. I will read Proust I think. I will go backwards and forwards" ("A Writer's Diary" 138). She sums up the five modes of truth through a synchronic comparative study of Western novels, with a focus neither on their respective features, nor on selecting the best, but on the wholeness of life, on the revelation of different levels of the life globe.

Woolf's perception differs from the conventional hypotheses of truth in Western poetics. In traditional Western poetics, the essential criterion of truth is "the agreement of knowledge with its object,"[6] which is still elaborated on by many contemporary critics. M. H. Abrams' influential exploration of truth in *The Mirror and the Lamp*, for example, reveals thoroughly the convergent process of the concept of truth, from many small streams of opinions to several dominant rivers of theories: mimetic theories, pragmatic theories, and expressive theories,[7] with the thought of "agreement" as its fundamental criterion.

Woolf's summary of modes transcends the paradigm of "agreement," which regards literary truth as the truth of life, beyond the artificial split of facts, imagination, emotion, psychology and mind. Similar opinions can be found in Chinese poetics. Although from the time of the Han dynasty until the Southern and Northern dynasties (206 B.C.—581), "faithful recording" is highly praised by scholars, such as Wang Chong, Ban Gu, Zuo Si, yet the highest state of art is always regarded to be "true to emotions, scenes, facts and consciousness concurrently,"[8] and "to merge naturally the truth of facts, scenes, emotions and intelligence into one."[9] Woolf's parsing of truth into five distinct categories is, perhaps not surprisingly, entirely concurrent with this classical Chinese view.

An Insight into the truth

By refining the five modes, Woolf gains an insight into the essence of truth. As she puts it,

> It is the gift of style, arrangement, construction, to put us at a distance from the special life and to obliterate its features; while it is the gift of the novel to bring us into close touch with life.

The two powers fight if they are brought into combination. The most complete novelist must be the novelist who can balance the two powers so that the one enhances the other.

("Phases of Fiction" 143-144)

Woolf holds that literary truth is neither the truth of a thing nor the truth of spirit merely; it is the truth of life expressed through a balance between form and life. To achieve such a truth, one not only needs to perceive and look beneath the depths of life, but also needs to possess the power of style, arrangement, and construction so as to shape his work. Her perception of truth is similar to the gist of *Zhenhuan* disclosed by Cengliang Mei, a Chinese scholar of the Qing dynasty: "There is no poem without me, and there is no poem without the thing. When the thing moves me, there comes the poem…A poem is something which expresses me and represents the thing. Considering the sounds, weighing the words, perceiving it a poem of me and a poem of me and the thing, then *Zhen* exists in it."[10] To Cengliang Mei, *Zhen* is a unification of "me" and "the thing" in a "poem," or a unity of the *Zhen* of life perceived by me from the thing and the *Huan* of a poem shaped by sounds and words. Both Woolf and Cengliang Mei seek balance among art, the thing and the spirit.

To achieve such a balance, Woolf makes an appeal for future fiction in "The Narrow Bridge of Art," analyzes the nature of fiction in *A Room of One's Own*, and depicts poetic novels in "Phases of Fiction." What she repeatedly emphasizes are three viewpoints, which aim to transcend the split among the thing, the spirit, and the form.

The first is to keep a distance between literature and life. She writes:

…it will differ from the novel as we know it now chiefly in that it will stand further back from life. It will give, as poetry does, the outline rather than the detail. It will make little use of the marvelous fact-recording power, which is one of the attributes of fiction…with these limitations it will express the feeling and ideas of the characters closely and vividly, but from a different angle. It will resemble poetry in this that it will give not only or mainly people's relations to each other and their activities together…but it will give the relation of the mind to general ideas and its soliloquy in solitude ("The Narrow Bridge of Art" 18-19).

Here Woolf asserts that a distance from life enables literature to transcend the particularity of things and to focus on the relation of human beings to nature, to fate, to their imagination, to their dreams, in the way that Shakespeare transcends Hamlet's relation to Ophelia to raise questions about the state of being of all human life. A similar opinion is stated by Chinese poets and scholars, with the most influential statement by Xie Zhen as follows: "Poetic writing should not be verisimilitude to life; [what is more] appropriate is to be like viewing scenes from afar, which can be lovely, illusive and beyond words, with blue hills and changing clouds; yet if we walk nearer to the hills, the wonderful vision disappears, with nothing but a few stones and trees left alone. What is seen afar and near are different, the most important [thing] is to remain ambiguous."[11]

Woolf's second principle is to see human beings in their relationship to the world of reality, apart from the world of men and women. This is the conclusion of *A Room of One's Own*, after Woolf clarifies the need to transcend the mere truth of facts, imagination, emotion, mind and self-conscious respectively in five chapters:

> ...if we have the habit of freedom and the courage to write exactly what we think; if we escape a little from the common sitting-room and see human beings not always in their relation to each other but in relation to reality; and the sky, too, and the trees or whatever it may be in themselves...our relation is to the world of reality and not only to the world of men and women....   (*A Room of One's Own* 118)

Here she suggests Western literature break through limiting itself to the human world only and to envision human beings in relation to the world of reality, as an effective means to transcend the blindness of human beings themselves. Woolf's modernist vision here correlates with the fundamental stance of Chinese literature, which holds "the truth of poetry is between things and consciousness."[12]

The third point is to regard literature as a poetic expression of life itself. "It may be," she points out, "that the perfect novelist expresses a different sort of poetry, or has the power of expressing it in a manner which is not harmful to the other qualities of the novel" ("Phases of Fiction" 137).

For Woolf, great works express poetic significance beyond language and form. They present a vision in relation to love, death, or nature, rather than to human beings themselves, which is of a poetic significance that insinuates without ceasing to be itself. Such a belief is what Chinese critics consider as the most important, or as they put it, "the novelist holds truth as the principal, illusion as the vision,"[13] and the best poem is the one "with illusion in its truth, the static in the dynamic, sound in its silence, spirit in its peace, sentence beyond sentence, taste beyond taste."[14]

In general, the function of all three viewpoints is to diminish the obstacle between the truth of life and the form of art. "To keep a distance between literature and life" helps break through the visual block of the thing, in order to realize the unification between limited vision and limitless imagination; "to see human beings in their relation to the world of reality" helps achieve a sublimation by transcending the limitation to subjectivity; "to regard literature as a poetic expression of life itself" helps stress the recovering nature of art by foregrounding its poetry beyond language and form. All three points create a balance between the truth of life and the illusion of art, which is Woolf's ultimate response to her question about truth and illusion quoted above.

In ten years, Woolf goes a long way in exploring truth. Setting out from her intuitive consciousness of the truth in literary tradition, Woolf questions and argues against the long-lasting notion of truth in Western poetics, and gradually she develops her own view by unifying the spirit with the material and truth with illusion. Her progressive disclosure of truth parallels her intuitive penetrating of the wholeness of life, which is very similar to Lily Briscoe's ten-year-long painting process. Life itself is the essential stance of her theory of truth, which makes possible a display of the infinite complexity of wholeness in her modes, and makes possible a balance of three substantial elements of art (the thing, the spirit and the form) by reducing the intensity of each. Distance is taken to dissolve the solid shape of things, its relation to the world is held to deconstruct the centrality of the human spirit, and poetic significance is emphasized to transcend the certainty of sign.

The essential difference between Woolf's "truth" and the truth of traditional Western poetics is that they are based on different philosophical stances, and therefore on different paradigms. The philosophical stance of traditional truth is epistemological. Originating in Aristotle's statement that the soul's representations are likenesses of things, the essence of truth has long been formulated as the "agreement" of the judgment with its object, or as "the agreement of knowledge with its object." In traditional poetics, the "agreement" gets broken asunder into two directions, by realism and by idealism. The former holds that literary truth is an agreement of representations with the things depicted, for the external world is present-at-hand in itself, while the latter insists that literary truth is an agreement of expressions with an understanding of Being, for Being and Reality are only in the consciousness, and cannot be explained through entities. The replacement of these two criteria of truth is described by Abrams as a transfer from the "mirror" to the "lamp."[15] In the 20th century, after the advent of linguistics, literary truth is regarded as the truth of language itself, pure simulacrum, after a successive phase of reflection, denaturing, and absence of a profound reality, and it turns out to be the dominant principle (Baudrillard 6). From the thing through the spirit to the language, a linear replacement of literary criterion is completed, and what they share in common is that the locus of truth is judgment, with an isolated subject as the starting point and knowing as the only mode of access to truth.

Unlike such an epistemological position, Woolf's truth is both ontological and aesthetic, similar to *Zhenhuan* in Chinese poetics.

Essentially, the truth of art is to uncover the truth of life itself, which is the common position of both Woolf's and Chinese poetics. After years of literary writing and theoretical meditation, Woolf thus summarizes her understanding of the novel: "the novelist may vary his scene and alter the relations of one thing to another…one element remains constant in all novels, and that is the human element; they are about people, they excite in us the feelings that people excite in us in real life. The novel is the only form of art which seeks to make us believe that it is giving a full and truthful record of the life of a real person" ("Phases of Fiction" 141). The belief that "art originates in the human soul" is a fundamental and essential view that has been rooted deeply in Chinese poetics for thousands of years.

To express the truth of life, art must be aesthetic, transcending the illusive entities of existence. On the one hand, all things are changing and uncertain, illusive yet natural; as a result, an imitative representation of things or emotions can only record appearances rather than the essential; on the other hand, things and emotions are the only way to reveal the primordial, so they are the fundamental items of art. The only way out is to transcend things and emotions, and to express the truth between the real and the unreal. Woolf repeatedly expresses, in novels and articles, that the truth of art is "between things, beyond things," and artistic form expresses the illusive image of the truth of life, with her intentional balance between Briscoe's vision and Mr. Ramsay's reality as a good example. Chinese poetics holds that art is an uncovering of the primordial through imagery, a primordial which is beyond the spirit and the thing. The following are only a few statements of many that affirm this conviction. Su Shi believes that art is "beyond Lihuang,"[16] Xu Wei insists that art is "to obtain unreal imagery at the sacrifice of the real shape of the thing," Yan Yu emphasizes that the best art is "beyond marks of the thing," and Sikong Tu holds that the truth of art is to pursue that which is "beyond images."[17]

To examine Woolf's truth in comparison with *Zhenhuan* offers a surprisingly new insight into the distinctive form of her aesthetics.

Notes

1   See, for instance, Selden 7-8: "what might be called the 'materialist' view is that literature is most truthful when it represents objects 'as they are' ('things in themselves') outside the human mind…At the other end of the spectrum is the mythopoetic view that literature creates its own reality…In simple terms, the first three views may be called 'mimetic' and can be traced back to Aristotle. The second group may be called 'idealist' and can be traced back to Plato."

2. See Lukacs 51: "…the modernist writer identifies what is necessarily a subjective experience with reality as such, thus giving a distorted picture of reality as a whole (Virginia Woolf is an extreme example of this)."

3. Xu Shen 168: "仙人变形而登天也。"

4. Lao Tzu 44-45: "道之为物，惟恍惟惚。惚兮恍兮，其中有象；恍兮惚兮，其中有物。窈兮冥兮，其中有精；其精甚真，其中有信。"

5. Zhuangzi 286: "真者，精诚之至也。不精不诚，不能动人……真在内者，神动于外，是所以贵真也……礼者，世俗之所为也；真者，所以受于天也，自然不可易也。"

6. Qtd. in Heidegger, *Being and Time* 258.

7. See Abrams 263-335.

8. Chen Yizeng 241: "情真，景真，事真，意真。"

9. Fan Dongshu 252: "事真景真，情真理真，不烦绳削而自合。"

10. Mei Cengliang 35: "无我不足以见诗，无物亦不足以见诗，物与我相遭，而诗出于其间也……肖乎吾之性情而已矣，当乎物之情状而已矣。审其音，玩其辞，晓然为吾之诗，为吾与是物之诗，而诗之真者得矣。"

11. Xie Zhen 242: "凡作诗不宜逼真，如朝行远望，青山佳色，隐然可爱，其烟霞变幻，难于名状；及登临非复奇观，惟片石数树而已。远近所见不同，妙在含糊，方见作手。"

12. Lu Shiyong 241: "诗贵真，诗之真趣，又在意似之间。"

13. Zhang Wujiu 248: "小说家以真为正，以幻为奇。"

14. Wu Leifa 255: "真中有幻，动中有静，寂处有音，冷处有神，句中有句，味外有味，诗之绝类离群者也。"

15. See Abrams 30-69.

16. "beyond Lihuang": "求于骊黄之外"，"Lihuang" here refers to the things.

17. Zhu Liangzhi 16-29: "求于骊黄之外"（苏轼）；"舍形而悦影"（徐渭）；"无迹可求"（严羽）；"象外之象"（司空图）

Works Cited

Abrams, M. H. *The Mirror and the Lamp: Romantic Theory and the Critical Tradition*. Oxford: Oxford UP, 1953.

Barzilai, Shuli. "Virginia Woolf's Pursuit of Truth." *Virginia Woolf: Critical Assessments,* vol. 2. Ed. Eleanor McNees. Sussex: Helm Information Ltd., 1994. 19-30.

Baudrillard, Jean. *Simulacra and Simulation*. Trans. Sheila Faria Glaser. Ann Arbor: U of Michigan P, 1994.

Chen Yizeng. "Poetry Pedigree." *Selected Texts of Classical Chinese Theory of Art, vol.*2. Ed. Hu Jingzhi. Beijing: Beijing UP, 2001. 241.

Fan Dongshu. "Speech of Zhaomeizan." *Selected Texts of Classical Chinese*

Theory of Art, vol. 2. Ed. Hu Jingzhi. Beijing: Beijing UP, 2001. 252.

Heidegger, Martin. *Being and Time*. Trans. John Macquarrie and Edward Robinson. San Francisco: Harper, 1962.

Hussey, Mark. *The Singing of the Real World: The Philosophy of Virginia Woolf's Fiction*. Columbus: Ohio State UP, 1986.

Lao Tzu. *Tao Te Ching*. Trans. Arthur Waley. Beijing: Foreign Language Teaching and Research P, 2009.

Lu Shiyong. "On the State of Poetry." *Selected Texts of Classical Chinese Theory of Art*, vol. 2. Ed. Hu Jingzhi. Beijing: Beijing UP, 2001. 241.

Lukacs, Georg. *Realism in Our Time: Literature and the Class Struggle*. Trans. John and Necke Mander. New York and Evanston: Harper and Row, 1964.

Mei Cengliang. "Preface to Selected Poems of Ziling Li." *Selected Essays of Chinese Poetics: Late Qing Dynasty*. Shanghai: Shanghai Education P, 2008. 35-37.

Selden, Raman. *The Theory of Criticism from Plato to the Present: A Reader*. Essex: Longman Group, 1988.

Woolf, Virginia. "Character in Fiction." *The Essays of Virginia Woolf*, vol. 3. Ed. Andrew McNeillie. London: Hogarth P, 1988. 420-437.

___. "Half of Thomas Hardy." *The Captain's Death Bed and Other Essays*. London: Harcourt Brace Jovanovich, 1978. 62-68.

___. "Modern Fiction." *The Essays of Virginia Woolf*, vol. 4. Ed. Andrew McNeillie. London: Hogarth P, 1994. 157-164.

___. "Phases of Fiction." *Granite and Rainbow: Essays*. London: Harcourt Brace Jovanovich, 1958. 93-145.

___. "Reading." *The Captain's Death Bed and Other Essays*. London: Harcourt Brace Jovanovich, 1978. 151-179.

___. *A Room of One's Own*. San Diego: Harcourt Brace Jovanovich. 1957.

___. *To the Lighthouse*. London: Penguin Books, 1996.

Wu Leifa. *Selected Texts of Classical Chinese Theory of Art*, vol.2. Ed. Hu Jingzhi. Beijing: Beijing UP, 2001. 255.

Xie Zhen. "Siming Poetics." *Selected Texts of Classical Chinese Theory of Art*, vol. 2. Ed. Hu Jingzhi. Beijing: Beijing UP, 2001. 242.

Xu Shen. *Interpreting Words*. Beijing: Zhonghua P, 2010.

Zhang Wujiu. "A Preface to Northern Song Sanshupingyao." *Selected Texts of Classical Chinese Theory of Art,* vol.2. Ed. Hu Jingzhi. Beijing: Beijing UP, 2001. 248-249.

Zhu Liangzhi. *True Water is of No Fragrance.* Beijing: Beijing UP, 2009.

Zhuangzi. *Zhuangzi.* Beijing: Zhonghua Book Company, 2007.

Re-Orienting Impersonality:
T. S. Eliot and the Self of the Far East

Christian Kloeckner

In the spring of 1883, a young Bostonian named Percival Lowell traveled to Japan, determined to learn the language and explore the culture of that far-away country. After his return late in the following year, Lowell began to work on a book that would become one of the most influential and popular narratives of comparative cultural anthropology in the late nineteenth century. Today, *The Soul of the Far East* (1888) stands as a prime example of what Edward Said has called Orientalism, a "style of thought based upon an ontological and epistemological distinction between 'the Orient' and (most of the time) 'the Occident'" (2). Setting the stage for sharp contrasts between the West and the Far East, the first few pages alone characterize that foreign world with adjectives such as "upside down," "topsy-turvy," "antipodal," "inverted," "reversed," "oblique," "diametrically opposed" (1-2). To the newcomer, Japan appears as "one huge, comical antithesis" of the West, in which even its citizens speak, write, and read "backwards" (2). Although Lowell expresses his wish to command respect for an "equal but opposite" foreign culture and affirms that only by new perspectives gained through intercultural understanding mankind can "realize humanity" (3), his book's opening also prepares the ground for assessments that ultimately prove the West's superiority. According to Lowell, Far Eastern societies are less dynamic because they imitate— rather than incorporate and assimilate—foreign influences, and thus represent a case of "partially arrested development" (8).

At the center of this divide and the Far East's stagnant culture, are diverging conceptions of individuality. Lowell claims,

the sense of self grows more intense as we follow in the wake of
the setting sun, and fades steadily as we advance into the dawn.
America, Europe, the Levant, India, Japan, each is less personal
than the one before. We stand at the nearer end of the scale, the
Far Orientals at the other. If with us the *I* seems to be the very
essence of the soul, then the soul of the Far East may be said to
be Impersonality. (15)

If individuality were "but the transient illusion the Buddhists would
have us believe it," Lowell argues, there could no more be any faith
nor action (16-17). Convinced that individualization was part and
parcel of modernization efforts, he embraces the notion that Western
development is "the natural course of evolution" (25) and that *the
degree of individualization of a people is the self-recorded measure of
its place in the great march of mind*" (195). The lack of individuality in
Eastern cultures thus proves their backwardness:

> [T]hese people are now, at any rate, stationary not very far from
> the point at which we all set out. They are still in that childish
> state of development before self-consciousness has spoiled the
> sweet simplicity of nature. An impersonal race seems never to
> have fully grown up. (25)

In the remainder of the book, Lowell seeks to validate his thesis
with examples from language, everyday thought and practices, and
religion. Commenting on Japanese's lack of personal pronouns, plural
forms, gender markers, and the frequent use of sentences without
subjects (81-105), Lowell claims that impersonality is the essence of
an extremely restrained language. In society, impersonality manifests
itself in arranged marriages and the Confucian, patriarchic family
structures that rule over the individual (29-59). And while Lowell
points to many similarities between Christianity and Buddhism, it is
the idea of the self that opens up a "fathomless abyss" between the two
religions, a "separation more profound than death": "Christianity tells
us to purify ourselves that we may enjoy countless æons of that bettered
self hereafter; Buddhism would have us purify ourselves that we may
lose all sense of self for evermore" (184-85). Lowell's contribution to
the ongoing debates on the vogue of Buddhism in the late nineteenth

century thus furthered the image of a deeply pessimistic, impersonal creed in which "personality, this sense of self, is a cruel deception and a snare" (186).[1]

If there is one area where Lowell allows the Far Eastern subject to be superior to the Westerner, it is in matters of taste and appreciation of beauty. But their "most affectionate intimacy" with art, Lowell maintains, "implies of itself impersonality in the people" (111). Since Japanese art invariably speaks of nature, religion, and humor in a "universal tongue which all can understand," it remains for him fundamentally unoriginal (122-23, 216). Their lack of originality and imagination—which Lowell deems even more important for scientific progress—prevents them from becoming more individualized and helping their societies to advance more rapidly. Thus, the Far Eastern people are collectively "nearer, just as a stream, in falling from a cliff" (217). A book that began with benignly calling the Far East "equal but opposite" thus ends with a chilling warning with Social Darwinist overtones:

> That impersonality is not man's earthly goal they unwittingly bear witness; for they are not of those who will survive. Artistic attractive people that they are, their civilization is like their own tree flowers, beautiful blossoms destined never to bear fruit; for whatever we may conceive the far future of another life to be, the immediate effect of impersonality cannot but be annihilating. If these people continue in their old course, their earthly career is closed. Just as surely as morning passes into afternoon, so surely are these races of the Far East, if unchanged, destined to disappear before the advancing nations of the West. Vanish they will off the face of the earth and leave our planet the eventual possession of the dwellers where the day declines. Unless their newly imported ideas take root, it is from this whole world that Japanese and Koreans, as well as Chinese, will inevitably be excluded. Their Nirvana is already being realized. (225-26)

Many years later, Percival Lowell's younger sister must have disagreed. In fact, Amy Lowell, along with other modernists, turned her poetic attention to the Far East. Kathleen Flanagan, Robert Kern, Zhaoming Qian, and other critics have convincingly argued that modernist writers turned to Oriental cultures as a means of reinvigorating and purifying their poetic practice (Kern ix) and "achieving an artistic 'revolution'" (Flanagan 115). In Emily Haddad's formulation, the Orient had for a long time functioned as an "alternative aesthetic space," which European and American poets perused for poetic experimentation. Orientalism here served "as a diffuse avant-garde, a matrix for the re-examination of both preexisting conventions and contemporary expectations in poetry and poetics" (2). In the case of modernist poets, Far Eastern themes and forms thus became a "pretext" and "a model for aesthetic dissent" (Flanagan 127) against the literary modes of Romantic and Victorian poetry. Verse forms influenced by Japanese *haikus* and *tankas* or Chinese Tang and Sung dynasty verse turned into "a revolutionary tool, an exotic means of dissenting from prevailing poetic techniques in English" (Flanagan 119). The central figure in this movement was surely Ezra Pound, according to T. S. Eliot "the inventor of Chinese poetry for our time" (Introduction 14). In this essay, however, I focus on Eliot, born in the year when *The Soul of the Far East* was published, and who today is not only remembered for his modernist poetry but for an aesthetic model that employs the same terms with which Lowell describes the "soul" of the Far East: Eliot's theory of impersonality.

While I do not claim that Eliot developed his aesthetic theory specifically in response to Oriental poetics or Far Eastern cultures, I argue that their literary and cultural traditions supplied Eliot with role models worth emulating in his poetic practice. Even if Eliot was predominantly concerned with Western philosophical and religious traditions and would reject pantheism as "not European" ("Function" 28), his engagement with Buddhist and Brahminist texts at Harvard and beyond contributed to an understanding of world literature as an organic whole, to which the individual poet owed allegiance. Crucially, I maintain that the impersonality attributed to Far Eastern cultures and the impersonality sought in modernist poetry are not entirely unrelated concepts or simply coincidental. And I do no simply base this claim on the high likelihood that by the time Eliot left Boston for Europe, he had learned about Lowell's portrayal of an impersonal Far East in the context of an ongoing scholarly debate on Buddhism's rejection of the self.

In highlighting the non-European sources of Eliot's impersonality theory, I wish to draw attention to the concept's appropriation of a rhetoric that had been firmly implicated in imperialism and Orientalism. A brief analysis of the significance and functions of the Eastern voices in Eliot's *The Waste Land* will then allow me to address my main concerns: What are the ethical dimensions of Eliot's impersonal poetics, and what roles do Buddhist thought and the Far Eastern interventions in Eliot's poetry play in it? Does Eliot appropriate and assimilate these 'other' voices in order to aggrandize himself? Or does his criticism and poetry open up spaces for the (foreign) 'Other' at a time when imperialism has begun to crumble? One aim here is thus to show that precisely because impersonality is such an aesthetically and politically contested concept, it can tell us much about the ways in which modernist writers explored Eastern "alternative aesthetic spaces." Additionally, the history of impersonality's contested meanings can reveal much about our own practice as literary scholars.

Eliot's concept of impersonality is, of course, related to other terms with which critics have described key elements of modernist poetry. Zhaoming Qian has counted "objectivity" among the features of Oriental poetry that proved attractive to modernists (3). Pound's poetic precept of the "direct treatment of the 'thing,'" for instance, must be understood in the context of Ernest Fenollosa's essay on the ideogrammic nature of the Chinese written character. Fenollosa thought that Chinese poets faced fewer problems of representation because their language's signs always combined nouns and verbs into "things in motion" (364). As he understood Chinese, subject, act, and object were always interrelated and formally inseparable. With respect to poetry, Fenollosa concluded that "the moment we express subjective inclusion, poetry evaporates. The more concretely we express the interactions of things the better the poetry" (382-83). Chinese language and classical poetry thus offered modernists examples of how to avoid letting personalities intrude on their poem's worlds. Christine Froula understands Fenollosa's vision to entail "Western thought's awakening to the limits of the objectivist modalities its grammars inscribe and its search for a poetics not trapped within subject/object dichotomies, whether at the level of grammar or of international, interracial, intercultural, and geopolitical interchange" (60). Consequently for Pound, as Karen Jackson Ford notes, one of the haiku's allures was that it was grounded in impersonality with which Western poetry could be purged of its "obsession with the self and thus [...] of Victorian and Georgian verbosity, sentimentality, abstraction, and vagueness" (59). Seemingly, at least for some modernists, impersonality had become an enviable cultural trait of Far Eastern cultures.[2]

In his escape from the "'sincere' ego of romantic poetry and the 'righteous ego' of Victorian moralizing discourse" (Altieri 4), T. S. Eliot traveled a somewhat different route. Just like Pound, he faulted humanism and liberalism for creating a pompous self, and he was equally concerned with creating a more scientific poetry through a process of "depersonalization." Yet, Eliot's suggestion is that the poet first of all needs to submit and surrender to an organic and dynamic literary history. In his 1919 essay "Tradition and the Individual Talent," Eliot writes of a "mind of Europe" (51), encompassing everything from Shakespeare to Homer to the "rock drawing of the Magdalenian draughtsmen," which propels the true artist to a "continual self-sacrifice, a continual extinction of personality" (53). Eliot constructs a paradoxical play of individuality and conformity, in which a poet's originality manifests itself precisely where she lets her "ancestors [...] assert their immortality most vigorously" (48). The poet's role, therefore, is not that of the inspired genius but that of a "catalyst" of emotion, a "receptacle" for feelings, phrases, and images, and a "medium" for the voices of the dead (54, 55, 56). And in this almost technical, scientific transmutation of emotion lies the true artist's skill and responsibility: "Poetry is not a turning loose of emotion, but an escape from emotion; it is not the expression of personality, but an escape from personality. But, of course, only those who have personality and emotions know what it means to want to escape from these things" (58).

These bold statements stand in tension to the way Ezra Pound, just two years earlier, introduced Eliot to the readers of *The Egoist* in a commendatory review of *Prufrock and Other Observations*: "He has been an individual in his poems. [...] 'I have tried to write of a few things that really have moved me' is so far as I know, the sum of Mr. Eliot's 'poetic theory'" ("Drunken Helots" 73). One may ask: Did Pound in 1917 simply get Eliot wrong? Or what let Eliot develop a poetic theory that seems to clash with the quotation Pound attributed to him? The fact that the essay has its own share of inconsistencies— for instance, in its use of the terms "feelings" and "emotions"—and that Eliot later called it a "product of immaturity" (cit. in-Ellmann 35) makes the concept of impersonality not less difficult to handle. His clarification in 1923 that the essay pointed to "something outside of the artist to which he owes allegiance, a devotion to which he must surrender and sacrifice himself in order to earn and to obtain his unique position" ("Function" 24), only helps to underline the paradox.

Most scholars, indeed, understand impersonality to intensify paradoxically the personal by rendering its emotive states in more universal terms.[3] Others, like Louis Menand, claim that the essay's effectiveness lay in tacitly using widely shared nineteenth-century aesthetic values, wrapping them in a new idiom, and remaining purposely reductive: "For the higher degree of particularity a theory of art has, the more it exposes itself to critique [...]. It is part of the peculiar design of Eliot's early criticism that the received language of aesthetic theory is used to make arguments whose theoretical content is practically zero" (150-51). Maud Ellmann, author of the influential study *The Poetics of Impersonality* (1987), agrees that the concept is so vague and contradictory that "it can mean anything from the destruction to the apotheosis of the self" (ix). For her, some of the questions that remain open are: "Does it mean decorum, reticence, and self-restraint? Does it imply concealment or extinction of the self? Or does it mean the poet should transcend his time and place, aspiring to universal vision?" (4).[4]

In their quest to solve these mysteries, critics have tried to identify the sources for Eliot's theory of impersonality and usually found them in Eliot's philosophical education and other European contexts.[5] In the following, however, I focus on Eliot's engagement with Eastern thought and texts that contributed to his theory of impersonality. Even if the "Tradition" essay speaks of "the mind of Europe" and even if *The Waste Land* is fundamentally a poem about Europe's decay (Rabaté 221), his embrace of impersonality was underpinned by his study of Sanskrit and Pali texts in his Harvard years, by his attraction to Buddhism, and by an internationalist attitude evident in his articles and essays between 1917 and 1919.

A short article Eliot published in *The Egoist* under the pseudonym Apteryx begins to illustrate this last aspect: "The serious writer of verse must be prepared to cross himself with the best verse of other languages and the best prose of all languages" ("Verse Pleasant and Unpleasant" 43). In another article of 1918, Eliot reiterates the importance of such "cross-breeding in poetry" in terms that would resurface later in the "Tradition" essay: "A poet, like a scientist, is contributing toward the organic development of culture: it is just as absurd for him not to know the work of his predecessors or of men writing in other languages as it would be for a biologist to be ignorant of Mendel or De Vries." Foreign influences may be "disturbing," even "terrifying," but, he emphasizes, "[t]hat is the test of a new work of art" ("Contemporanea" 84). Significantly, it is through these intimate engagements with other (most often dead) authors that poets become "bearers of a tradition" ("Reflections" 39).

Although Eliot is mainly writing here about European, particularly French, traditions, his essays on Pound's engagements with the Far East suggest that these views encompass non-Western sources and traditions, as well. In *Ezra Pound: His Metric and Poetry* (1917), Eliot argues that an increasing scope and diversity of literary influences have had a liberating effect on Pound's poetry. Predicting that it will always rank among Pound's most original works, Eliot calls *Cathay* a preliminary climax in his friend's oeuvre. It is "original" because its language is not "due to the Chinese" but to Pound's own evolving poetry whose language "was ready for the Chinese poetry." In turn, these Chinese poems will now be "important for English." Pound's translations of Noh plays may be less significant, but again Eliot finds passages which "are different both from the Chinese [*sic*] and from anything existent in English" (*Ezra Pound*). In a review of these Noh plays in *The Egoist*, Eliot elaborates how translation can fertilize a literature "by importing new elements which may be assimilated, and by restoring the essentials which have been forgotten in traditional literary method." What such "rejuvenation" of literature requires is not literal translation but a "happy fusion between the spirit of the original and the mind of the translator" (102). Therefore, "when the writing is most like Mr. Pound," Eliot declares, "it also presents the appearance of being most faithful to the original" (103). Eliot's judgment here foreshadows the "Tradition" essay's paradox that poetry is the most "individual" when it lets dead poets "assert their immortality most vigorously" (48).

However, the Japanese Noh plays may in their own right be relevant for Eliot's impersonality theory. Eliot cites the stage directions of one such play, in which a red kimono placed on the stage epitomizes the protagonist's struggles and death. The Noh's "image character" and its symbolic use of the stage compare favorably with European drama, Eliot asserts, as it makes the plays brief, prevents rhetoric, and better stimulates the audience's imagination. It is also less personal: Whereas in Western plays like *Macbeth*, a haunted person's "ghost is given in the mind of the possessed," in the Noh "the mind of the sufferer is inferred from the reality of the ghost. [...] In fact, it is only ghosts that are actual; the world of active passions is observed through the veil of another world. But these passions are just as real" (103). This, in fact, would describe very well the other-worldliness of *The Waste Land*. Likewise, the Noh's inverted method of dramatizing mental states is consistent with an impersonal poetry that avoids openly expressing emotion and personality.[6]

Turning to the other main Eastern sources of Eliot's poetics of impersonality, his study of Sanskrit texts and Buddhist thought at Harvard has been well documented. Eliot himself acknowledged the influence of Indian thought and sensibility on his poetry (Murray 125) and called the *Bhagavad-Gita* the "next greatest philosophical poem to the *Divine Comedy* within my experience" ("Dante" 258). At the time of writing *The Waste Land*, he reportedly once said, he seriously considered becoming a Buddhist (Spender 20). While this claim may not have been entirely sincere (Kearns, "T. S. Eliot" 128), Eliot elsewhere explains that the price of such a move would have been too high: "I came to the conclusion [...] that my only hope of really penetrating to the heart of the mystery [of Eastern philosophical thought, C.K.] would lie in forgetting how to think and feel as an American or a European: which, for practical as well as sentimental reasons, I did not wish to do" (*After Strange Gods* 40-41). Scholars have often grappled with how to harmonize these Eastern influences with the orthodox Christian positions Eliot would take after his conversion to the Anglican Church in 1928. The authoritative account of Eliot's use of Hindu and Buddhist traditions to that effect is Cleo McNelly Kearns's *T. S. Eliot and Indic Traditions: A Study in Poetry and Belief* (1987). In her book, Kearns argues that not only did Indic texts serve Eliot as a "repository of images" but they posed "valuable challenges to established points of view" on religion, philosophy, and writing, and thus acted as a "catalyst for fundamental changes in his thought and style" (vii, viii). While scholars disagree on the degree to which Brahminist and Buddhist thought made a lasting impact on Eliot,[7] it is obvious that one of its main attractions lay in its radically divergent notion of the self.

Buddhism's rejection of an illusionary self and its association of human desire with pain can therefore serve as a key to Eliot's criticism and poetry. Kearns maintains that the "Tradition" essay's terms such as "transmutation of emotion," "self-sacrifice," and "extinction of personality" have Buddhist overtones grounded in the belief that the self does not represent any eternal essence but a fleeting, ever-changing assemblage of constituent and interrelated parts (*T.S. Eliot* 62, 74). Eliot's attack against the "metaphysical theory of the substantial unity of the soul" ("Tradition" 56) then finds its aesthetic correspondence in his presentation of a tradition that will be recast and remodeled with the advent of any new work of art. Understood in the context of Buddhist thought, Eliot's concept of "tradition" thus is far more fluid and "multivocal," full of "discordant truths" and "a multitude of perspectives" (Perl and Tuck 124, 125) than its staunch critics would have it be.

Moreover, this perspective helps us tackle the impersonality of the "Eliot voice" (Hugh Kenner) or what A. David Moody has called Eliot's "wisdom mode." Wisdom, for Eliot, consists in simplicity and openness, and does not, as Kearns writes, "juxtapose sharp and opposed positions, but subsumes many lines of argument under an embracing stance or point of view." Manifested in proverbs, aphorisms, and silence, such wisdom appeared to Eliot "feminine, multivalent, and communal rather than masculine, univocal, and individual." Kearns adds:

> The wisdom mode of the logos is also, for Eliot, a crucial strategy for achieving the impersonal, ruminative, yet intimate voice that transforms the injured self into the wholeness of a member of a community. The emergence of this wisdom voice

is almost inconceivable in Eliot's work without the continuing influence of Indic traditions. (19-20)

Significantly, Kearns's chain of logic suggests that for Eliot not only wisdom is female, but also that impersonality and the Orient are femininely gendered concepts, as well. I will come back to the implications of this analysis at the end of this essay. First, however, I need to consider Eliot's seminal *The Waste Land* in order to highlight how he deploys impersonality and Eastern voices in his poetry.

Even a severe critic of Eliot's poetics of impersonality like Maud Ellmann concedes that the poem is impersonal insofar as it "violates the very notion of a private self, for its speaker is invaded by the dead, hypnotically repeating the voices of the past. Caught in an infinite quotation, the 'I' is exposed as a grammatical position, rather than the proof of the presence of an author" (15). The poem is a radical assemblage of multiple voices and draws on utterly diverse materials, ranging from the myth of the dying and resurrected heathen Gods, the quest for the Holy Grail, to Jacobean drama, pop and pub culture, and the occult practices of fortune-tellers. This mix of voices, languages, styles and genres can hardly be unified, the pronouns remain highly unstable, and the supposedly unifying consciousness of Tiresias is perhaps more properly to be understood as an intersexual, sterile, and prophetic "*osmosis* of identities" (Ellmann 97). The poem's shattered references and broken surfaces, its world populated by urban waste, body waste and decrepitude, and a palpable sense of a culture's degradation, may— in line with many critics' understanding of impersonality—intimate deeply felt psychic conflicts of a disturbed self.[8] Interestingly, however, fragments from two Eastern texts, namely Buddha's Fire Sermon and the Fable of the Thunder in the *Brihadaranyaka Upanishad*, interfere to release the self from its despair.

At the end of Part III, "The Fire Sermon," Eliot juxtaposes a fragment of Buddha's exhortations with fragments from St. Augustine's *Confessions*:

To Carthage then I came

Burning burning burning burning
O Lord Thou pluckest me out

O Lord Thou pluckest

burning   (*Waste Land* 34: ll. 307-11)

As Eliot writes in his notes on *The Waste Land*, "the collocation of these two representatives of eastern and western asceticism, as the culmination of this part of the poem, is not an accident" (44n.309). Certainly it is not. The juxtaposition mutually reinforces the significance of the fragments, as it signals a turn away from the temptation of the outward beauties of Carthage, a renunciation of worldly experience and sense impressions, and a purification by fire from "burning" passions. In fact, the fragment from Buddha's Fire Sermon drastically sharpens the Christian asceticism by gradually consuming the agents of the Western text: At first, the "I" who has come to Carthage becomes "me," the object of God who "pluckest" him out; in the next line, the personal pronoun is gone; at last, even the "Lord" seems to have disappeared into or behind the "burning." Buddha's sermon preaching liberation through estrangement from one's self and passions is enacted here in what Eloise Knapp Hay has called Eliot's exploration of the void, his "negative way," in this case towards the Buddhist *sunyata* (199-200). In Eliot's poetics of impersonality, the artistic relief that the "escape from emotion" and "escape from personality" brings is perhaps reminiscent of the release that Buddha's Fire Sermon promises.

The title of Part V, "What the Thunder said," refers to the Fable of the Thunder, whose key terms serve as a leitmotif in the poem's conclusion. It is introduced in the following way:

Ganga was sunken, and the limp leaves
Waited for rain, while the black clouds
Gathered far distant, over Himavant.
The jungle crouched, humped in silence.
Then spoke the thunder
Da
Datta: what have we given?
My friend, blood shaking my heart
The awful daring of a moment's surrender
Which an age of prudence can never retract
By this, and this only, we have existed
                                      (*Waste Land* 38: ll. 395-405)

According to the *Brihadaranyaka Upanishad*, the creator Prajapati's injunction of "DA" is interpreted differently by gods, men, and demons to respectively mean "*damyata*" (control yourself), "*datta*" (to give), and "*dayadhvam*" (be compassionate, sympathize). All these interpretations signify moments of self-surrender, but Eliot changes the sequence of the interpretations so that the first one is man's obligation to "give," and the last one is the injunction to the gods to "control" themselves. In *The Waste Land*'s first interpretation of "DA," to "give" means to expose and submit one's self to another person, which may run counter to a culture that above all else values individualism, pragmatism and expediency—"to give" may thereby subvert a way of life that cannot reciprocate such a gesture ("never retract"). Most importantly, "to give" is our only way to live meaningfully. Compassion and self-restraint have the same goal: through the former, we can realize and respond to each other's "prison" (*Waste Land* 39: ll. 413-14); through the latter, we create consensus and acceptance, and are able to do good ("your heart would have responded / Gaily, when invited, beating obedient / To controlling hands," (*Waste Land* 39: ll. 420-22).

The ending formula of the Upanishads, "Shantih shantih shantih," which Eliot in his notes translates as 'The Peace which passes understanding' (46n.433), points to the desired state of enlightenment, free of the self and its painful passions. Hay explains that this ending, "[s]poken in stark, impersonal severity," shuns the "Christian" peace that the experience of World War I seems to have discredited. Horrified at the anarchy of his internal as well as the external world, the speaker "asks relief from consciousness itself" (202). The referential turmoil of the poem's last lines supports this reading; thus, the peace formula may indeed represent a moment of total exhaustion, annihilation, or, in the words of Balachandra Rajan, "a termination rather than an ending" (195).

Given that *The Waste Land* ends with apparently ethical concerns, what interests me in particular is the question whether Eliot's poetics of impersonality and his ostensible renunciation of the self makes room for the Other, or whether he in fact appropriates these multiple voices, including the Eastern ones just cited, in highly self-centered fashion. This is related to the question in what ways *The Waste Land* represents, to speak with Frank Kermode, an "image of imperial catastrophe" (233). Although these questions can hardly be settled conclusively, a look at the contrasting ways in which Eliot's impersonality theory and *The Waste Land* have been read reveals not only the concept's pliability and the poem's openness, but at least as much about the critical concerns that scholars have brought to the poem over time.

I will focus on two diametrically opposed positions to stake out the terrain of critical discourse. On the one hand, for Maud Ellmann the case is clear: Eliot's impersonality is a deeply anti-liberal, conservative, authoritarian concept that "conceals its iron hand by sentimentalising its paternalism." Eliot employs a "rhetoric of organicism" that disregards a hegemonic canon's "social, economic and political exclusions" (37-38). In Eliot's comment that poetry begins "with a savage beating a drum in a jungle" (cit. in Ellmann 52), she finds betrayed "his foreign as well as his domestic policy, and in particular a nervous admiration for imperialism" (52). And although she does not elaborate on her claim, its implication is clear: the rhetoric of impersonality should be related to the promise of Empire that only through submission colonized countries and cultures can achieve civilization, and hence immortality. In Ellmann's equation, impersonality is a self-serving ruse of the ego that functions exactly like the imperialist center's preferred mode of expression, the deceptively benevolent paternalism à la *The Soul of the Far East.*[9]

In Tim Dean's rendering, on the other hand, the impersonal poet becomes "a more or less pliant instrument for 'the other voice'" ("The Other's Voice" 472). As mentioned above, Eliot had called the poet a "medium" in the "Tradition" essay, and Dean points to the fortune-telling occult medium Madame Sosostris in *The Waste Land* to claim that for Eliot poetry significantly involves forms of "*speaking through* or *being spoken by*" an Other ("The Other's Voice" 472). Rejecting Ellmann's assessment of impersonality, Dean asserts to the contrary that impersonality "clears a space for otherness at the expense of the poet's self," and thus "should be considered ethically exemplary" ("T. S. Eliot" 44). It also points to "more progressive ways of imagining social relations" (49). Dean obviously draws on Emmanuel Levinas's philosophy when he writes that impersonality compels Eliot "to embrace a passivity and openness that renders him vulnerable to what feels like bodily violation" (45). The raped bodies and violated figures in *The Waste Land*, he concludes, therefore "represent Eliot's poetic ideal" (45): just like the rape of Philomela precedes and preconditions her transformation into the "inviolable voice" of a nightingale, poets need to be possessed by "souls and consciousnesses far beyond the realms of their own knowledge and experience" in order to create truly ethical art ("The Other's Voice" 489).

Tim Dean's queer studies-inflected Levinasian reading of impersonality seems to me as much a product of contemporary scholarly trends as Maud Ellmann's leftist-poststructuralist position in the early 1980s. Ellmann's claims indeed seem too facile and one-sided; it is no wonder that she must ignore Eliot's embrace of Eastern thought. Even A. David Moody, who generally downplays the significance of Buddhism for Eliot's poetry and prose, argues that Eliot recognized difference as the "basis for any genuine cross-cultural understanding" and that he refrained from an Orientalist appropriation of Eastern cultures for his own ends (Moody 19). Kearns points out that precisely because Eliot understood Buddhism and Hinduism to be "highly evolved, historically conditioned, culturally rooted forms of life and religious practice," his ultimate rejection "perhaps paid Buddhism a higher compliment" by preserving its otherness and not "allowing himself the illusion of assimilation" ("T. S. Eliot" 131, 135).

If I am not completely sold on Dean's "ethical Eliot," either, it may have to do with the fact that Eliot always seems to be very much in control over which voices enter his poetry and when they do so. And if we think of the Buddhist and Brahminist interventions in *The Waste Land*, these are not exactly, as Dean would have it, voices beyond Eliot's knowledge or experience, but ones he has studied quite well. Yet, Dean's notion that Eliot's "conception of the poet as a passive medium for alien utterances tacitly feminizes the poet's role" (45) poses an even bigger problem. Dean surely draws a compelling conclusion from his reading, a conclusion that furthermore is compatible with Kearns's attribution of femininity to Eliot's concepts of wisdom, impersonality, and the Orient discussed above. However, keeping the context of imperialism with its attendant characterizations of the Far East in mind, this is precisely the point where the "ethically exemplary" concept of impersonality gets compromised: in Dean's construction, Eliot's impersonality begins to sound uncannily identical to the Orientalist conception of Asia as female, passive, and at least imaginatively, rapable. It is almost as if Dean "orientalizes" Eliot's poetic ideal of impersonality to the point where it morphs into Lowell's description of the impersonal soul of the Far East.

There is an important difference, however: For the Western modernist self, impersonality—much like Orientalism—offered release and the exploration of "alternative aesthetic spaces." It allowed Eliot to free Indic materials from the strangling grip of nineteenth-century poetry and translate the "Oriental Renaissance" (Raymond Schwab) into "the idioms and rhythms of his own place and time" (Kearns, *T. S. Eliot* 164). The concept of impersonality was so fluid and vague that it even enabled Eliot sometimes to endorse and at other times to challenge Western imperialism. If this is true for his criticism, it is all the more so for his poetry: *The Waste Land* simply does not fit any narrow ideological boxes that some of its readers have occasionally built for it. Indicative of Eliot and his fellow modernists' implication in the tangled history of imperialism, however, these poets usually preferred to deal with the Orient of the past or the imagination (Flanagan 125). Most often, Asia was constructed as a "timeless, ethereal, utopic space" that remained "removed from the reality of contemporary Asia" (Yoshihara 106).

One aspect of that new reality was that since the establishment of the Meiji reign in 1868, Japanese poets had already adapted their haikus to explore the modern self in more personal and formally less rigid ways (Atsumi 103). More importantly still, while Lowell wrote about the impersonal Far Eastern self and ruminated about their culture's eventual annihilation, Chinese immigrants had already become the targets of racist legislation such as the Chinese Exclusion Act of 1882. At the time Eliot was devising his concept of impersonality, the "Asiatic Barred Zone Act" of 1917 had already made most Far Eastern subjects ineligible to immigrate into the United States. Detained in the San Francisco Bay at Angel Island and awaiting their deportation, some of these immigrants, most of them Chinese, asserted their identities in deeply personal poems. As the editors of *Island* (1991) point out, these poems express "a vitality of indomitability never before identified with the Chinese Americans" (Lai 27). Poems like the following neither fit the stereotype of the passive and complacent Asian subject nor the modernists' ideal of impersonal poetic expression:

> Leaving behind my writing brush and removing my sword, I came to America.
> Who was to know two streams of tears would flow upon arriving here?
> If there comes a day when I will have attained my ambition and become successful,
> I will certainly behead the barbarians and spare not a single blade of grass. (84)

Thus, for Far Eastern selves, impersonality is quite a different affair. Their impersonality is not freely chosen but externally attributed, and a highly tenuous position to be in: Bereft of power and reduced to passivity, their depersonalization as impersonal souls all too often paved the road to their eventual dehumanization.

Notes

1. In fact, Lowell deemed the Far East to have become even more impersonal than the place and religion from which Buddhism emerged—India and Brahmanism. Perhaps drawing on James F. Clarke's concept of Buddhism as the "Protestantism of the East" (1869), Lowell constructs an analogy between Catholicism and Brahmanism on the one hand, and Protestantism and Buddhism on the other: rejecting external spiritual authority, the two reformed movements were much more concerned with individual salvation, but to opposite effects: "The Protestant, from having tamely allowed himself to be led [by Catholic churchmen, C.K.], began to take a lively interest in his own self-improvement; while the Buddhist, from a former apathetic acquiescence in the doctrine of the universally illusive, set to work energetically towards self-extinction. […] Not content with being born impersonal, a Far Oriental is constantly striving to make himself more so" (191-92). On the "vogue" of Buddhism in the late nineteenth century and contemporary discussions of Buddhism, see Jackson 141-56.

2. Some Western explorers of the Far East had already shared this sentiment. One significant example is Lafcadio Hearn, otherwise an admirer of *The Soul of the Far East*, who soon after his arrival in Japan in 1890 found Lowell's preference for the West's individuality over Far Eastern impersonality mistaken. In a letter to his

friend Basil Hall Chamberlain, Hearn deplored that the ideal of individuality lay at the root of many problems in the West: "Much of what is called personality and individuality is intensely repellent, and makes the principal misery of Occidental life" (cit. in Jackson 236).

3. Marianne Thormählen and Ronald Bush concur that Eliot calls on poets to cast off their "Ego" or their socially conditioned self, while leaving intact an underlying "true self" (Thormählen 125) or an unconscious "authentic personality" (Bush 44). Bush follows: "The truly personal work must be composed of material free of the artist's superficial attitudes. To act as the 'definite token' of uncontaminated feeling or as a magnet that will attract the deepest impulses of the self, it must be composed of elements that are objective, foreign, other" (47).

4. Interestingly, Carl T. Jackson has leveled the same charge against Percival Lowell's use of these terms: "His Impersonality thesis is difficult to accept—or to rebut—because one is unsure what he meant by impersonality and individuality" (208).

5. Eliot's engagement with F.H. Bradley's idealist philosophy (Drexler 66-72, Brooker 22), his growing dissatisfaction with Bergsonian time-philosophy of the *durée* (Ellmann 10-14, Goldman 153-54), and his acquaintance with Bertrand Russell's analytical empiricism (Kearns, *T. S. Eliot* 110-17) may all have been instrumental in forming the ideas behind impersonality. Ronald Bush has claimed that Eliot derived his notion of personality from the writings of Rémy de Gourmond (44-45). Maud Ellmann adds that Eliot disdained psychological readings of poetry, whose proliferation Sigmund Freud's discoveries at the turn of the century had provoked (5). Furthermore, the ideal of an impersonal poetry is itself a tradition in Western literature that one could, for instance, trace to classicism or to the French Symbolists' search for a pure art, as in Mallarmé's formulation: "L'œuvre pure implique la disparition élocutoire du poète, qui cède l'initiative aux mots, par le heurt de leur inégalité mobilisés; ils s'allument de reflets réciproques comme une virtuelle traînée de feux sur des pierreries, remplaçant la respiration perceptible en l'ancien souffle lyrique ou la direction personnelle enthousiaste de la phrase" (cit. in Yu 264-65).

6. This claim can be supported by another article on the Noh plays that appeared during Eliot's assistant editorship of *The Egoist*. Yone Noguchi emphasizes that the Noh's stories and the acting are subordinate to the creation of poetic harmony and the expression of an eternal order. Good actors, she goes on, rarely break their restraint and "make a rupture of the general harmony of the plays, suddenly

falling into the bathos to expose shabbily their own selves" (99). Much like the Noh for its actor, poetry means for the artist "a continual self-sacrifice, a continual extinction of personality" ("Tradition" 53).

7. Kearns, Eloise Knapp Hay, Harold E. McCarthy, Jeffrey M. Perl and Andrew P. Tuck belong to the group of scholars emphasizing the significance of Eastern thought in Eliot's criticism and poetry. Hay warns against reading Eliot's poems retrospectively through the prism of his later conversion to Christianity (191). McCarthy calls Buddhism's belief in being's essential impermanence, perpetual change and suffering "precisely the intuition which underlies the poetry of T. S. Eliot" (41). Dissatisfied with Western philosophy, Eliot found in the Buddhist concept of salvation a model of liberation from received presuppositions, Perl and Tuck claim (124). A. David Moody, on the other hand, calls the attempts to "assimilate" Eliot with Buddhism "a reverse form of 'orientalism,'" and argues that it represented to Eliot a "primitive wisdom" that he could use to rediscover "the basis of a Christian vision for a secularised Western society" (19). A middle position is taken by scholars like Marianne Thormählen and Jewel Spears Brooker who hold that the tensions between Christianity and Buddhism were not important for Eliot. Thormählen thus speaks of "a point of confluence for Indic and Christian traditions in Eliot's verse" (129), while Brooker gracefully draws a parallel to the European mind in the "Tradition" essay: Eliot's is "'a mind which changes, and … this change is a development which abandons nothing en route,' which does not superannuate either humanism or aestheticism or Buddhism, but includes them, at least residually, in an ever increasing complexity of intelligence and feeling" (26).

8. As is well known, Eliot suffered a nervous breakdown in 1921 and produced the first full draft of *The Waste Land* while receiving treatments by Roger Vittoz, a well-known doctor in Lausanne (Moody 116, 127).

9. Of course, Eliot would have refuted this argument. In "A Romantic Patrician," he suggests instead that the real roots of imperialism were to be found with Romanticism ("Imperfect Critics" 32).

Works Cited

Altieri, Charles. *The Art of Twentieth Century American Poetry: Modernism and After*. Malden: Blackwell, 2006.

Apteryx [T. S. Eliot]. "Verse Pleasant and Unpleasant." *The Egoist* 5.3 (March

1918): 43-44.

Atsumi, Ikuko. "New Epics of Cultural Convergence." *Asian and Western Writers in Dialogue*. Ed. Guy Amirthanayagam. London: Macmillan, 1982. 101-14.

Brooker, Jewel Spears. "Substitutes for Religion in the Early Poetry of T. S. Eliot." *The Placing of T. S. Eliot*. Ed. Jewel Spears Brooker. Columbia: U of Missouri P, 1991. 11-26.

Bush, Ronald. *T. S. Eliot: A Study in Character and Style*. New York: OUP, 1983.

Dean, Tim. "The Other's Voice: Cultural Imperialism and Poetic Impersonality in Gary Snyder's *Mountains and Rivers without End*." *Contemporary Literature* 41.3 (Autumn 2000): 462-94.

___. "T. S. Eliot, famous clairvoyante." *Gender, Desire, and Sexuality in T. S. Eliot*. Ed. Cassandra Laity and Nancy K. Gish. Cambridge: CUP, 2004. 43-65.

Denney, Reuel. "The Portable Pagoda: Asia and America in the Work of Gary Snyder." *Asian and Western Writers in Dialogue: New Cultural Identities*. Ed. Guy Amirthanayagam. London: Macmillan, 1982. 115-36.

Drexler, Peter. *Escape from Personality: Eine Studie zum Problem der Identität bei T. S. Eliot*. Frankfurt: Lang, 1980.

Eliot, T. S. *After Strange Gods: A Primer of Modern Heresy*. London: Faber, 1933.

___. "Contemporanea." *The Egoist* 5.6 (June-July 1918): 84-85.

___. "Dante." 1929. *Selected Essays*. 2nd ed. London: Faber, 1934. 237-77.

___. *Ezra Pound: His Metric and Poetry*. New York: Alfred Knopf, 1917. *Project Gutenberg*. January 1, 2005. December 4, 2010. <http://www.gutenberg.org/ebooks/7275>.

___. "The Function of Criticism." *Selected Essays*. 2nd ed. London: Faber, 1934. 23-34.

___. "Imperfect Critics: A Romantic Aristocrat." *The Sacred Wood: Essays on Poetry and Criticism*. 2nd ed. London: Methuen, 1928. 24-32.

___. Introduction. *Selected Poems*. By Ezra Pound. Ed. T. S. Eliot. 1928. London: Faber, 1973. 7-21.

___. "The Noh and the Image." *The Egoist* 4.7 (August 1917): 102-03.

___. "Reflections on Contemporary Poetry (IV)." *The Egoist* 6.3 (July 1919): 39-40.

___. *The Sacred Wood: Essays on Poetry and Criticism.* 2nd ed. London: Methuen, 1928.

___. "Tradition and the Individual Talent." 1919. *The Sacred Wood: Essays on Poetry and Criticism.* 2nd ed. London: Methuen, 1928. 47-59.

___. *The Waste Land and other poems.* London: Faber, 1999.

Ellmann, Maud. *The Poetics of Impersonality: T.S. Eliot and Ezra Pound.* Cambridge: Harvard UP, 1987.

Fenollosa, Ernest. "The Chinese Written Character as a Medium for Poetry." *Instigations.* By Ezra Pound. New York: Boni and Liveright, 1920. 357-88.

Flanagan, Kathleen. "The Orient as Pretext for Aesthetic and Cultural Revolution in Modern American Poetry." *Cohesion and Dissent in America.* Ed. Carol Colatrella and Joseph Alkana. Albany: SUNY P, 1994. 114-29.

Ford, Karen Jackson. "The Lives of Haiku Poetry: Self, Selflessness, and Solidarity in Concentration Camp Haiku." *Cary Nelson and the Struggle for the University: Poetry, Politics, and the Profession.* Ed. Michael Rothberg and Peter K. Garrett. Albany: SUNY P, 2009. 59-74.

Froula, Christine. "The Beauties of Mistranslation: On Pound's English after *Cathay.*" *Ezra Pound & China.* Ed. Zhaoming Qian. Ann Arbor: U of Michigan P, 2003. 49-71.

Goldman, Jane. *Modernism, 1910 – 1945: Image to Apocalypse.* Basingstoke: Palgrave Macmillan, 2004.

Hay, Eloise Knapp. *T. S. Eliot's Negative Way.* 1982. Rpt. in *Critical Essays on T. S. Eliot's The Waste Land.* Ed. Lois A. Cuddy and David H. Hirsch. Boston: G. K. Hall, 1991. 190-204.

Jackson, Carl T. *The Oriental Religions and American Thought: Nineteenth-Century Explorations.* Westport: Greenwood, 1981.

Kearns, Cleo McNelly. "T. S. Eliot, Buddhism, and the Point of No Return." *The Placing of T. S. Eliot.* Ed. Jewel Spears Brooker. Columbia: U of Missouri P, 1991. 128-35.

___. *T. S. Eliot and Indic Traditions: A Study in Poetry and Belief.* Cambridge: CUP, 1987.

Kermode, Frank. "A Babylonish Dialect." *The Sewanee Review* 74.1 (Winter 1966): 225-37.

Kern, Robert. *Orientalism, Modernism, and the American Poem*. Cambridge: CUP, 1996.

Lai, Him Mark, Genny Lim, and Judy Yung. *Island: Poetry and History of Chinese Immigrants on Angel Island, 1910-1940*. Seattle: U of Washington P, 1991.

Lowell, Percival. 1888. *The Soul of the Far East*. New Illustrated Ed. New York: Macmillan, 1911.

McCarthy, Harold E. "T. S. Eliot and Buddhism." *Philosophy East and West* 2.1 (Apr. 1952): 31-55.

Menand, Louis. *Discovering Modernism: T. S. Eliot and His Context*. New York: OUP, 1987.

Moody, A. David. *Tracing T. S. Eliot's Spirit: Essays on his poetry and thought*. Cambridge: CUP, 1996.

Murray, Paul. *T. S. Eliot and Mysticism: The Secret History of Four Quartets*. New York: St. Martin's P, 1991.

Noguchi, Yone. "The Japanese Noh Play." *The Egoist* 5.7 (August 1918): 99.

Perl, Jeffrey M., and Andrew P. Tuck. "The Hidden Advantage of Tradition: On the Significance of T. S. Eliot's Indic Studies." *Philosophy East and West* 35.2 (Apr 1985): 115-31.

Pound, Ezra. "Drunken Helots and Mr. Eliot." *The Egoist* 4.5 (June 1917): 72-74.

Qian, Zhaoming. *Orientalism and Modernism: The Legacy of China in Pound and Williams*. Durham: Duke UP, 1995.

Rabaté, Jean-Michel. "Tradition and T. S. Eliot." *The Cambridge Companion to T. S. Eliot*. Ed. David A. Moody. Cambridge: CUP, 1994. 210–22.

Said, Edward. *Orientalism: Western Conceptions of the Orient*. With a new afterword. London: Penguin, 1995.

Spender, Stephen. *T. S. Eliot*. New York: Viking, 1975.

Thormählen, Marianne. "'My Life for This Life': T. S. Eliot and the Extinction of the Individual Personality." *T. S. Eliot at the Turn of the Century*. Ed. Marianne Thormählen. Lund: Lund UP, 1994. 120-32.

Yoshihara, Mari. *Embracing the East: White Women and American Orientalism*. Oxford: OUP, 2003.

Yu, Pauline. "The Poetics of Discontinuity: East-West Correspondences in Lyric Poetry." *PMLA* 94.2 (March 1979): 261-74.

"Young Willows" in Pound's *Pisan Cantos*:
"Light as the Branch of Kuanon"

Ronald Bush

I. Introduction

Starting from the period of his earliest Canto drafts, Ezra Pound became fascinated by the complex symbolic resonance of the Buddhist Bodhisattva of compassion whose avatars, according to his principal sources (Laurence Binyon's *Painting in the Far East* and *The Flight of the Dragon*, and Ernest Fenollosa's *Epochs of Chinese and Japanese Art*) included the Chinese Kwan-yin (or Guanyin), the Japanese Kanon and the Korean Kwannon.[1] Following Fenollosa's usage, Pound glancingly alluded to "Kwannon" in the rejected early version of Canto I. But it was in the Pisan Cantos (and in the pre-Pisan Italian drafts and in the manuscript version of the poem even more explicitly than in the published sequence itself) that Pound's imagination of the figure that Canto LXXIV Italianizes as "Kuanon of all delights" really flowered (C74 / 498).[2] These wartime texts enlist elements of Kuanon's traditional iconography to portray heaven's compassionate intercession and nature's healing power. And although studies during the last decade by Zhaoming Qian, Britton Gildersleeve and Rupert Arrowsmith have argued for affiliating various works of Asian painting and sculpture with Pound's representation of Kuanon, the strong verbal echoes in Pound's drafts of his previous reading suggest that Kuanon in the *Pisan Cantos* had as much to do with Pound's written sources as with any actual or reproduced piece of visual art.

Pound first encountered the figure of Kuanon in London in 1909 through fellow poet and the British Museum's then Assistant Keeper of Prints and Drawings, Laurence Binyon.[3] Their ongoing conversations

involved among other things Binyon's already published work on
Chinese art, including *Painting in the Far East* (1908), which refers to
the figure frequently (e.g., 65, 162, 188). They later discussed Ernest
Fenollosa's legacy, *Epochs of Chinese and Japanese Art*, a book that
was finished and edited with Binyon's substantial help after Fenollosa
applied to Binyon in 1908 "for guidance through the British Museum's
collection . . . having heard 'most pleasant things said of you by [his
previous client] Mr. Freer'" (Beasley, 59). Fenollosa died suddenly in
1908 and his widow Mary Fenollosa, with help from Binyon and others,
published the book in 1912. As Rupert Arrowsmith has shown, Binyon
selected the book's illustrations (emphasizing images of Kuanon over
representations of the Buddha himself) and tailored Fenollosa's text
accordingly (Arrowsmith 212). Pound read Binyon's 1911 *The Flight
of the Dragon: An Essay on the Theory and Practice of Art in China and
Japan* and reviewed it in the second number of *Blast*. And at Binyon's
instigation by 1913 he began to read and then swallowed Fenollosa's
book (Qian, *Response* 233), fixing in his mind the always lyrical and
frequently Christianized language Fenollosa employed to affirm
Kuanon's transcultural appeal.

Though sometimes colored by contemporary religious and
aesthetic attitudes, the studies Pound read in the early teens conveyed
a reasonably balanced account of Kuanon in Asian culture. Fenollosa,
for example, in the first volume of *Epochs of Chinese and Japanese
Art* explains the idea of a "Bodhisattwa" in the tradition of Northern
Buddhism as "a being who has advanced so far in the scale of wisdom
and insight, and the renunciation of fleshly ties, as to be just on the
point of entrance into Nirvana and salvation," only to then "*deliberately
renounc[e] it*, electing to work . . . for the love of one's fellow-man." On
the same principles, Fenollosa continues, a "perpetual Bodhisattwa,"
has become "a great spirit making for love and righteousness, invisible
to man, but assisting him, whose answer to man's prayer comes with
every accelerating throb of human devotion." Such a being "would
become worshipped as a sort of personification of the great moral or
spiritual principle for which he specially stood"—as, for example,
"Kwannon, the Bodhisattwa of providence, sustenance and salvation
from physical evil" (I.106-107).

About the way the ungendered Indian figure of Kuanon evolved across centuries of Asian culture, the emphases of Fenollosa and Binyon differed. In *Painting in the Far East,* Binyon's account describes the historical stages in which the Indian Bodhisattwa Avalokitesvara (whose name means among other things he of compassion who hears the voices of suffering) evolved into a feminine form of Kuan-yin or Guanyin beginning in the time of the Tang dynasty (618-905) and complete by the time of the Song (960-1280), when it became common to render the figure in white porcelain as a mother with a babe in her arms (65). Fenollosa on the other hand was sceptical of the linear model of this narrative and explains that "a great Bodhisattwa is in its own nature indeterminate as to sex, having risen above the distinction, or rather embodying in itself the united spiritual graces of both sexes. It is a matter of accident which one it may assume upon incarnation." Fenollosa does allow, however, that while the "Tang thought . . . of Kwannon as a great demiurge or creator, [the] Sung preferred to lay stress upon the element of motherhood." (I. 124).[4] But Binyon and Fenollosa in their most enthusiastic moments wax equally lyrical about Kuanon's feminine graces and advert to her Western analogue, the image of the Madonna.[5] Fenollosa, for example, notes in *Epochs* that "millions of Chinese and Japanese have for seven centuries looked up to, and prayed to [Kwannon] with the same sort of passionate confidence in the divine motherhood that the millions of European believers have to the Holy Virgin, Mother of Christ." Commenting especially on the great Mu Ch'i painting of Kwannon in the Daitokoji temple of Kyoto, Fenollosa adds that "The purity and weakness of the form, the beautiful lines like a marble statue, the splendid dominance of the hood and crown, and the sweetness of the face, stand as high for a world's aesthetic type as do the great Madonnas of Italian work, say the sweet half-length Bellini at the Venice Academia. In 1886 I took our own John LaFarge to Daitokoji . . . Mr. Lafarge, devout Catholic as he is, could hardly restrain a bending of the head as he muttered, 'Raphael.' Indeed, the Mokkei [Mu Ch'i] Kwannon challenges deliberate comparison with the sweetest mother types of the great Umbrian" (II.50).

As the last citation suggests, Pound's sources also discovered in Asian representations of Kuanon a proto-abstract aesthetic of decorative line. So Fenollosa points out that "Chinese painting of the great school of Tang" teaches the lesson that "[i]t is not things that we want in art, but the beauty of things; and if this beauty dwells largely in their *line*, their boundaries of space, their proportions and shapes, and the unity and system of the line rhythms, it is a glorious convention that can seize on just that and make supreme music out of it . . . For the aim of real art evolution is not to come nearer and nearer to a coloured photograph, but if possible to put more and more grandeur and refined beauty into our spaces, our proportions, and our systems of line rhythm" (*Epochs* I.130-31). Binyon's 1913 monograph *Botticelli* —on which Pound silently collaborated (Arrowsmith 201)—similarly links "masterpieces of the early Buddhist art in China and Japan" with the "singular power of line" and the "imagination for rhythmical movement" to be found in Botticelli (32-34), and therefore with the Florentine's "Relation to Modern Painting" (19).

It was with these contemporary Western applications in mind that Pound's interest in the Kuanon first emerged. So in his 1914 essay "The Renaissance" he writes that "this century may find a new Greece in China" (LE 215) and in the first of his *Three Cantos* (1915-17) he asks himself how to "begin the progress" of a new Renaissance and entertains the thought that it may begin "with China" and with the figure of "Kwannon / Footing a boat that's but one lotus petal" (EW 149). What follows, though, will concentrate on a second stage of Pound's involvement concentrated in the 1930s and 1940s—years when a renewed correspondence with Laurence Binyon (Arrowsmith 200-1) returned Pound to Chinese materials, first in Cantos XLIX and LII-LXI and then in his wartime preparations for what become the *Pisan Cantos*.[6]

II. Kuanon in Pound's Unpublished Wartime Italian Drafts

Preceding the Pisan Cantos

The *Pisan Cantos* had a longer gestation than is usually acknowledged. Pound composed the sequence proper in the U.S. Army Detention Training Center between late June and mid-November 1945, but the sequence also drew on wartime Italian drafts that began as early as 1941. The so-called Fascist Cantos LXXII and LXXIII, written in Italian in late 1944 and early 1945, have now been integrated into the published text of the poem, but equally influential Italian typescripts that Pound composed immediately afterwards have yet to be fully published. The latter include two further Cantos in Italian left in a provisional state and the equivalent of an entire sequence of notebook and typescript drafts, many of which directly anticipate elements of the *Pisan Cantos*.[7] These along with the notebook manuscript version of the *Pisan Cantos* that grew out of them contain unexpectedly explicit and extremely suggestive representations of Kuanon. A useful way of getting at their significance is to examine the way these Italian and English manuscripts develop four attributes traditionally associated with Kuanon in Asian art, all of which had been drawn to Pound's attention by Binyon and/or Fenollosa. These include instances in which Kuanon (1) holds a lotus flower, or (2) holds a vessel full of pure water, or (3) holds a willow branch, or (4) displays the moon in her tiara. In 1944 and 1945 Pound appropriated this iconographic material in an effort not only to deepen the synthesis of Christian and Buddhist traditions he had discovered in Fenollosa, but also to attempt a synthesis of Confucian and Buddhist strains of Eastern thought.

The substance of Pound's wartime elaboration of Kuanon survives in two of the unpublished Italian texts just mentioned. The second, which I will examine presently, fuses the Madonna of the Transfiguration with her Eastern counterpart Kuanon in a more general figure, "la Luna," an image of compassionate feminine intercession. Before that, however, Pound drafted a vision of Buddha and Confucius, silently allied through a relation to an unmentioned Kuanon and standing side by side as guides to human enlightenment. This vision constitutes the second page of a polished Italian draft written in December 1944 and early 1945, in which the three Asian figures introduce their Western counterpart, the Neoplatonic medieval philosopher Scotus Erigena.[8] The typescript draft is provisionally entitled "Cunizza":

> Ogni beato porta con sé il cielo / il suo dal qual egli dipende
> e qu[a]le egli nurte della fiamma
>
> in su son troni
>   (ch'io vidi)
> seguendo quella forma po[rge]/ che come nube a spasso
> soav[e]mente, e senza parer determinata : ma dolcemente

leggiadra salì, come ~~nebbia~~ sta str[a]le di nebbia
   che monta l'Eos/ l'aurora :; e che i miei occhi seguir[o]no
mi pareva mezz' ora/;
                                        in su, in su sempre/
         finché io vidi il Loto /
               e sul Loto, Buddha Gautama
            sogna bellezza eterna l'Indiana
         nel sempiterno sogno / a sinistra di dove guardai
e a destra/ a col nor[d] di dosso: sedeva
Confucio, che dava eterna legge: per chi in terra
vive già beato o fond[a] o regge dinastia duratura/
            sopra l'acqua dolce, che mai s'infanga /
ma dall' eterno fonte, d'Eraclito / corre nel infinito
            e mai non lascia buco in sete/; non appianato/
               della misura d'ogni uman condotta

      il bel pensar / e bel agire son due in questo aspetto/
               ma io: se sono i due veri / come nell' asse
   che per questa passa/
         il verticale: ma loro come di orizzonte o sfera/

         / voice with brogue /
      un asse; c' è: dove tu non stai ancora/
            e quel che si vede da qui / sono riflessi/
      non son miraggi, nel senso grosso/ ma quel che
                     vedi,

               e come in specchio/
                                       apparecchio/

The following is offered as a rough English translation of Pound's
Italian:

   Every blessed one carries with him a heaven / of his own on
      which he depends
   and which he cultivates with flame

   above are thrones
      (that I saw)
   following this beckoning form / that like a cloud out for a stroll

suavely, and without appearing purposeful; but sweetly
lightly ascended, like a shaft of mist
   that mounts Eos/ the dawn; my eyes followed it
   it seemed to me a half-hour/;
                              upward, always upward
               until I saw the Lotus /
                  and on the Lotus, Gautama Buddha
                  he dreams eternal beauty, the Indian
               in an eternal dream / to the left I looked
         and to the right/ with the north at his back: was
                              sitting
Confucius, who was giving the eternal law; for he who on earth
already lives in bliss/ he founds and rules a lasting dynasty
      above the fresh water, that is never muddied
but rather springs from the eternal source, of Heraklitus/
                  and flows into the infinite/
      and never leaves you thirsty/; never flattened
               by the measure of all human conduct

beautiful thought / and beautiful action are two in this aspect
            but I: if they are the two truths / it is as though in
                           an axis
   that passes through this,/
               the vertical: but as if they were a horizon or sphere

         / voice with brogue /
         an axis; there is one: you are not there yet/
               and what one sees from here/ are reflections/
         are not mirages, in the gross sense. but what you see,

                  as in a mirror/
                              [rhyme:] an apparatus

   Rhetorically, this text positions the reader in space where Pound
finds himself intellectually: clued in but straining to focus. It proceeds
to seek unity where there first seems dualism, confronting paradoxes
that are perhaps natural, perhaps metaphysical. But the voice of an
instructor tells the poet that he is "not there yet," having reached a place
where "from here" all one can see are "reflections . . . as in a mirror"
or perhaps as in some scientific "apparatus." To be sure, the "axis" here

involves tendentious political associations: Pound uses Fascism's "axis" in parallel with a Confucian concept of what Pound's translation of Confucius's *Chung Yung* conceives of as a natural virtue that does not wobble, and would have us redefine our political conceptions so as to distinguish not between East and West but rather between Nordic and sub-Mediterranean Semitic cultures.[9] But the passage is concerned even more fundamentally to imply that the duality of sphere and point has already been resolved in medieval philosophy, in which, as for example in an account of Grosseteste by Etienne Gilson that Pound refers to in his essay "Cavalcanti," light first presents itself as a point *or* line but engenders itself as an immense luminous sphere (LE 160).

To be sure, the way this text presents its conundrum is somewhat strained, but the success of the passage relies less on clarity than on a productive uneasiness generated by the poetry's push toward a more sweeping perspective, from which conflicting views of the world can be reconciled. Also, the text quickly reinscribes its opposition into global philosophical forms—first between Buddhist and Confucian and then between Eastern and Western ideals. The larger truth, Pound implies, is unitary, to be found in what Pound's translation of Confucius's *Chung Yung* calls a *medium* in which "the celestial [spiritual] and earthly [perceptual] process can be defined in a single phrase" (*Confucius* 183).

In the present context the "Cunizza" draft's attempt to resolve an opposition between Confucian and Buddhist thought—defined first as between "eternal law" and an "eternal dream" and then as between "beautiful action" and "beautiful thought"—is at least as interesting as the parallel it draws between East and West. For the poem affects the first stage of its reconciliation by silently linking Confucius and the Buddha within a unified iconographic scheme whose most prominent features are the lotus and a vessel of pure water—both of which Pound knew as standard attributes in Asian painting and sculpture of Kuanon. "Cunizza" sites the Buddha and/or Confucius "sul Loto" (on the Lotus), which, as Pound had read in Laurence Binyon's *Painting in the Far East*, is both associated with Kuanon and "sacred in Eastern art as the flower which from mud and ooze rises to unfold unsullied blossoms on the peaceful water, type of the soul aspiring from the muddy passion of gross nature" (115). And the first part of the passage's vision concludes with a phrase that seems to refer only to Confucius but which when examined in fact ambiguously describes the way the Buddha also arises from "l'acqua dolce, che mai s'infanga / ma dall' eterno fonte, d'Eraclito / corre nel infinito / e mai non lascia buco in sete" ("the fresh water, that is never muddied / but rather springs from the eternal fountain of Heraclitus / flows into the infinite / and never leaves you thirsty"). These phrases can be traced to Binyon's accounts of Kuanon, both in a 1908 reference to "a Buddhist text [that] says that he who prays to her even though his mind be on fire, shall feel the flames turn into a fountain of fresh water" (Binyon, *Painting* 162), and in a 1910 commentary on an image of Kuanon in which she holds the "living water" of the spirit in an extended vessel while she sits beside a waterfall helping the sinner see his "flames turned into living water" (Binyon, *Guide* 23; Qian, *Orientalism* 184).

Soon after finishing "Cunizza," moreover, Pound went on to compose several versions of a second Italian text that gestures toward similar iconography. Consider: (1) a fragment that represents part of the provisional typescript of an eventually unpublished Italian Canto 75, along with (1a) a fuller and more advanced state of the same text that probably dates from April 1945 and survives as part of a typescript made by Pound's companion Olga Rudge[10]:

> (1)   Ave Maris Stell[a] mi suonò all' orecchio, per l'aria ser[a]le
> e col ramo di   . io la vidi
> come Kuanina, col ramo [d]i salce/   vidi l'eterna dolcezza
> formata: di misericordia la madre, dei mari protettrice
> so[c]corso in naufragio/   manifesto/

Translation:

> Ave Maris Stella sounded in my ear through the evening air
> and with a branch of   . I saw her
> like Kuanon, with a branch of willow/ I saw the eternal sweetness
> fully formed: mother of pity, protectress of the seas
> succor in shipwreck /   manifest/

> (1a)   ASSUNTA (?dopo Cunizza)
>   <u>dopo ascesa</u>

> Il ragg[i]o di Citera fa stella in quel punto
> "Mai coi codini sarà l'arte monda"

senti[i] a mezz' orecchi, da bocca incerta
e poi in altro tono
            "Maris Stella" suonò si dolcemente,
con Ave, Ave, per l'aria serale
   e lascia che [i] Dei tornaran fra di voi/
   e fra le due vidi, ed era come Kuanon nel aer
~~ma poi~~   col ramo di salce
      colla verghetta/ deliziosa/
                  stava calando per la diafana
            calava lentamente come cala una foglia
Vidi l'eterna dolcezza / formata
di misericordia la madre / dei mari protettrice
soccorso in naufra[g]io / come sempre rivista a Prato, e
   a Monte Rosa/ "il fano delle grazia é rovina[ta]" mi disse
   a Pantaleo mi rifu[g]io , la sfollata /
sotto la Dorata mi sempre cacciata/ duratura / dei bachi
      protettrice/ umile
      Il pargoletto mi ama, che nutro. Io son la Luna/
   non sono la Sofia, anzi la temo; così mosaicata / così
   ieratica/ Hecate nemmeno conosco / mai incoronata nell' alta
      sfera
      sono l'assunta / Io mi chiamai, da Giove amata
   mesta errante. Europa mi chiamai, sotto le stelle dell' ors[a]/

   sotto gli ulivi: vista da te l'altr' anno
   mio marito vangava al clivo; mio sp[o]so novello
   col pargoletto sedevo, tu m' hai visto..
   non sono Sofia, anzi la temo.

      troppo spiegar sarà presuntuoso
            Pietà mi chiamai anche, mio figlio è morto

      Io son l'assunta/   son la sfollata
                  sea imbronza; dec.
                  lake of light/

Translation:

         ASSUNTA (? after Cunizza)
          after the ascent

The ray of Cythera becomes a star in that point

"Never with fanatics will art be pure"
  I half heard, from an uncertain mouth
and then in another tone
    "Maris Stella" sounded so sweetly,
with Ave, Ave, in the evening air
  and let the Gods return among you/
and between the two I saw, and she was like Kuanon in the air
          but then   with a branch of willow
    with the little branch/ delicious/
        she was descending through the diafana
      she descended slowly the way a leaf falls
  I saw the eternal sweetness   /formed
of compassion the mother / protectress of the seas
aid in shipwreck / as she is always seen again in Prato, and
  in Monte Rosa/ "the Delle Grazie shrine is ruined" she said to
    me
    at Pantaleo I take refuge, the evacuee/
  under the Dorata I am always driven/ enduring/ of cocoons
    the protectress/ humble
  The little boy loves me, whom I feed. I am la Luna
I am not la Sofia, in fact I fear her; so mosaiced/ so
hieratic/ Nor do I know Hecate / never crowned in the high
    sphere
    I am l'assunta / Io was I called, Jove's beloved
sad wandering. Europa I was called, under the stars of Orsa

    under the olives: seen by you last year
my husband hoed the earth on the rising path; my new
    bridegroom
I sat with the little boy, you have seen me.
I am not Sofia, rather I fear her.

    to explain too much would be presumptuous
        Pietà I was also called, my son is dead

    I am the Assunta/ the evacuee

                    sea imbronzes; dec[ember]
                    lake of light

  The second and more advanced version of this text (1a) identifies
its provenance in its title, which tells us that in Pound's sequence it

belongs "dopo Cunizza? dopo ascesa"—i.e., after the "Cunizza" text just examined, which limns the "ascesa"—the rising—of Buddha and Confucius. These two sages are referred to in "ASSUNTA" as "le due vidi"—the two visions—"fra"—among which—the female figure of "l'eterna dolcezza" (eternal sweetness) is at first perceived. However, whereas in "Cunizza" the Buddha and Confucius are located so high that it takes strenuous effort to discern them, the female figure with the "little," "delicious" branch of willow easily descends from the sky oblivious to the speaker's exertions, "through the diafana"—the translucent mist that registers the existence of her light—"slowly the way a leaf falls," toward the water of the "seas." The very manner of her appearance, that is to say, speaks not of striving but of the ease of unbidden comfort. Pound's core conception here—"l'eterna dolcezza" of the figure's descent—can be traced to Fenollosa's *Epochs*, which describes the way a painted representation, the "Standing Kwannon," "descends from Heaven upon a cloud-like mass that breaks into the actual foam of water as it pierces space." This descent, Fenollosa writes, "makes the figure seem more like an actual revelation, as in the Sistine Madonna of Raphael," and answers to the image's representation of "the great gracious figure, looking down upon . . . unconscious children with the hint of a beneficent smile, bears for them salvation and spiritual sustenance" (I.132-33). Later in the study, remembering this description in reference to the "Famous Kwannon" of Mu Ch'i, Fenollosa points to "Kwannon's gracious figure, sweetly bending forward, as if listening with inner ear" (II.49) and remarks especially upon the "sweetness" of her "face." He goes on to note "the pure line used to express the most tender divinity of womanhood," and, reiterating the word "sweet," compares in a passage already cited Mu Ch'i's Kwannon to "the great Madonnas of Italian work, say the sweet half-length Bellini at the Venice Academia" (*Epochs* II.50).

Pound's "ASSUNTA" carries on Fenollosa's religious syncretism. In the draft Pound invokes the figure of Kuanon as an idealized Eastern counterpart to the Christian Madonna of the Assumption ("Assunta") just as Fenollosa had called her a counterpart to Raphael's Sistine Madonna. Pound's phrase "misericordia" in the line "di misericordia la madre / dei mari protettrice / soccorso in naufra[g]io" furthermore recalls the language of Binyon's admiration in *The Flight of the*

Dragon, which depicts "the image of Kwannon" as "the impersonation of Mercy and Loving-kindness"(43) and "the conception of a divine pity in the core of things"(44). And Pound's "soccorso in naufra[g]io" once again echoes Fenollosa's account of the Kuanon of Mu Ch'i, in which he informs his reader that Kwannon "is especially the Mother of Waters, the Providence who guards the travellers upon ships. Here the goddess is plainly feminine . . . [and] typifies, in a general way, the great human . . . category of 'motherhood' in a manner, Fenollosa says, that is comparable to the Holy Virgin, Mother of Christ" (*Epochs*, II.49).

Following in Fenollosa's footsteps, Pound, who in the 1940s had himself become a devoté of local Italian Madonnas in seaside churches and the votive offerings of rescued sailors, in "ASSUNTA" follows Fenollosa in drawing on parallel traditions of Asian and Italian art.[11]

A third attribute of Kuanon in the "ASSUNTA" draft had been anticipated in "Cunizza" but would grow ever more prominent as Pound's writing progressed. In the earlier version of the text reproduced above as (1), it is not the lotus flower or a vessel of water but a willow branch that Kuanon holds in her arms. Pound intended to include this image just after the passage begins, but was forced to leave a blank in his line because for a moment he forgot the Italian word for willow. In leaving the blank as placeholder, he indicated that he was resolved to retrieve the missing word, whatever its sound might be. Then he straightaway remembered the word and inserted it into the text. But he did not use the cumbersome process of moving the typewriter roll and trying to align the word into the blank. Instead he typed a new version of the line immediately below, where he employs a variant ("salce" instead of "salice") of the common Italian word for willow: "come Kuanina, col ramo [d]i salce/   vidi l'eterna dolcezza." A version of the same line survived into his more advanced text (1a).

Pound owed Kuanon's willow branch to Fenollosa's *Epochs of Chinese and Japanese Art*. Writing about a great Song "Standing Kwannon," for example, Fenollosa notes that the "salvation and spiritual sustenance" that Kwannon expresses is symbolized in the form of a "wisp of willow" in the figure's "raised left hand" ("which," Fennolosa tells us, "in other pictures sits in a vase," but here it is as if "he were actually sprinkling his protégés with the water of baptism" [I.133]). And in reference to the "Famous Kuanon" of Mu Ch'i, Fenollosa observes the importance of "a crystal vase with a sprig of willow (both sympathetic with the elements of water and ether, which Kwannon symbolizes) [that] stands on a rock at her left" (II. 49).

But where Fenollosa assimilates the willow to Christian baptism, Pound jumps to a poet's intuition of a distinct Asian genre of representing Kuanon. The Yoryu Kuanon, worshipped ever since the T'ang dynasty in China and the Kamakura period in Japan, holds a willow branch as symbol of her healing powers (Yu 14, 78). (Conversely, the streaming branches of the weeping willow are considered to represent the tears shed by Kuanon as the deity of compassion.) According to C.A.S. Williams, "Buddhists consider that water, sprinkled by means of a willow branch, has a purifying effect" (402). And, perhaps because acetylsalicylic acid (aspirin) is a product of willow, esoteric Japanese Buddhist texts suggest that willow wood can cure various illnesses, and recommend willow branches specifically for the ritual expulsion of plagues (Shinku).

Pound seems to have instinctively understood not only these symbolic associations but other suggestions of the willow in Chinese and Japanese painting as well. For instance, the willow is frequently "regarded as a sign of spring" and by implication as linked to the first, innocent erotic stirrings of the season. It is therefore a Buddhist "symbol of meekness," and in more secular art "owing to its beauty, suppleness, and frailty" in Tang poetry and Song painting, the willow became "the emblem of the fair sex" (Williams 402). In Pound's poetry, these last associations, which derive the theme of healing from the delicate sway of the willow tree, come close to a core intuition. The "ASSUNTA" draft shows him beginning to expand his early fascination with the importance of line in Asian painting by connecting it with its appropriate emotional subject. So in his draft he employs "ramo di salce" to objectify both Kuanon's beauty and her compassion, employing the phrase "the way a leaf falls" to mimic the sway of the willow in the wind:

> col ramo di salce
> colla verghetta/ deliziosa/
>> stava calando per la diafana
>> calava lentamente come cala una foglia
> Vidi l'eterna dolcezza[12]

Finally, Pound's "diafana" in this passage suggests a fourth key attribute of Kuanon—her luminescent identity with the moon. Pound was deeply invested in a primal mythological distinction between the feminine moon and the masculine sun, and so seems to have paid particular attention to a brief and relatively unusual reference to the moon in *Epochs of Chinese and Japanese Art*. Fenollosa dramatically describes how the Korean Yumedono Boddhisattwa preserved at Horiugi, Japan, was unveiled for him by the priests at Horiugi for the first time in "more than two hundred years" in the "summer of 1884" and notes that one of its distinctive features was a crown whose curved lines were "twine[d] about the focus of a crescent moon" (I.50-1). (Fenollosa also observes the hands of the Yumedono Boddhisattwa "holding between them a jewel or casket of medicine," an image that Rupert Arrowsmith suggests may well be the origin of Pound's line in Canto 74: "Kuanon, this stone bringeth sleep" [C74 / 455, Arrowsmith 211].)

Remembering Fenollosa's words, Pound's "ASSUNTA" draft clothes a composite Madonna / Kuanon in light, calling her "Maris Stella" (the star of the sea), and emphasizing her proclamation: "Io son la Luna" (I am the moon). This connection between Kuanon and "la Luna" was in fact essential to the Neoplatonic Paradiso Pound had kept in mind ever since his study of Cavalcanti's poem "Donna mi prega" (Bush, "*La filosofica*"). At the heart of his conception was a sense that the divine emanation of ideal form enables us to actualize our understanding of the world in the way that light lets us actualize it in our vision. In this regard, the word "diafana" (translucencies) with its implication that matter is destined to be illuminated, has associations with Plotinus[13] by way of Grosseteste. And so Pound cites the latter's disquisition *De Luce* in his essay on Cavalcanti (LE 161) to gloss Cavalcanti's: 'Prende suo stato / si' formato / chome / Diafan dal lume / d'una schuritade' ("Donna mi prega").[14] Carroll Terrell also points to Albertus Magnus' *De Anima*: "For we see light not by itself, but in a certain subject, and this is the diafane" (142).

It is also worth noticing here that Pound in his representation of Kuanon's interactive descent through the "diafana" appropriates a delicate Chinese atmospherics of cloud and mist—an aesthetic that would soon become (cf. Canto LXXXIII's "the phantom mountain

above the cloud") one of the guiding principles of the *Pisan Cantos*
(C83 / 550).

III. Kuanon in the Pisan Cantos Manuscript Notebook

Pound's fascination with Kuanon did not end with the Italian
drafts we have just examined. Pound felt the pull of the compassionate
Bodhisattva much more powerfully during the two and a half weeks of
his internment in an open cage in the U.S. Army Disciplinary Training
Center near Pisa, where he was under the constant oppression of
an imminent trial and possible execution for treason. Following a
breakdown and a fragile recovery, he was transferred to the relatively
benign conditions of an officer's tent in the camp's medical compound
and left to commune with the Tuscan sky. It was then, with his
unpublished Italian drafts still in his head, that he began the *Pisan
Cantos*. Pound's manuscript notebook records that the first three words
of the poem Pound recorded were "La sorella luna," followed quickly
by a note about spiritual "intercessors" of the kind he had marked in
the pages of the *Catholic Prayer Book for the Army and Navy* he was
issued when he first entered the camp (Flory, Kraus).[15] In marginal
comments in the Prayer Book, Pound again constructed these
"intercessors" as composite figures of East and West. For example, he
marked a prayer to the "immaculate Virgin Mary" with ideograms (純
亦 不 已), taken from the end of Chapter 26 of the Confucian *Chung
Yung*: "The <u>unmixed</u> functions [in time and space] without bourne.
This unmixed is the tensile light, the Immaculata. There is no end to
its action" (Pound, *Confucius* 187; Flory 160). And he augmented the
Prayer Book's mention of "invisible presence of assisting angels" with
marginal characters 洋乎 如 在 其 上 如 在 其 左 右 drawn from
the *Chung Yung* XVI [洋should have been but wasn't repeated]: "the
spirits of the energies and of the rays" that "make bright the vessels for
the sacred grain . . . seem to move above . . . as water wool-white in a
torrent" (Pound, *Confucius* 131; Flory 159). Also, next to the phrase,
"Thou hast revealed them Who canst neither deceive nor be deceived,"
Pound inserted the name of the Japanese moon-nymph, "Hagoromo"
(Kraus 244).

Given the crucial role played by the felt presence of the moon
in Pound's inception of the poem, it is hardly surprising that his
notebook manuscript of the *Pisan Cantos* turns early and often both to
"ASSUNTA" and Kuanon. In my discussion below I refer to five explicit

and one implied notebook references to Kuanon, each included in the following transcription followed by the published version of the text:

(1)
C74, MS pp. 22-3
in this day the air was made open
[23] for the ~~ever blessed~~ Kuanon ~~mother~~ of all delights the ~~Immaculate~~
Lynus cletus clement ~~& for all the saints = = ==~~
~~&~~ whose prayers.

C74 / 448
> and this day the air was made open
> > for Kuanon of all delights,
> > > Linus, Cletus, Clement,
> > > > whose prayers,

****

(2)
C74, MS pp. 82-3
& the pleiades sit in her mirror.

To reign unto Kuanon gold bough or the willow twig – "for this
    stone bringeth sleep"
till faceted stone give way before seal stone
"as the two halves of one tally"
that mortal man lay with immortal goddess.
~~or offered Apollo the wine bowl~~
[83] ~~or offered wine bowl to his sun god.~~
or offered the wine bowl
> 配
> 上
> 帝 [16]

"grass nowhere out of place"

C74 / 455
Kuanon, this stone bringeth sleep;
    offered the wine bowl
        grass nowhere out of place

****

(3)
C74, MS p. 109
with the mast held by the left hand.
or this air is of Kuanon
enigma. forgetting the times & seasons.
but this air brought her ashore a La Marina.
with the gt shell borne on the seawaves
nautilis biancastra

C74 / 463
      ΧΑΡΙΤΕΣ possibly in the soft air
      with the mast held by the left hand
      in this air as of Kuanon
enigma forgetting the times and seasons
but this air brought her ashore a la marina

****

(4)
C77, MS p.151
above which the lotus, white nenuphar,
Kuanon. the mythologies. & the willow twig
      樂 ， 知 不 如 樂 　 知 [17]

C77 / 492
above which, the lotus, white nenuphar
Kuanon, the mythologies

****

(5)
C81, MS, p. 243
Light as the branch of Kuanon!

C81 / 539
      Light as the branch of Kuanon

****

(6)
C83, MS pp. 266-70
[266] in the drenched tents there is quiet
sered eyes are @ rest,

[..........................]

樂
pax, υδορ 水 the sage
    "delighteth in water"

[........................]
[267] as he was standing below the altars.
        of the spirits of rain

[268] ^when^ every hollow is full,
it moves forward.
to the phantom mountain
    ~~of water~~ above the cloud.

[.............................]

[270] Plura diafana. ~~the~~
~~The~~ Heliads ~~move~~ lift the mist from the ~~valleys.~~ ^plain,^
~~& the young oaks~~ ^elms oaks poplars^ ~~are entangled.~~
young willows are caught in the veil
there is no base seen under Taishan.
but the brightness of ύδορ
the poplar tips float in brightness,
only the stockade posts stand.

C83 / 549-551
        in the drenched tent there is quiet
                sered eyes are at rest
            [............]
                the sage
    delighteth in water
            [............................]
    as he was standing below the altars
            of the spirits of rain
            "When every hollow is full
                it moves forward"

to the phantom mountain above the cloud
    [..............................]
Plura diafana
    Heliads lift the mist from the young willows
there is no base seen under Taishan
    but the brightness of '**udor**   ὕδωρ
the poplar tips float in brightness
only the stockade posts stand

Perhaps the most striking feature of these notebook passages has to do with their regular return to Kuanon's willow. Pound would in revision excise some of these instances, but I want to argue that this was not because he thought them misconceived. Rather his emendations show him superimposing associations of the willow branch on companionate images and then simplifying. Regarding (2), for example, the manuscript notebook text presents moonlight illuminating the Pleiades and includes the "willow twig" to intimate the healing properties of that phenomenon. In the manuscript version, Pound goes on to add a "stone" that "bringeth sleep" (probably derived from Fenollosa's praise of the Yumedono Kuanon's "jewel or casket of medicine" mentioned above) and then to supplement the sequence by inserting Chinese characters (配 上 帝) drawn from *The Great Digest* X.5, which suggests the mating of heaven and earth in the ritual observance of a deserving sovereign (*Confucius* 71). Pound then removed the willow, likely because he sensed his additions were by themselves sufficient to suggest the moon's medicinal properties. Nevertheless, the deletion effaced some of the passage's deep affiliations with (4) and (6).

Pound's emendation of Passage (4) follows a similar logic. Pound's manuscript follows a vision of the lotus with a glimpse of willow to suggest the comfort of the ideal, and then appends Chinese characters (不 如 樂) drawn from *Analects* 6.18. (In Pound's translation: "He said: Those who know aren't up to those who love; nor those who love, to those who delight in" [*Confucius* 216]). Pound probably then removed the willow because he thought the passage from the *Analects* (which unfortunately was later allowed to drop out of the text) effectively communicated the comfort that accompanies intellectual delight. Without the willow, though, the poem's growing chain of associations that links beauty to compassion and healing loses some of its clarity, and the logic behind the reappearance of "young willows" in Canto LXXXIII becomes harder to follow.

These excisions, along with the disappearance of the Italian "Cunizza" and "Assunta" texts, significantly mute the resonance of (5), a key to the suite's denouement. In Canto LXXXI Pound famously experiences a release from oppression caused by a sudden lightening of spirit. In the Canto this is linked both to an influx of the English lyric tradition and to the unexpected appearance of the "new subtlety of eyes" of a visionary guest. Pound, however, presages the entrance of the guest by a brief and enigmatic reference to Kuanon ("Light as the branch of Kuanon"), whose implication became obscure when deletions to (2) and (4) stripped the word "branch" of its associations with the graceful form of the willow. (I will return to this passage below.)

Passage (6)—excerpted from Canto LXXXIII—belongs to what Pound initially conceived as the sequence's concluding Canto and brings together many of the poem's most important themes (Bush, "Quiet"). With regard to Kuanon, the passage develops Fenollosa's account of the willow's "sympathetic" relation to "the elements of water and ether" (spirit and compassion) and refines the sense of earlier passages that concern the effects of light on mist. These include a series of references to *Analects* 12.21.1, where Confucius walks amid "rain altars." Pound glances at this text first in Canto 78 / 501, but only in reference to its interrogation of passion in politics ("how to discover delusions [confusions]"). He reiterates the image of "rain altars" at 80 / 532, however, in a context in which the Confucian phrase is affiliated with Paradise and focused by the trees (perhaps poplars, perhaps willows) in Lévy-Dhurmer's portrait of Rodenbach (Kenner 479). At 80 / 532, we learn that "those trees are Elysium" and that the "rain altars" are connected to the "grey stone" in one of Pound's Paradisal places, the Aliscans, whose name (as Dante had observed) condenses the French words for Elysian Fields.

The culmination of the *Pisan Cantos'* array of references to Confucius's "rain altars," though, occurs in passage (6) at 83 /549-51. The manuscript version enlarges the basis of Elysium by bringing the altars together with Chinese characters (樂 水) that reprise the theme of "delight" in *Analects* 6.18. And although the ideograms were eventually allowed to drop out of the text, their English translation ("the sage / delighteth in water") sustains a new reference to the neighboring text of *Analects* 6.21: "the wise delight in water . . . the knowing are active . . . The knowing get the pleasure" (Pound, *Confucius* 217; Bush, "Confucius Erased" 188):

> in the drenched tent there is quiet
>   sered eyes are at rest
>   [............]
>   the sage
> delighteth in water
>   [.............................]
> as he was standing below the altars
>   of the spirits of rain
>   "When every hollow is full
>   it moves forward"
>   to the phantom mountain above the cloud

The lines "as he was standing below the altars / of the spirits of rain" add still another dimension by telescoping the sacred altars with willows (water-trees), thereby affirming that the willow's healing power is the natural consort of ritual purification.[18] The next two lines ("When every hollow is full / it moves forward") further thicken the chain Elysium-delight-reverence-willows-rain by invoking Mencius's discourse on the "passion-nature" from *Mencius* II.1.2.13-5 and suggesting that the rain-trees are transfigured by spiritual sustenance.[19] (The manuscript and typescript versions of the continuation of this text go on to cite much more of this text, both in English translation and—in now missing ideograms—in the original Chinese [Bush, "Confucius Erased" 188-89].)

The final lines of passage (6) cap this chain of increasingly rich appositions by linking "young willows"—figures of innocence and natural grace—to the phrase "plura diafana" (many translucencies), which the poem recalls from the "ASSUNTA" draft to suggest a multiplex illuminated world:

Plura diafana
    Heliads lift the mist from the young willows
there is no base seen under Taishan
    but the brightness of 'udor   ὕδωρ
the poplar tips float in brightness
only the stockade posts stand

Homing in on one of its central mysteries, the *Pisan Cantos* here register Kuanon's spiritual benevolence descending from the heavens to the earth. Her light illuminates "plura diafana"—many translucencies —the first and most beautiful of which constitute water-trees and mist. It is a passage that realizes itself brilliantly as both naturalist observation and myth. Pound succeeds in presenting a painterly *tour-de-force*, bringing to life the moment when the "brightness" of the sun joined with the moon dispels the morning mists from the ground up. But he also charges the scene with what can only be called religious energies by supplying "Heliads"—sun-nymphs—to "lift the mist"—in other words, to reveal the essence of the "young willows." Echoing Fenollosa's account of the way Kuanon's willows are "sympathetic with the elements of water and ether," the lines magically dissolve the oppressive gravity of the quotidian as they unveil the spiritual clarity of the earth. Here only the stockade posts, alone maintaining their oppressive gravity, succeed in "standing" while every other element in the scene communes like the willow with water and air. And behind all this presides Kuanon, no longer a humanized shape but an infused luminescence. Transformed into an elevating power that is in itself Paradise ("those trees are Elysium"), she transfigures all but the stockade posts themselves. The implication here is that Pound like the world around him has been temporarily liberated and for an instant has become (to quote the presage to this moment) "Light as the branch of Kuanon."

Notes

1. Pound's representations of Kuanon in the *Pisan Cantos* have been discussed previously by Zhaoming Qian (*Response* 10-13), Britton Gildersleeve, and, in a recent book based on the British Museum archives, Rupert Arrowsmith (especially chapters 5 and 9). All of these recognize the influence of Binyon and Fenollosa,

and most recently Arrowsmith (chapter 9) has succeeded in identifying the images that Pound first encountered in Binyon's unpublished March 1909 lectures "Art and Thought in East and West," attended by Pound at Binyon's invitation (Qian, *Orientalism* 182). For the various forms of the Bodhisattva's name, see Binyon, *Painting* 65.

2. References to the *Cantos* in this essay are to the 13th printing, 1995, and abbreviated in the text as Canto / page number. Also, *Literary Essays* are abbreviated LE, *Idee fondamentali* IF, and *Early Writings* EW. All previously unpublished material by Ezra Pound, Copyright © 2012 by the Trustees of the Ezra Pound Literary Property Trust; used by permission of New Directions Publishing Corp., agents for the Trustees. All published material by Ezra Pound used by permission of New Directions Publishing Corp.

3. Binyon entered the British Museum in 1893, but was transferred in 1895 from the Department of Printed Books—his William Blake catalogue appeared in 1906—to the Department of Prints and Drawings. By 1905 he had turned his attention to Far Eastern Art and by 1908 had been appointed Assistant Keeper of Prints and Drawings (Qian, *Response* 6). In 1912 he was put in charge of the newly created Sub-Department of Oriental Prints and Drawings (Beasley 59). The publisher Elkin Matthews introduced Binyon to Pound in February 1909, and Qian has suggested that the two poets discussed the Kuanons that appeared in the 1910-1912 British Museum Exhibition of Chinese and Japanese Paintings, which Binyon curated and whose catalogue he wrote (Binyon, *Guide*). Some of these images were subsequently included in Binyon's *The Flight of the Dragon* (1911), which Pound reviewed in the second number of *Blast* ("Chronicles," Qian, *Orientalism* 183-4). Pound and Binyon continued their discussions of Chinese art until Pound left London in 1920, and afterwards kept up an intense though intermittent correspondence.

4. For recent and more extended commentary on this history, see Crim 79-81; Palmer and Ramsay; and Yu.

5. In *The Flight of the Dragon*, Binyon informs his readers that "the main force of Buddhist art was spent in the creation of sublime figures . . . and that the paradigm of these figures could be found in "the image of Kwannon." It is "her gracious form," he continues, that we frequently find "seated lost in tender meditation alone upon a rock by solitary waves" (43-44). Binyon goes on to assert that "the substitution of such tenderness for the conception of ruthless power shows us the change wrought by Buddhism" to Asian culture (*Dragon* 44).

6. In yet a third period, which involves the composition of the three last volumes of the Cantos—*Rock-Drill, Thrones, and Drafts and Fragments*, all written or drafted in Washington D.C. in the fifties—Pound extended his elaboration of Kuanon by exploring her affiliation with more esoteric mythological figures such as the Egyptian-Roman figure of Isis (Elliott).

7. See Bush, "Quiet," "Towards Pisa" and "Remaking," as well as Bacigalupo, "Cantos 72 and 73."

8. This typescript produced by Olga Rudge can be found in the Olga Rudge Papers at the Beinecke (YCAL MSS 53, Series ii, Box 29 Folder 627). For previous commentary, see Bush, "Towards Pisa" 113-4, 116" and "Science."

9. So Pound writes in "European Paideuma," "Sound ethic we have from Confucius via Mencius . . . The tradition[al] portrait of Confucius shows him a nordic. . . . How far South of the 38th parallel can we go without . . . unsleeping suspicion of every belief. . . ?" (Bacigalupo, "European Paideuma" 226).

10. As with the "Cunizza" typescript, the second of these can be found in the Beinecke Library's Olga Rudge Papers (YCAL MSS 53, series ii, Box 29, Folder 627), while the first comes from the Beinecke's Ezra Pound Papers (YCAL MSS 43 Box 76, Folder 3387).

11. In one of his contemporary essays, Pound notes that "sea-board shrines to the Madonna" "at points commanding a view of the sea" "are filled with votive offerings of ship models and pictures of shipwrecks from which the votators have been saved" (Bacigalupo, "European" 229). An associated essay in Italian notes that the Madonna in these shrines is in fact an expression "della maternità. E l'antica 'Charitas' . . . . Superfluo accenare alle chiese costruite sulle basi dei templi pagani; alla *Stella Maris* patrona dei marinai" (of motherhood. She is the antique 'Caritas' . . . . It would be superfluous to add that these churches are built on the foundations of pagan temples, and to the survival of the figure of 'Stella Maris' patroness of mariners) (IF 134). The text goes on to invoke a confused series of Italian votive shrines to the Madonna, all of which appear in Pound's wartime drafts: "Monte Rosa" (Montallegro, a church situated on limestone cliffs above Rapallo); the Sanctuario (or Fano, shrine) "Delle Grazie" on slightly lower cliffs near Rapallo at Chiavari; and a chapel of the Madonna at Prato, near Florence.

12. These associations would continue to haunt Pound and would emerge again ten years later in *Drafts and Fragments*: "Foam and silk are thy fingers, / Kuanon, / and the long suavity of her moving, / willow and olive reflected / Brook-water

idles, / topaz against pallor of under-leaf / The lake waves Canaletto'd / under blue paler than heaven" (C110 / 798).

13. See also C100/ 742: "thus Plotinus / per plura diafana / neither weighed out nor hindered."

14. Pound translates these lines in the Cavalcanti essay as "Formed there in manner as a mist of light / Upon a dusk" (LE, 155), and in Canto XXXVI as "Formed like a diafan from light on shade" (C36 / 177).

15. Pound's annotated copy of the Prayer Book is owned by his daughter Mary de Rachewiltz. The handwritten manuscript of the Pisan Cantos can be found in the Beinecke Library at Yale (YCAL MSS 183).

16. "The Great Digest" X.5:

"The *Odes* say:

Until the Yin had lost the assembly...

They could offer the cup and drink with

The Most Highest.

—*Shi King*, III, i, i, 6.

"We can measure our regard for equity by the Yin. High destiny is not easy. Right action gains the people [*I think this ideogram has an original sense of the people gathered at its tribal blood rite.] and that gives one the state. Lose the people, you lose the state" (Pound, *Confucius* 71). (Pound has crossed out the last two ideograms in his manuscript, and left only the 配 ideogram, meaning "mate" or "harmonize" with Heaven, on the typescript.

17. From *Analects* 6.18. The repeated appearances of the first and second characters represent Pound practicing to draw them properly.

18. This moment of softening also has for Pound a personal application: attempting to moderate his rage against the Americans, he remembers in the "rain altars" passage of *Analects* 12. 21 that Confucius asks: "For one morning's temper to jeapord one's life and even that of one's relatives, isn't that hallucination" (Pound, *Confucius* 248).

19. "Being nourished by rectitude, and sustaining no injury, it fills up all between heaven and earth" (Legge, *Mencius* 190).

Works Cited

Arrowsmith, Rupert. *Modernism and the Museum: Asian, African, and Pacific Art and the London Avant-Garde*. Oxford: Oxford UP, 2010.

Bacigalupo, Massimo. "Ezra Pound's Cantos 72 and 73: An Annotated Translation." *Paideuma* 20 (1991): 11-41.

___. "Ezra Pound's 'European Paideuma.'" *Paideuma* 30 (2001): 225-245.

Beasley, Rebecca. *Ezra Pound and the Visual Culture of Modernism*. Cambridge: Cambridge UP, 2007.

Binyon, Laurence. *The Art of Botticelli: An Essay in Pictorial Criticism*. London: Macmillan,1913.

___. *The Flight of the Dragon: An Essay on the Theory and Practice of Art in China and Japan, Based on Original Sources*. London: John Murray, 1911.

___. *Guide to an Exhibition of Chinese and Japanese Paintings*. London: British Museum, 1910.

___. *Painting in the Far East: An Introduction to the History of Pictorial Art in Asia Especially China and Japan*. London: Arnold, 1908.

Burke, John J., C.S.P, ed. *Catholic Prayer Book for the Army and Navy*. New York: The Paulist Press, 1917.

Bush, Ronald. "Confucius Erased: The Missing Ideograms in *The Pisan Cantos*." *Ezra Pound and China*. Ed. Zhaoming Qian. Ann Arbor: U of Michigan P, 2003:163-92.

___. "Ezra Pound's Fascist 'Europa': Toward the *Pisan Cantos*." *Europa! Europa? The Avant-Garde, Modernism and the Fate of a Continent*. Ed. Sascha Bru. Berlin: De Gruyter, 2009: 210-28.

___. "*La filosofica famiglia*: Cavalcanti, Avicenna, and the 'Form' of Ezra Pound's *Pisan Cantos*." *Textual Practice* (Special Issue: "Thinking Poetry") 24.4 (August 2010): 669-705.

___. "'Quiet, Not Scornful'?: The Composition of the *Pisan Cantos*." *A Poem Including History: The Cantos of Ezra Pound*. Ed. Lawrence Rainey. Ann Arbor: U of Michigan P, 1996: 169-212.

___. "Remaking Canto 74." *Paideuma* 32.1-3 (Spring-Fall-Winter 2003): 157-86.

___. "Science, Epistemology, and Literature in Ezra Pound's Objectivist Poetics (With a Glance at The New Physics, Louis Zukofsky, Aristotle,

Neural Network Theory, and Sir Philip Sidney)." *The Idea and the Thing in Modernist American Poetry*. Ed. Cristina Giorcelli. Palermo: Ila Palma, 2001: 147-72.

___. "Towards Pisa: More From the Archives about Pound's Italian Cantos." *Agenda* 34 (1996/97): 89-124.

Crim, Keith, ed. *The Perennial Dictionary of World Religions*. New York: Harper and Row, 1981.

Elliott, Angela. "Pound's 'Isis Kuanon': An Ascension Motif in the *Cantos*." *Paideuma* 13.3 (1984): 327-56.

Fenollosa, Ernest F. *Epochs of Chinese and Japanese Art: An Outline History of East Asiatic Design*, 2 vols. London: Heinemann, 1913.

Flory, Wendy. "Confucius against Confusion: Ezra Pound and the Catholic Chaplain at Pisa." *Ezra Pound and China*. Ed. Zhaoming Qian. Ann Arbor: U of Michigan P, 2003: 142-62.

Gildersleeve, Britton. "'Enigma' at the Heart of Paradise: Buddhism, Kuanon, and the Feminine Ideogram in *The Cantos*." *Ezra Pound and China*. Ed. Zhaoming Qian. Ann Arbor: U of Michigan P, 2003: 193-212.

Kenner, Hugh. *The Pound Era*. Berkeley: U of California P, 1971.

Kraus, James. "Ezra Pound's Catholic Prayer Book: Pro Patria Et Deo." *Ezra Pound and Referentiality*. Ed. Hélène Aji. Paris: PUPS, 2003: 239-48.

Legge, James. *The Works of Mencius*. 1895; rpt. New York: Dover, 1970.

Palmer, Martin, and Ramsay, Jay. *Kuan Yin: Myths and Revelations of the Chinese Goddess of Compassion*. London: Thorsons, 1995.

Pound, Ezra. *The Cantos*. 13th printing. New York: New Directions, 1995.

___. "Chronicles, III: Rev. of Laurence Binyon, *The Flight of the Dragon: An Essay on the Theory and Practice of Art in China and Japan, Based on Original Sources*." *Blast* 2 (1915): 86.

___. *Confucius*. New York: New Directions, 1969.

___. *Early Writings: Poems and Prose*. Ed. Ira Nadel. New York: Penguin, 2005.

___. *Idee fondamentali: "Meridiano di Roma" 1939-1943*. Ed. Caterina Ricciardi. Rome: Lucarini, 1991.

___. *Literary Essays*. New York: New Directions, 1954; rpt. 1968.

Qian, Zhaoming, ed. *Ezra Pound and China*. Ann Arbor: U of Michigan P,

2003.

___. *The Modernist Response to Chinese Art: Pound, Moore, Stevens.* Charlottesville: U of Virginia P, 2003.

___. *Orientalism and Modernism: The Legacy of China in Pound and Williams.* Durham: Duke UP, 1995.

Shinku, Matsuo. "Kannon shinko no susume: Saikoku sanjusansho tohojunrei o hete." *Diahorin* 8 (1991): 112-62.

Terrell, Carroll. *A Companion to The Cantos of Ezra Pound.* 1980; rvd. Berkeley and Los Angeles: U of California P, 1993.

Williams, C.A.S. *Chinese Symbolism and Art Motifs.* 1974; rpt. Vermont: Tuttle, 2006.

Yu, Chung-fang. *Kuan-yin.* New York 2001.

Mai-mai Sze, The Tao, and Late Moore

Zhaoming Qian

In the "Foreword to *A Marianne Moore Reader*" (1961), Marianne Moore refers to a lecture entitled "Tedium and Integrity," which she gave at Mills College in Oakland, California, on 16 October 1957: "What became of 'Tedium and Integrity,' the unfinished manuscript of which there was no duplicate? A housekeeper is needed to assort the untidiness." Not the entire manuscript was lost after all, for she clarifies two paragraphs below: "Of 'Tedium and Integrity' the first few pages are missing—summarized sufficiently by: manner for matter; shadow by substance; ego for rapture" (*Complete Prose* 525).

Speaking of the surviving pages of Moore's typescript kept at the Rosenbach Museum and Library, Linda Leavell claims: "this may have been one of Moore's most important essays along with 'Feeling and Precision' and 'Humility, Concentration, and Gusto' had she not lost the first four pages" (Leavell 157). Is the opening of "Tedium and Integrity" really lost? With this question in mind I traveled to Mills College in May 2010. Thanks to the assistance of Janice Braun, Curator of the Mills College F. W. Olin Library Special Collections, a recording of the 1957 lecture was found. Leavell's speculation proves correct. This lecture provides essential clues about the development of Moore's late modernist poetic manifest in her last two books of verse, *O to Be a Dragon* (1959) and *Tell Me, Tell Me* (1966). It brings to light what inspired her October 1957 lecture—a book about the Tao, which she had read earlier that year. The aesthetic concepts and forms she had learned from that book and then elucidated in the lecture would lead to her sudden renewal of experimental modernism in old age. Without access to the entire lecture, the Taoist influence in Moore's late modernist poetry could well remain lost to readers. Indeed, in her final decade, Moore could have turned this lecture into an essay as important as "Feeling and Precision."

I

As the recording attests, Moore began her 40-minute lecture at Mills College with a brief explanation of what she meant by "Tedium":

> Tonight our topic is "Tedium and Integrity." How are we going to express it, a creative principle? It should in any case be the opposite of the uninstructed teaching the lesson, the unnecessary. It should be the initiate making explicit the intangible. What kind of poetry is not tedious? What is tedium? One of my compositions is entitled "Poetry," and I said, "I, too, dislike it." What did I mean by that? I mean that we dislike . . . manner for matter, shadow for substance, and ego for rapture.
>
> ("Tedium and Integrity")[1]

For Moore modern poetry should be like modern painting that "centers much less on seeing the real world than on making of it another world" ("Tedium and Integrity"). Accordingly, she would consider tiresome when reading any poetry with no vision of "another world" or no "sensibility and imagination" that created "another world." With this elucidation, Moore shifted to "Integrity," which idea she credited to Mai-mai Sze's *The Tao of Painting* with a translation of *The Mustard Seed Garden Manual* 1679-1701:

> Now this whole theme of integrity, for I would like to dispatch tedium for good, was suggested to me by *The Tao of Painting* edited and with a translation by Mai-mai Sze. It's published by the Bollingen Foundation in 1956, and anything I say that is worth the hearing should be attributed to Ms. Mai-mai Sze. Well, Hsieh Ho, whose six canons of painting were formulated about AD 500, said, "The terms ancient and modern have no meaning in art." And I indeed felt that art is timeless when I saw in the Book Review Section of the *New York Times* last winter, a reproduction of a plum branch, a blossoming branch entitled "A Breath of Spring."
>
> ("Tedium and Integrity")

As I have noted elsewhere, Moore received her copy of *The Tao of Painting* along with two other books from the Bollingen Foundation in

January 1957. Just how thrilled she became by possessing these books in the Bollingen series is evident in a letter she wrote John Barrett on 22 January 1957: "You cannot imagine my excitement in possessing these books. The exposition of subjects and the terminology in discussing 'the Elements of a Picture' in the Chinese text is pleasure enough for a lifetime" (Marianne Moore Collection).[2] Her admiration for *The Tao of Painting* is further revealed in her letter of 5 September 1957 to Barrett, in which she ordered five more copies of *The Tao* for her friends:

> Now!—I need five copies of the TAO and for two, enclose a check for fifty dollars and a memorandum of what I owe for conveyance will have to be made. I seem to make a salesman of you … I have been talking to my friend Bryher [Annie Winifred Ellerman] about my so-called lecture in California TEDIUM AND INTEGRITY about how the Tao makes study charming and I cannot rest till she has this treatise—of all my friends the one perhaps who deserves it most. (Marianne Moore Collection)

What first caught Moore's eye were no doubt the book's expertly chosen plates of Chinese paintings. She alluded to one of them, *A Breath of Spring*, in her 1957 lecture, and she extravagantly praised another, *Early Autumn* by Qian Xuan (fig. 1), in her first letter to Barrett:

> If I were in a decline mentally, the insect and frog color-print in Volume I of the Tao would, I think, help me to regain tone.

Qian Xuan (1235-1305), Early Autumn. Courtesy, Detroit Institute of Arts.

> The accuracy without rigidity of the characterizations is hard
> to credit; the emerald of the leopard-frog and its watchful eye,
> the dragon-flies, sanguine, brown and greenish gray against
> the fragile beetle of some kind, the climbing katydid and
> grasshopper on the move, the plausibility of all this life above
> the pumpkin-leaves and lace of lesser leaves, the bumble-bee
> so solid despite frail violet wings and trailing legs with thorny
> rasps, are something, I suppose, that one could learn by heart
> but never become used to. (Marianne Moore Collection)

For decades Chinese art had held a well-known fascination for
Moore. Yet until she read *The Tao* she had no objective understanding
of what made Chinese art eternally fascinating. And more importantly,
she discovered to her amazement that much of the Tao or the aesthetic
behind Chinese art appeared akin to her own modernist poetic. She
could invigorate her poetry by deliberately applying the Tao. She
wished fervently to share her new insights with others, and precisely
at that moment she received a lecture invitation from Mills College. It
provided her with that opportunity.

"Tedium and Integrity" is thus Moore's homage to *The Tao*.
Whereas "tedium" is Moore's term for Sze's locution "egotism," or
siyu in Chinese (Sze 31), "integrity" is her expression for the Tao. In
Chapter 1 on the Tao, Sze stresses the indefinable nature of the Tao by
quoting Laozi as saying "The *Tao* that can be called the *Tao* is not the
eternal Tao . . ." (Sze 15). "In Chinese writing, which is pictographic, of

course," Moore observes in her lecture, "a tao is a pair of legs, whereas the Tao has legs, arms, and a head – it's a total harmony, from head to foot" ("Tedium and Integrity"). Moore derives this symbolic meaning from Sze's analysis of the character 道 (*dao* in pinyin) as depiction of a head on top of depiction of a foot, representing wholeness of head and foot, heaven and earth, body and soul (Sze 16).

We can now see why Moore has chosen "integrity" as the term for the Tao. The English word, too, emphasizes both aspects of the Taoist concept symbolized in the character道—wholeness of all things (Heaven and Earth) and wholeness of character (individual from head to foot). Since her college days, as Cristanne Miller has noted, Moore was known for her avowed objection to "egotism" (Miller 26), what the Buddhists call "ignorance," which underlies her attraction to the Taoist insistence on clearing away all *siyu* or obscurings (Sze 31).

Just as Sze in Chapter 2 of *The Tao* turns attention to the first of the Six Canons of Painting formulated by Xie He 500 AD, Moore does the same in the second part of her lecture. The Six Canons plays a key role in Chinese art criticism. Laurence Binyon in *The Flight of the Dragon* (1911) deals with the Six Canons in its opening chapter. In reference to the first canon, "rhythmic vitality," he states, "We are probably nearer to its essence when we speak of the rhythmic movements of the body, as in games or in the dance. We all know, by experience, that in order to apply the energy of the body to the utmost effect, we must discover a certain related order of movements" (Binyon 15).

Ezra Pound reviewed *The Flight of the Dragon* in *Blast 2* (1915). In it he calls attention to the First Canon by capitalizing every word of its definition: "FOR INDEED IT IS NOT ESSENTIAL THAT THE SUBJECT-MATTER SHOULD REPRESENT OR BE LIKE ANYTHING IN NATURE, ONLY IT MUST BE ALIVE WITH A RHYTHMIC VITALITY OF ITS OWN" (Pound 99). Moore, too, had read Binyon's *The Flight of the Dragon*.[3] However, it was Sze's summary of the First Canon—"the idea that *Ch'i* (the breath of Heaven, the spirit) stirs all of nature to life" (33)—rather than Binyon's statement about it that opened her eyes to its importance. In her lecture she, drawing on Sze, observes: "In China Six Canons of Painting were formulated, as has been said, about AD 500 by Hsieh Ho [Xie He]. Of these the first— basic to all—[which] controls the other five and applies to all kinds of painting is spirit. The word *ch'i*—in Cantonese version pronounced *hay*, is almost like exhaling a breath, cognate in meaning to *pneuma* and the word *spiritus*" ("Tedium and Integrity").

The Tao was evidently present in Moore's thought throughout her October 1957 lecture. Drawing to its close, she swiftly turns back to the beginning, that is, the symbol of the Tao described by Sze as a circle whose "beginning (the head) and end (the foot) are the same" (Sze 16). "Everything must be in relation to the Tao, the center," Moore observes echoing Sze. "A circle's beginning, its head, and its end, or foot, are the same, unmoving and continually moving." "As a symbol of the power of heaven," she adds, "the dragon, slumbering or winging its way across the heavens, has movement as a main characteristic" ("Tedium and Integrity"). Unsurprisingly, the dragon is to be the central symbol of Moore's next book of verse, *O to Be a Dragon* (1959).

II

In September 1957, when Moore was musing on *The Tao*, *The Tao*'s author Mai-mai Sze (1909-92) (fig. 2), a fellow New Yorker, was attracted to Moore's *Like a Bulwark*. Coming across a review of this 1956 book of verse in *The Listener*, Sze could not resist clipping it out and sending it to Moore with a note: "You may perhaps not see this enclosed review in the London B.B.C. weekly The Listener. I thought that you might wish to have it" (Marianne Moore Collection). This note of 28 September 1957 was followed by a correspondence between the two that lasted for twelve years.

Mai-mai Sze (1909-92). Photo by Carl Van Vechten. Courtesy, Van Vechten Trust; courtesy, Yale Collection of American Literature, Beinecke Rare Book and Manuscript Library.

Mai-mai Sze was the oldest daughter of Alfred Sao-ke Sze (1877-1958), the Republic of China's ambassador to Washington, 1934-1937. Educated in England and the U.S. and holding a degree from Wellesley College (1931), Sze began her career both as a painter and a writer. As a painter, she was better known for her portrait of Eugene O'Neill to be printed on the cover of the 17 July 1957 *Newsweek* than for her landscapes exhibited in London, Paris, and New York. As a writer, her first book was *Echo of a Cry: A Story Which Began in China* (1945), an autobiographical novel, and her second book was *Silent Children* (1948), a novel about refugee children in post-World War II Europe. But it was her third book, *The Tao of Painting*, that won her a lasting friendship with Moore.

The Tao not only gave an impetus to Moore's 1957 lecture on "Tedium and Integrity," but it also inspired her 1959 book of verse *O to Be a Dragon*. In April 1959, upon the publication of *O to Be a Dragon*, Moore sent Sze an inscribed copy. In an enclosed letter, she acknowledged her debt to Sze by calling Sze "Angel to me and friend of the dragon-symbol": "Just please realize my gratitude, the fond thoughts you evoke—the celestial reveries for which you are responsible; my universe [is] enlarged and ever expanding by receiving from Mr. Barrett TAO OF PAINTING—the mustard-seed garden and above all Volume II" (Marianne Moore Collection).

How *The Tao* impacted *O to Be a Dragon* is the topic of a chapter of my 2003 study, *The Modernist Response to Chinese Art*. I am not returning to any *O to Be a Dragon* poems examined there except the opening piece, "O to Be a Dragon." Before her trip to Mills College, Moore had been asked to read a few of her poems after the lecture. The first poem she read that night was an early version of "O to Be a Dragon." "Before I read this," she explains in her lecture,

> I want to say what I forgot to say last night at Stanford. The editors of *the Sequoia* were really very unusually persevering about my contributing to *Sequoia*.[4] They said they'd be very glad to publish this; they'd heard I was to give a lecture. And I said, well it belonged, it was the property of President White. "Well we'd be glad to publish it too." "No," I said. And then I thought, and I will say this obliging, that I thought of this: I was at a party the other night, and a gentleman who seemed to

be an expert in every field, we're talking about the Chinese and these symbols, and he said, "O, to be a dragon!" Symbol of the power of heaven! So I thought, there's something.

> If I had, like Solomon,
> my wish ... O to be a dragon,
> of silkworm
> size or immense; or at times invisible.
> Felicitous phenomenon!
>
>   ("Tedium and Integrity")

In the published version of the poem, "could have my wish—" is inserted as a second line and "a symbol of the power of Heaven—" is added to "of silkworm" to form the new fourth line (*Complete Poems* 177).

Among the distinguishing characteristics of Moore's poetry are the juxtaposition of observations and quotations, the omission of quotation marks around quotations, and the use of end notes to acknowledge sources of quotations. While the first two of these are evident in "O to Be a Dragon," the last is hardly seen. In other words, here Moore has experimented with unacknowledged quotations in the true sense. The poem is a collage of observations and quotations. Sandwiched between an opening statement and an exclamation are three quotations, two of which I have identified in *The Modernist Response to Chinese Art*: "a symbol of the power of Heaven" is a quotation from Sze's *Tao* (Sze 81) and "of silkworm / size or immense; at times invisible" derives from the sixth century B.C. philosopher Guanzi translated by Sze (82-83). What I did not know previously is that "O to be a dragon" is also a quotation. As is revealed first in the lecture and then in the "Foreword to *A Marianne Moore Reader*," at a party Moore described to a friend, "an authority on gems, finance, painting, and music," how the Tao led her to the dragon as its symbol, the symbol of the power of heaven. When she "concluded a digression on cranes, peaches, bats, and butterflies as symbols of long life and happiness," the friend exclaimed, "O to be a dragon!" (*Complete Prose* 551). That exclamation inspired Moore to improvise her 1957 dragon poem.

Moore's admiration for the Chinese dragon may be traced to 1923 when she in separate letters to her brother John Warner Moore and friend Bryher paid tribute to "a dragon in the clouds" in the Metropolitan

Museum Exhibition of Chinese Paintings (*Selected Letters* 194, 197).
The dragon resurfaces in her 1932 poem "The Plumet Basilisk": "As
by a Chinese brush, eight green / bands are painted on / the tail—"
(*Complete Poems* 22). One thing that distinguishes her 1957 dragon
poem from "The Plumet Basilisk" and other lyrics is its compact form.
Moore's poems are typically medium-sized. Her occasional short
pieces consist of eight to ten lines. By contrast the 1957 dragon poem
has only six lines.

The new dragon poem echoes what she observes in her lecture on
"Tedium and Integrity": "Symbolism, as I said, is a characteristic of
Chinese thinking, and as a symbol of the power of heaven, the dragon,
slumbering or winging its way across the heavens, has movement as a
main characteristic. At will, it can change, be the size of a silkworm,
or swell so large as to fill the heaven and earth, thus representing
totality" ("Tedium and Integrity"). The Tao "responsible" for "O to Be
a Dragon" was also "responsible" for many other "celestial reveries":
"To a Chameleon," "A Jelly-Fish," "The Arctic Ox (or Goat)," and
"Leonardo da Vinci's," to name but a few that have been considered in
The Modernist Response to Chinese Art.

III

Moore and Sze continued to correspond after *O to Be a Dragon.*
In the early 1960s, Sze made several trips to Europe and North Africa
with her companion, the costume designer Irene Sharaff, for the
filming of *Cleopatra.* After each of these trips, she would send Moore
a souvenir (Sze to Moore, 14 July 1962, Marianne Moore Collection).
On a 1963 visit to Italy, Moore bought Sze a "ceremonial bronze" in
return (21 November 1963, Marianne Moore Collection). After living
in Brooklyn for thirty-six years, Moore moved back to Manhattan in
the winter of 1965. Sze was among the first to be invited to visit her
new home. As a result of that visit, Sze began addressing Moore as
"Dear Marianne" (Sze to Moore, 17 February 1966, Marianne Moore
Collection).

For Moore Sze's most precious gifts were not souvenirs from
her European and North African trips, nor her 1968 Christmas gift
of a custom-designed violet shirt (Sze to Moore, 18 December 1968,
Marianne Moore Collection). They were her book *The Tao of Painting*

and a subscription to the *Times Literary Supplement*. Shortly after the two began exchanging letters, Sze found that Moore had no access to *TLS*. The London weekly literary review soon found its way to Moore's Brooklyn apartment, and it was renewed year after year. In the decade of 1958-1968, *TLS* provided the two writers with numerous interesting discussion topics. In a letter to Sze of 20 November 1963, for instance, Moore referred to a *TLS* review ("The Elephant and the Mouse") that compared Dr. Johnson to the elephant and Boswell to the mouse: "'Comparing all our acquaintance to some animal or other,' wrote Mrs. Thrale, 'we pitched upon the elephant for [Johnson's] resemblance, adding that the proboscis of that creature was like his mind most exactly, strong to buffet even the tyger, and pliable to pick up even the pin'" (Marianne Moore Collection). Moore was an avowed elephant fan. In a 1917 poem, "Black Earth," she assumes the personae of a dark elephant called "Melanchthon," characterizing him as witty, selfless, and generous. Reading the above *TLS* review, Moore naturally approved its likening of Dr. Johnson's wit and generosity to an elephant's.

Sze never worked together with Moore on any poems, but by passing onto her the spirit of the dragon through *The Tao of Painting* and giving her a subscription of *TLS*, she became Moore's collaborator in a special way. In her letter of 16 November 1963, Moore acknowledged Sze as an educator/inspirer in her life: "Affording me luxury week by week —educating me …… in the Tao of Painting—of which I never tire, permanent gifts, they have been, that I have for *all time*" (Marianne Moore Collection). To say that she carried the spirit of the Tao in her mind is an understatement. Indeed, the Tao continued to be prevalent in Moore's final book of verse, *Tell Me, Tell Me*.

The opening poem of *Tell Me, Tell Me*, "Granite and Steel," celebrates the Brooklyn Bridge designed by the German immigrant John Roebling (1806-1869) and completed in 1883. Spanning the East River, it connects the two boroughs of New York City, Manhattan and Brooklyn, where Moore had homes in different time periods. To Moore, the bridge is not so much a hub of communications as it is an artwork. It looks like a Chinese dragon in ink painting, blending the designer's personality with the blue sky and the brown river. In "celestial reveries," she envisions the bridge as changing from image to image—from a "seagull's wing" to "a double rainbow" and "Caged

Circe" (*Complete Poems* 205). In the third stanza, lines borrowed from
Hart Crane and Dorothy Beall echo the spirit of the Tao—modern
architecture united with nature, and heaven united with earth:

> "O path amid the stars
> crossed by the seagull's wing!"
> "O radiance that doth inherit me!"
> —affirming inter-acting harmony! (205)

The *TLS* account of Dr. Johnson and Boswell provided Moore with
a new way of admiring the elephant. In "Charity Overcoming Envy"
the elephant appears as a carriage for Charity in her battle against Envy.
Instead of trampling the dog-riding Envy, it only "scarcely stretched"
his cheek (*Complete Poems* 216). In lines 23-25, "The elephant, at no
time borne down by self-pity, / convinces the victim / that Destiny
is not devising a plot." Moore's characterization of Charity on the
elephant and Envy on the dog in "Charity Overcoming Envy" could be
partially patterned on the *TLS* sketches of Samuel Johnson and James
Boswell.

In "Old Amusement Park" Moore describes a pair of pachyderm
statuary:
> The park's elephant
> slowly lies down aslant;
>
> a pygmy replica then rides
> the mound the back provides. (210)

The description is reminiscent of Boswell in the *TLS* review. When
the elephant falls "aslant," the pygmy tumbles with it, as his fortunes
are inseparable from the elephant's. According to the review, Boswell
would often ask the impelling question: "'What would Johnson say of
this?'" ("The Elephant and the Mouse"). He, like the pygmy in "Old
Amusement Park," was unable to act without Johnson's elephantine
intellect.

In "To a Giraffe" the giraffe is a metaphor for T. S. Eliot and the
modernist ideal of impersonality he upholds. As Ruth Carrington
has noted, in the mid-1940s Moore already began referring to Eliot
as a giraffe (148-49). In a letter to Eliot of 16 November 1946, Moore

wrote: "Dear San Tomas (as you appear in the Morley classification of American fauna, under giraffes), For a giraffe to cook a gosling does not seem very kind, but it is; and I shall not hamper you further with impractical considerations" (Marianne Moore Collection). In his reply, Eliot refuted: "Dear Marianne: But it was very mischievous of him to classify me under Giraffes, unless anybody is a Giraffe who has dwelt in the Giraffe house; my proper classification is under Elephants" (Marianne Moore Collection). Yet Moore continued to think of Eliot as a giraffe.

The poem can be interpreted as Moore's commentary on the changing poetic style in the late 1950s to the early 1960s. In those years, Moore witnessed her aesthetic values, the values of modernist poetry, being challenged by those of postmodernist poetry. Lawrence Ferlinghetti's City Lights Bookstore published Allen Ginsberg's *Howl*, the landmark poetry of the Beat Generation, 1 November 1956. The rawness of Ginsberg's language did not impress Moore; nor did his repeated references to drug use and hetero/homosexual lovemaking. Moore's disapproval of Ginsberg's poetry is visible in a letter to him of July 1952: "I have been thinking about this manuscript [Empty Mirror] which you left me....... Your disgust worries me and I can't make clear without being objectionable...... (Self-pity is bad, friend.) ...... Can't you be grateful for *that*? If not, Not. *But try*" (*Selected Letters* 499, 501).

It was two years after Ginsberg's reading of *Howl* at Six Gallery in San Francisco and one year after its publication by City Lights of San Francisco that Moore went to Mills College in Oakland, East Bay, to give the lecture "Tedium and Integrity." While "Integrity" is her tribute to the Tao, "Tedium" implies her critique of the Beat Generation and their very personal and literal poetry. Moore makes this clear in her lecture:

> Chinese philosophy [Ms. Mai-mai Sze observed] might be said to be psychology, a development of the whole personality. And egotism, or what the Buddhists call ignorance, obscures a clear view of the Tao. It is unusual, in my experience at least, to come on a book of verse which has not a tincture of [animosity,] sarcasm, grievance, or some sense of injury, personal or [impersonal] – general. And I feel very strongly what [Señor] Jimenez,[the Spanish poet], says in referring to something else to what is not poetry: "There is a profounder profundity," than

wistful egocentricity.

("Tedium and Integrity")

Moore's theme of "Tedium and Integrity" is reaffirmed in "To a Giraffe." The opening of the poem might be interpreted as saying: "If the artist is not to be personal or literal, and should be innocent, he or she is required to work always at the highest reach, like the giraffe, an animal that pleasures us because it is 'unconversational.'" Certainly the speaker had in mind Eliot (a giraffe) and herself (an elephant) when stating this. Both became aware of the threat of extinction of their kind of poetry in the early 1960s.

The poem thus continues: "When plagued by the psychological, / a creature can be unbearable // that could have been irresistible; / or to be exact, exceptional // since less conversational / than some emotionally-tied-in-knots animal" (*Complete Poems* 215). Carrington convincingly argues that these lines allude to Moore's friend, Robert Lowell, who was "certainly 'plagued by the psychological' when he was writing his 'not cooked, but raw' poems of this period about his recurring bouts with mental illness, his periodic hospitalizations, and his conflicts with family members (152).

Would the giraffe, or modernist poetry, become extinct in face of the rise of very personal and literal contemporary poetry? The speaker offers an answer in the next stanza: "After all / consolations of the metaphysical / can be profound" (*Complete Poems* 215). Her choice of the word "metaphysical" further reveals that she had in mind Eliot and Eliot's brand of modernism. To her, no poetry, neither modern nor postmodern, neither impersonal nor personal, can be perfect, as "In Homer, existence // is flawed." Despite their respective shortcomings, she predicts, modernist poetry and postmodernist poetry will journey side by side "from sin to redemption, perpetual" (*Complete Poems* 215).

Sze devotes a chapter of *The Tao* to the Six Canons of Painting formulated by Xie He 500 AD. The First Canon of Painting, "rhythmic vitality," is illustrated in sensual imagery in "Blue Bug," a poem immediately inspired by a photograph of polo ponies printed on the 13 November 1961 *Sports Illustrated*. In the speaker's imagination, one of the ponies, nicknamed "Blue Bug," is galloping with rhythmic vitality.

In this camera shot,
from that fine print in which you hide

(eight-pony portrait from the side),
you seem to recognize
a recognizing eye,
limber Bug.

(*Complete Poems* 218)

All of a sudden, the spirited pony is metamorphosed into the African American ballet dancer Arthur Mitchell in the role of Puck: "bug brother to an Arthur / Mitchell dragonfly, / speeding to left, / speeding to right; / reversible . . ." (*Complete Poems* 218).

While envisioning the dancer in the pony, the speaker seems also to hear what Daniel Albright calls the "music of the body": "like 'turns in an ancient Chinese / melody, a thirteen / twisted silk-string three-finger solo.'" Is the speaker imagining the *guzheng* music, *guzheng* being an ancient Chinese plucked string instrument? The rhythmic vitality in the polo pony, the ballet dance, and the *guzheng* melody further calls up in the speaker's mind's eye the clouds and waves in the Qing dynasty Yellow-River scroll: "There they are Yellow River- / scroll accuracies." This miraculously shifts to "the acrobat Li Siau Than, / gibbon-like but limberer / defying gravity, / nether side arched up, / cup on head not upset— / China's very most ingenious man."

No Western poem has elucidated the workings of the First Canon more vividly than "Blue Bug." Appropriately, all illustrations except Arthur Mitchell are from the Orient: Chinese *guzheng* music, Chinese scroll painting, and Chinese acrobat. What about polo popular in many European countries? From *Encyclopedia Britannica* (1911) Moore could have learned that polo was first played in Persia, fifth century B.C. It became popular in Tang-dynasty China in the seventh century A.D., as is depicted in murals unearthed from Tang Prince Zhanghuai's tomb in Qianling Mausoleum in Shanxi, China.

The African-American ballet star in "Blue Bug" reappears as a central figure in "Arthur Mitchell" as Puck dancing the dragon dance:

Slim dragonfly
too rapid for the eye
      to cage—
contagious gem of virtuosity—
make visible, mentality.
Your jewels of mobility

    reveal
        and veil
            a peacock-tail. (*Complete Poems* 220)
Puck is the clever, mischievous elf in Shakespeare's *A Midsummer
Night's Dream*. In the 1964 Lincoln Kirstein's and George Balanchine's
City Center ballet production of the play, Mitchell miraculously
captures the rhythmic vitality of Puck dancing the dragonfly dance.
In her poem "Arthur Mitchell," Moore likewise catches the rhythmic
vitality of the African-American ballet dancer in that role. Once more
the modernist poet proves that she herself is capable of being the
powerful and changeable Chinese dragon.

In the same collection where these poems appear, the title poem,
"Tell Me, Tell Me," begins with a rhetorical question, reaffirming the
theme of her October 1957 lecture:
    where might be a refuge for me
    from egocentricity
    and its propensity to bisect,
    mis-state, misunderstand
and obliterate continuity?"
                        (*Complete Poems* 231)
"Egocentricity" is precisely what Moore in her Mills College
lecture refers to as "tedium," or what the Buddhists call ignorance. For
Moore as for traditional Chinese artists, egocentricity obscures a clear
vision of the Tao and makes profound art impossible. What helped
Henry James and Beatrix Potter remain exempt from egocentricity? To
the speaker it is their "Chinese / 'passion for the particular'" (*Complete
Poems* 231). Miss Potter's Tailor of Gloucester, despite sickness and
fatigue, "finished / the Lord Mayor's cerise coat" (232). He set a fine
example for all artists and poets. What else besides devotion to "passion
for the particular" can fight away egocentricity? The speaker tells us
her own defense, which is deference. "Passion for the particular" is a
professional tip whereas "deference" offers moral advice. How can the
two go together? Moore in her October 1957 lecture calls our attention
to what Mai-mai Sze has emphasized, the Chinese view "that painting
is not a profession but an extension of the art of living" (Sze 5). "Tell
Me, Tell Me" thus verifies what Moore has said to Sze: "in the Tao of
Painting—of which I never tire, permanent gifts, they have been, that I

have for *all time*. Possessions that I carry with me in my mind—along with some incurable ignorances" (Marianne Moore Collection).

Modernism arose not out of the effort of a single genius but the collective efforts of numerous avant-garde artists and poets working closely together. Just as the collaboration of Pablo Picasso and Georges Braque ushered in Cubism, which broke ground for revolutionary artistic concepts, the gathering together of Ezra Pound, Hilda Doolittle, and Richard Aldington brought about Imagism, which changed the nature of poetry written in English. Among Pound's collaborators were also Mrs. Mary Fenollosa and Pao Swen Tseng. Had not Mrs. Fenollosa provided her late husband's Chinese poetry notes, Pound could not have made *Cathay* (1915). Similarly, had not Miss Tseng interpreted the Chinese manuscript poems of a screen-book from Japan, Pound's memorable Seven Lakes Canto would have been out of the question.[5] T. S. Eliot's most notable collaborator was Pound, whose radical revisionary efforts helped make Eliot's *The Waste Land* the modernist masterpiece it is. Marianne Moore's collaborators included H. D., Bryher, Eliot, and her mother. Whereas H. D. and Bryher were responsible for the publication of Moore's first book of verse, *Poems*, in 1921, Eliot personally selected the poems for the 1935 *Selected Poems of Marianne Moore*, arranged them, and wrote the introduction. As to Mrs. Moore, she was for decades the first reader and critic of Moore's draft poems, contributing in her way to her daughter's poetic style. Her death in 1947 left a void in Moore's career. Arguably, Moore's friendship with Mai-mai Sze not only satisfied her lifelong thirst for Chinese culture but filled the void in Moore's career. Sze's *The Tao of Painting* literally excited her into new creativity, resulting in two volumes of astonishing, experimental late modernist lyrics.

Notes

I would like to thank Douglas Barry for helping research a *TLS* review and "Charity Overcoming Envy," Mary Bamburg for transcribing Mills College recording of Moore's 1957 lecture, and Qiaodan Lu for introducing me to the *guzheng*.

1. Permission for the use of the quotations from the "Tedium and Integrity in Poetry" lecture, given on 16 October 1957 by Marianne C. Moore, is granted

by the Literary Estate of Marianne C. Moore, David M. Moore, Administrator of the Literary Estate of Marianne Moore. All rights reserved. Courtesy, Special Collections, F. W. Olin Library, Mills College. "Arthur Mitchell," "Blue Bug," "Tell Me, Tell Me," "To a Giraffe," copyright © 2003 by Marianne Craig Moore, Executor of the Estate of Marianne Moore. Used by permission of Viking Penguin, a division of Penguin Group (USA) Inc.

2. Unpublished letters to and from Marianne Moore are cited by the writer, addressee, and date followed by (Marianne Moore Collection) where the unpublished letters are housed and catalogued.

3. Moore's copy of Laurence Binyon's *The Flight of the Dragon* is kept in the Marianne Moore Collection of Rosenbach Museum and Library, Philadelphia.

4. *Sequoia* was (and still is) the student literary journal of Stanford University. Lynn White was Mills College President, 1943-58. My thanks to Janice Braun for this information.

5. For an account of Pao Swen Tseng's contribution to Pound's "Seven Lakes Canto," see Qian, *Ezra Pound's Chinese Friends*, pp. 9-17.

Works Cited

Binyon, Laurence. *The Flight of the Dragon: An Essay on the Theory and Practice of Art in China and Japan Based on Original Sources.* London: Murray, 1911.

Carrington, Ruth. "Marianne Moore's Metaphysical Giraffe." *Marianne Moore: Woman and Poet.* Ed. Patricia C. Willis. Orona, ME: National Poetry Foundation, 1990. 145-52.

"The Elephant and the Mouse." *Times Literary Supplement* 16 Aug. 1963: 626.

Leavell, Linda. *Marianne Moore and the Visual Arts.* Baton Rouge: Louisiana State UP, 1995.

Marianne Moore Collection. Rosenbach Museum and Library. Philadelphia.

Miller, Cristanne. *Marianne Moore: Questions of Authority.* Cambridge: Harvard UP, 1993.

Moore, Marianne. *Complete Poems.* New York: Viking, 1981.

___. *Complete Prose.* Ed. Patricia C. Willis. New York: Viking, 1987.

___. "Foreword to *A Marianne Moore Reader.*" *Complete Prose of Marianne Moore.* Ed. Patricia C. Willis. New York: Viking, 1987. 550-54.

___. *Selected Letters.* Ed. Bonnie Costello, Celeste Goodridge, Cristanne Miller. New York: Knopf, 1997.

___. "Tedium and Integrity in Poetry." Rec. 16 October 1957. Mills College Olin Library Collection. 2010. CD.

Pound, Ezra. *Ezra Pound's Poetry and Prose Contributions to Periodicals.* Vol. 2. New York: Garland, 1991.

Qian, Zhaoming. *Ezra Pound's Chinese Friends.* Oxford: Oxford UP, 2008.

___. *The Modernist Response to Chinese Art: Pound, Moore, Stevens.* Charlottesville: U of Virginia P, 2003.

Sze, Mai-mai. *The Tao of Painting: a study of the ritual disposition of Chinese painting.* New York: Bollingen Foundation, 1956.

Louis Zukofsky's American Zen

Richard Parker

While the narrativization of second-generation Modernism has inextricably linked Zukofsky's career with Ezra Pound's, dubbed by T.S. Eliot "the inventor of Chinese poetry for our time" (Pound, *Selected Poems* xvi), little attention has been paid to Zukofsky's late engagement with the East. It would not be until Zukofsky's final florescence began in the early 1960s, and as he began to intensify his collaboration with the poets of the new generation, that he would begin an approach to a most unPoundian area of Orientalist interest—Zen Buddhism. This late approach to Zen encapsulates Zukofsky's complex relationship with Pound's Orientalism and his mentor's influence in general, as well as illuminating the surprising closeness of Zukofsky's collaboration with the younger generation of poets loosely affiliated with Donald Allen's *The New American Poetry* (1960).

Hugh Kenner wrote off Zukofsky and the Objectivists by writing in *A Homemade World* that "[t]he quality of their very youthful work is that of men who have inherited a formed tradition" (169).[1] This analysis is unhelpful to the extent that it simplifies the interaction between Pound and Zukofsky. That Zukofsky did, however, inherit a "formed tradition" is unarguable: Zukofsky, aged just 23, began his correspondence with Pound in 1927 after submitting "A Poem Beginning 'The'" to Pound for inclusion in his journal *Exile*. This poem, like much of his early work, is in large part a pastiche of Pound and Eliot; it displays its learning clearly, as well as its affinity with recent models such as *The Waste Land* (1922) and *Hugh Selwyn Mauberley* (1920). Beginning at this point of shared artistic interest, the two poets would collaborate closely for the next four years or so, with Pound generously guiding Zukofsky through a series of projects and offering him some important and pointed advice about artistic production in the Poundian vein, just as the younger poet's aesthetic understanding was forming and as such tasks as the initial planning of his life work "A" were broached. Central among the projects on which the poets would collaborate was Zukofsky's launching of the "Objectivist" brand in the February 1931 number of *Poetry*, with Pound taking a key role by persuading Harriet Monroe to allow Zukofsky guest-editorship of the issue and then extensively briefing Zukofsky on his strategy.

If, by a "formed tradition," Kenner means to imply that an awareness of the techniques of Imagism, Vorticism and Pound's other earlier modernist experiments were central to the Objectivist practice displayed in *Poetry* and its upshot, *An "Objectivists" Anthology* (1932), then he is correct. The example of Imagism, particularly in its Orientalist *Cathay* phase, is apposite throughout Zukofsky's Objectivist poetry and beyond, as it is in the poetries of other Objectivists such as George Oppen and Charles Reznikoff. The Objectivists were not, however, simply proponents of a High Modernist school of poetry, nor was Zukofsky, though Pound remained unchallenged in his centrality to the younger poet's work, a derivative Poundian. In fact the "formed tradition" they inherited gave Zukofsky and Oppen the opportunity to create a new poetry, one opposed to many of the tenets of modernism, drawn from the remains of the work of their forebears: the Objectivists would rewrite modernism from the inside.

The evidence of Zukofsky's intention to make the most of Pound's mentorship, at the same time as he was engaged in creating a poetics that went beyond the older poet's, can be detected early in their correspondence. Eliot commends Pound as an editor, stating that "[h]e was a marvelous critic because he didn't try to turn you into an imitation of himself" (Hall 206). However, as the 1930s began there were moments when a more complex form of influence was passed between Pound and Zukofsky than the unselfishness applauded by Eliot. This phase of Pound's mentoring began with an analysis of his own influence: in a letter dated 27 November 1930 Pound refers to "A"-1 to -7 as "one development or fugue [...] produced by Ludwig von Zuk and Sohn, on not always digested meat of his forebears," (Pound and Zukofsky 75-77) and then goes on to attack the "final contortion" of Zukofsky's canzone in "A"-7. In 1928 Pound had advised "[w]here accusation possibly false, that reminiscence of E.P. [...] alter, when possible" (25), a statement that simultaneously allowed that Zukofsky might not be influenced by "E.P." at all, yet Pound's influence might be so ingrained in the poetry of "A" that it would not be "possible" to remove it. By 1930 Pound is clearer about his own influence on Zukofsky, insisting that the structural procedures of "A," and particularly those of "A"-7, are derived from his own work, urging Zukofsky to desist from this imitation. However, the younger poet was not persuaded, and in "A"-9 he would approach Cavalcanti's "Donna mi priegha" in a similar fashion to that proscribed by Pound after his reading of "A"-7: thus Zukofsky would stubbornly retain the influence of Pound even as Pound attempted to influence him against doing so. For Zukofsky at this point in their relationship both writing like Pound and not writing like him seem to be the result of Pound's influence.

After a series of such crises Zukofsky would evaluate his position, writing in a letter to Pound in December 1930:

> The only things that might possibly save me would be the objective evaluation of my own experience [...] and a natural ability (or perverseness) for wrenching English so that (again, possibly) it might attain a diction of distinction not you, or Eliot, or Bill [William Carlos Williams], or anyone before me.
>   (Pound and Zukofsky 79)

This is a crucial moment for Zukofsky's development. The poet is set on creating his own style in contrast to his masters, one that will make ample use of his predilection for the "wrenching of English," a "perverseness" that many, including Pound, would come to criticize, but which would mark the battleground of Zukofsky's attempt to build a modernist poetics that would retain some integrity outside of the sphere of Pound's immediate influence.

We can see, then, in the light of the intense tutelage and apostasy of the late 1920s and early 1930s, that any move by Zukofsky into noticeably Poundian areas of practice immediately raises questions as to whether the younger poet is performing the role of dutiful and derivative heir, just as Kenner imagines. As a telling instance of this dilemma in thinking about Zukofsky's work, the use of the Orient as a subject and Orientalist techniques is one area where direct comparisons between Zukofsky's practice and his mentor's must inevitably be made.

It is difficult to imagine that Zukofsky was not conscious of Pound's use of the poetry and thought of the East. Pound was, as Eliot observed, the prime American interpreter of Chinese verse, and his example would have been paramount to almost any twentieth-century American poet, let alone to one who was as close a collaborator as Zukofsky.

The manner and the degree to which Zukofsky engages with the East must therefore be seen as emblematic of Zukofsky's encounter with Pound's influence. In fact, the degree to which Zukofsky engages with the East separates him from Pound's influence—with Zukofsky engaging with a specifically unPoundian aspect of American Orientalism in a manner which complicates the presence of those ghostly Chinese traces that find their way, via Imagism, into Objectivist verse. That this engagement with Zen happens simultaneously with, and is primarily mediated through, Zukofsky's collaboration with the poets of *The New American Poetry* also emphasizes how important a crux it represents in the narrative of his relationship with Pound's influence. Pound is the pre-eminent and ubiquitous Confucian of literary modernism, while Zukofsky's approach is far more in tune with American thinking and trends of the 1950s and 1960s, and is predicated upon an identifiably American version of Zen Buddhism. In an attempt to unpack this complex moment I will first describe the extent of Zukofsky's engagement with Zen; then suggest some of the ways in which Zukofsky's reaction against Pound is itself a quintessentially Poundian gesture, to the degree that it may suggest how Pound's anti-Buddhism in the 1930s and 1940s was not so antithetical to certain strands of Buddhism as it now seems. Finally, I will frame this moment as an attempted realignment with the poets of *The New American Poetry*.

From the outset Zukofsky's approach to the Orient suggests a conscious distancing from Pound's example. The younger poet's first approach to Zen Buddhism can be found in "(Ryokan's Scroll)," from the volume *I's (pronounced eyes)* (1963).[2] Its cover features a calligraphic rendering of a poem by the Japanese Soto Zen monk, calligrapher and poet Ryokan Taigu, photographed from a scroll lent to Zukofsky by Cid Corman, and mistakenly printed upside-down.[3] Corman was a key figure in Zukofsky's late re-emergence; the second series of his journal *Origin* (1961-1964) featured Zukofsky in every number (much as Charles Olson had been featured in the magazine's first run between 1951 and 1957), a signal moment in his Post-War rise in popularity. Corman published a wealth of Zukofsky material in *Origin*, including "(Ryokan's Scroll)," publishing him beside Black Mountain writers such as Paul Blackburn, but with the addition of a definite Eastern influence that was congruent both with Zukofsky's early Objectivist work and his drift in the 1960s. The last number of the second series of *Origin* (1964) makes an explicit connection between Zukofsky's work and a certain strand of Pound-influenced American Orientalism when Corman publishes the text of "A"-16 at the end of a number otherwise made up of Corman's own translations of Basho.

"(Ryokan's scroll)", the first poem in *I's (pronounced* eyes*)*, includes a translation of the text up-ended on the cover. The poem is essentially a collaboration with Corman; from its seventh line till the end the words of the poem are entirely Corman's literal translation of Ryokan (which is so unembellished as to be little more than a crib) (Corman, Letter to Zukofsky 13 December 1960), with Zukofsky's only contribution after the seventh line a typographical shift, when he sets lines 14 to 18 to the right and even through the first six lines Zukofsky's presence is studiedly minimal. The brackets in the title seem a visual representation of the curled ends of the scroll itself, though brackets, of course, also have a syntactical function, here suggesting that the title of the text is subordinate in some sense, auxiliary to the rest of the poem: Ryokan's text is so thoroughly subsumed into the texture of Zukofsky's poetry that its provenance is a secondary issue (and the fact that the words are predominantly Corman's becomes tertiary). Such an arrangement, in conjunction with the poem's subjects, offers a suggestion of the erasure of the authorial self that implies the denial of the self that is so central to Zen. The words also insist upon the physical, thingful, presence of the text and its source: "dripping / words // off // a / long / while" (203), recalling the ontologies of both Objectivist verse and Buddhism. The cover, though upended, must also be considered a part of this arrangement, with Zukofsky choosing to restrict his ideograms to the outside of his book in contrast to Pound's practice in *The Cantos*, while the lack of apparent authorial intervention around Ryokan's words and Corman's translation recalls, as well as Buddhism, a curtailed version of the Poundian reiteration of forms that is a primary organizational

principle of Pound's long poem. In its numinous simplicity Zukofsky's
poem stands as both a further re-imagination of that tradition and a
rejection of it, with the poet exchanging Zen and Japan for Confucius
and China—a substitution which must be considered central to
Zukofsky's commentary on Pound in this context.

Zukofsky would return to "(Ryokan's Scroll)" and the cover of *I's
(pronounced* eyes*)* in "A"-14 (1964), the fourteenth section of his long
poem "A." There Zukofsky writes,

> As at
> the scroll's
> first hanging
>
> found my
> own initials
> looking in
>
> Ryokan [;] (325)

a reinsertion of the authorial self and an apparent challenge to the
Buddhist sensibilities of the earlier poem. The self-effacing humor,
however, undercuts the challenge; the upending is "not / the worst /
erratum." Peter Middleton, writing about the American Buddhist poet
Philip Whalen, who was also active during the period of Zukofsky's
engagement with Zen, suggests that such self-mockery may in itself be
related to a Buddhist understanding. According to Middleton, Whalen's
work, habitually utilizing such a tone, "brings into being a somewhat
comic version of the humanoid unit of authenticity inflected by Buddhist
practice, which treats the pretensions to self-founding subjectivity as
a clumsiness of self that deserves to be seen for the comedy it presents
to the enlightened" (114). Applying Middleton's way of thinking about
Zen self-consciousness, we may also consider Zukofsky's irreverent
approach to Ryokan's calligraphy as a contradiction of Pound's
ideogrammania. Zukofsky foregrounds, in a way that Pound does
not, the poet's own distance from these unfamiliar signifiers: where
Pound wonders at the great capacity of the ideogram for capturing and
conveying the motion of meaning, Zukofsky relishes the, as it turns
out, upside-down figures' unreadability to both Western and Eastern

238   Parker

readers. The poet encounters this script as letters, privileged through their unreadability, not because of the ability to transmit pictorial sense beyond language in the way that Pound, with what Derrida refers to as his "irreducibly graphic poetics" (92), perceives. Where Henri Gaudier-Brzeska had been, according to Pound, able to "read the Chinese radicals and many compound signs almost at pleasure" (Fenollosa 59n.) with no prior knowledge of Chinese, Zukofsky can make out only a dim echo of his own initials and finds himself so fruitfully confounded by them that he has them printed upside down. The mistake itself, along with Zukofsky's self-denigration, confirms a Zen poetics through its suggestion of a Cagean aleatoriness, while the semiotically denuded calligraphic script emphasizes the existential parallels between Objectivist verse and Zen.

This testing of meaning, a Zukofskian trope that would find fullest expression in his homophonic translations of Catullus and that predicts the Language Poets' assault on reference, is perhaps the point when Zukofsky's early Objectivist theories meet and mesh with Zen. Thus, in the 1930s, Zukofsky had written of the experience of successful Objectivist verse that "[t]his rested totality may be called objectification – the apprehension satisfied completely as to the appearance of the art form as an object" (Zukofsky, *Prepositions* + 194). Zukofsky's youthful prose is never a model of clarity, but there is a definite, if not recognizably Buddhist, motion towards a mystical, quasi-religious experience of perception here. This tendency is more apparent when Zukofsky writes, via Spinoza, about the "rested totality" as "[p]erfect rest – Or nature as creator, existing perfect, experience perfecting activity of existence, making it – theologically, perhaps – like the Ineffable – "(Zukofsky, *Prepositions* + 207).

This is not Buddhism, but there is a mystical underpinning to Objectivist theory here that marks a definite moving away from Poundian modernism. As Norman Finkelstein points out, "[t]he poem ["A"] as a rested totality depends upon the particular balance it achieves between the acknowledged state of immediate existence and the desired state of unfolding futurity" (34), a statement that, with a little tweaking, motions towards the transcendent (or otherwise) "stillpoint" at the heart of Buddhism and Objectivist thinking.[4] There is, however, nothing here to suggest that Zukofsky was specifically considering Buddhism as a practice or as a poetics at the turn of the 1930s.

After I's, the volume that would follow *I's,* begins with a further exploration of those Zen themes implicit in "(Ryokan's Scroll)": it opens with "Daruma," a poem addressed to Will Petersen, one-time collaborator with Corman on *Origin* and somewhat of a ubiquitous figure in the circles of Beat-era Buddhism.[5] He, his wife Ami and his son Ren are identified and explicitly connected with Zen near the outset of the poem:

> Peter's sen
> Ami
> Ren
> Will[.]
>
> (Zukofsky, *Complete Short Poetry* 221)

An associate of Gary Snyder's, Petersen also appears as Rol Sturlason in Jack Kerouac's *The Dharma Bums* (1958). *Daruma* is an English representation of the Japanese transliteration of Dharma, the "way" of Buddhism. Here that constellation of ideas is connected to a fundamentally Zukofskian concern: Zukofsky begins, "Daruma / *found object* / that is art" (221). *Found Objects 1962-1926,* a brief selection of poems, would appear the following year. That collection's reference to "found objects" reinforces the idea that the process of Objectification that Zukofsky both had theorized in the early thirties and had been adapting to his work ever since had the potential to be linked to the practices of Zen Buddhism. The poetry in the volume is also printed in reverse chronological order (the poems run from 1962 back to 1926), an arrangement that places the beginning of the poet's career, namely, the creation of the process of Objectification, as a kind of telos for this work. Thus a bridge is created, linking the Zen-inflected poems of the early 1960s directly to the Objectivist period of the 1920s and '30s.

Petersen's work was primarily of interest to Zukofsky for his seminal essay on the Zen garden of Ryoanji, "Stone Garden." This article details a horticultural process and discipline equally related to Zukofsky's late poetics and Snyder's "Riprap": that focus on the mute object in Zen gardening, here "a bit / of rock," seems readily comparable to both the practice and the ideas behind Zukofsky's late work. Ryoanji is a very unconventional garden by Western standards:

> The garden consists simply of fifteen rocks – of various sizes and shapes, but of no odd or particular unusual quality – composed in five groups of 5-2-3-2-3 on a flat, rectangular area of carefully raked white sand, about the size of a tennis court. Except for a little moss at the base of each rock, serving to soften the transition between rock and sand, nothing grows in the garden.   (Petersen, "Stone Garden 127-30)

For Petersen the garden has a symbolic meaning and function:

> [T]he aim is not the creation of an imitation or miniature world, as decadent examples would lead us to assume, but to translate the elements of nature into comprehensible form – into art. By various means, without trace of artificiality, within the most intimate or limited space infinities could be realized.
> (Petersen, "Stone Garden 130)

Those "elements" turn up in the "air / fire / water" of "Daruma" (221). The methods and aims of such miniature maximalism predict Zukofsky's method, particularly in the short lyric poems of slight volumes such as *After I's*. For Zukofsky, too, the garden comes to represent Buddhist nothingness through the thingness of its minimal ingredients, much as Zukofsky's object-poem tries to get at "rested totality" through the interjection of language:

> It is at this point that we come to one of the basic paradoxes of Buddhist thought: only through form can we realize emptiness is thus considered not as a concept reached by the analytical process of reasoning, but as a statement of intuition or perception.   (Petersen, "Stone Garden 132)

Thus "[o]nly by filling the paper does it become empty" (132-33), a statement readily applicable to all stages of Zukofsky's career, but particularly appropriate to his late voice.

Centrally, the arrangements of the various sub-groups of rocks are held to represent a series of different meanings and symbolisms, their semantic interaction creating a complex layering of different possible meanings that suggests a Zukofskian multivalency:

> In declaring that the garden represents islands in the sea, etc., as is most commonly done, is to be held by form [sic]. To say, on the other hand, in more abstract terms, that the sand represents void, is to ignore the rock. All of these are merely equations in which the garden represents X, the unknown, and X is merely substituted. Regarded as a puzzle, the garden offers no solutions, but presents new questions to meet each answer.
> (Petersen, "Stone Garden 137)

The small, unconventionally linked stanzas in "Daruma" function in a repetition of this arrangement, suggesting that they exist together in as mutable a set of connections as the Ryoanji rocks. The *daruma* Petersen suggests fits well with Zukofsky's project and results in a poem that comes as close as Zukofsky would get to an open acknowledgement of Buddhism as an operating poetic in his work. While it is clear that Zukofsky was never a practicing Buddhist, "Daruma" shows us that Zukofsky both recognizes the comparable nature of his Objectivist project and Zen and that he then goes on consciously to work Buddhist elements into his poetry.

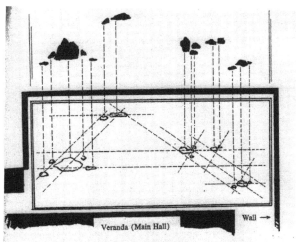

[Petersen's "[d]iagram of stone arrangement with projection in silhouette" at Ryoanji. (Petersen 129)]

In addition to an implicit deviation from Pound's Confucianism, then, Zukofsky's embrace of Zen also offered a late confirmation of the poet's earlier Objectivist theses and an assertion of his work's continued relevance to the young. It should also be remembered, however, that their indifference to Poundian Confucianism was also a significant motive for the younger poets Zukofsky was interested in, and a touchstone in *The New American Poetry*'s engagement with the East. Gary Snyder's essay, "Buddhism and the Coming Revolution," is a useful document for understanding how Zukofsky's approach to Zen is both a reaction against the Pound of the 1930s and 1940s and an example of the proximity of his practice to the poets of *The New American Poetry*. Snyder posits a radicalized Buddhism in which the abnegation of political activity is foresworn:

> Institutional Buddhism has been conspicuously ready to accept or ignore the inequalities and tyrannies of whatever political system it found itself under. This can be death to Buddhism, because it is death to any meaningful function of compassion. Wisdom without compassion feels no pain. (90)

Snyder, whose work is openly influenced by Objectivist fellow-traveler Kenneth Rexroth and whose "Riprap" with its "words / Before your mind like rocks" (404) suggests a renovation of Objectivist thought, here identifies and, to a certain extent, corroborates the violent criticism of the "goddam bhuddists" (Pound, *The Cantos* 284) of Pound's Chinese history cantos (published in the volume *Cantos LII-LXXI* in 1940). Pound's complaints against the Buddhists in that volume are various; they include a frustration with "muzzy language" (285), muzzy thought exampled by misrule ("False laws are that stir up revolt by pretense [sic] of virtue" [334]), a tendency towards decadence, and, centrally, the nefarious influence in Pound's view, the Buddhists' that alleged anti-Confucian passivity had upon the development of Chinese history ("poisoning life with mirages, ruining order" [318]). Snyder, however, turns Pound's criticism back on itself, and, through the dharma of compassion, vigorously connects Buddhism with political activism. Both Pound's particular interest in the East, Confucianism, and Fascism, his politics, are taken to task here in a way that appears a conscious rebuttal of his influence. Zukofsky would also make just such a connection between Buddhism and the politics of the New Left in "A"-18, wherein he includes excerpts from a *New York Times* article, entitled "THRONGS OF VIETNAMESE PILGRIMS VISIT POND OF MIRACULOUS FISH," that details anti-Buddhist South Vietnamese, and American, attempts to destroy a "giant fish apparently a / carp swimming in a pond the incarnate Buddha" (392). The division between Pound's Confucianism and Zukofsky's Zen is not, however, as clear as such rhetoric implies. Various critics have pointed out the centrality of Taoist beliefs to Pound's neo-Confucianism, including Kenner in *The Pound Era* and Zhaoming Qian in *Orientalism and Modernism* (who goes so far as to suggest a place for Taoism in Imagist practice [72])—a connection that Pound himself either did not realize or chose to ignore. Robert Duncan, prominent among the New Americans that collaborated with Zukofsky, insists of Pound that Buddhism is present in his anti-Buddhism:

> [I]n his blindness in regard to Lao-tzu Pound diminishes our view of Kung who shares with Lao-tzu the idea of cosmos as Tao, and that in this blindness in regard to Christianity (which he persistently sees in its aspect of the fetter) he diminishes our view of the gods. (91)

And, as Duncan goes on to point out, "[t]he Kuanon [who appears in canto 74] may enter *The Cantos* but not Mary; Helios, but not Christos." Duncan critiques Pound's eclecticism for its specificity; its arbitrary exclusions, in Duncan's view, contrast with his own characteristically freewheeling inclusivity. Recently, following Duncan's implicit point about the Kuanon, some critics have been adding specifically Buddhist flavors to the Taoist inheritance buried in Pound's poetics. Jonathan Stalling has convincingly set out the evidence for an integrally Buddhist strain in Ernest Fenollosa's "The Chinese Written Character as a Medium for Poetry" that came to color Pound's poetics at a foundational level. He quotes a memorandum from Fenollosa to himself:

> I must demonstrate my right to be a power in the world of philosophical opinion. I must go back to my work on Hegel. I must inform myself on present psychologic progress, and I must bring them together on the basis of Buddhist mysticism.
> (Fenollosa 12)

If, as Stalling goes on to suggest, Buddhism is a presence in the poetics of Imagism, then the intimations of Buddhism in Zukofsky's "rested totality" can be partially explained. Thus the "unique Hegelian Buddhism" (23) that Stalling detects in Fenollosa's thought remains a submerged but fundamental philosophical undercurrent through Imagism and its sequel Objectivism to reappear as allusions to Zen in Zukofsky's late work.

While their chosen Eastern mysticisms may seem opposed, primarily, as it turns out, because of Pound's adoption of an anomalously biased set of sources for his Chinese history cantos, perhaps even more pertinently a very similar, particularly American form of Orientalism is present in both writers. Neither poet ever traveled to the Orient; in fact notes held at the Harry Ransom Research Center at the University of Texas contain evidence that suggests that the impetus for Zukofsky's final Eastern pastoralism came from a 1969 visit to Kew Gardens in London (Leggott 325). Zukofsky's orient is noticeably modulated through a series of American intermediaries: Petersen, Corman, Snyder and Duncan, inheritors of an understanding of Buddhism formulated by such figures as D.T. Suzuki, Alan Watts, and, of course, Pound himself. These replace the Western sources of Pound's interest in China, which famously include not only Fenollosa, but also, as Qian has pointed out, such formative influences as Ralph Waldo Emerson, Herbert Allen Giles, T.E. Hulme, Laurence Binyon, and Allen Upward. There are plenty of moon-pointing fingers in both cases.[6] Both poets were also essentially collaborative Orientalists: at the outset of *Cathay* Pound writes that his volume is drawn "[f]or the most part from the Chinese of Rihaku, from the notes of the late Ernest Fenollosa, and the decipherings of the professors Mori and Agira" (Pound, *Poems & Translations* 247), and so would Zukofsky's interaction with Zen be drawn, for the most part, from the notes and decipherings of Corman and Petersen.

Finally, it should be noted that if Zukofsky's turn to Buddhism is in rejection of Pound's Confucianism, then this is a notably Poundian reaction that recalls Pound's recommendation in 1928 to remove Pound's influence through Poundian means. Just such a dynamic persists into Zukofsky's final works; his repeated adoption of fundamentally unPoundian sources (which are not limited to Zukofsky's admittedly peripheral forays into Buddhist thought) nonetheless are presented via a recognizably Poundian practice. Thus at the end of both poets' careers they turn to the East as part of a conscious attempt at framing paradisal visions. Zukofsky briefly adopts an American Buddhism and, in *80 Flowers*, his final completed work, and "Gamut: 90 Trees," the sequence he was working on at his death, a heavily mediated Oriental pastoralism, as well as the texts of the Hindu Vedas, respectively. Pound employs a somewhat partial view of Confucianism and, in his final cantos, an ethnic Chinese pastoralism through his very late interest in the peoples of the Na'Khi (again mediated, in this case via the anthropological work of Joseph Rock). Both of them, and Duncan too, though he demurs, employ an eclectic esotericism that relies on closely allied conceptions of the privileged status of sacred texts and belief. The division, then, reveals more about the poets' own works than it does about Buddhism, the East, or even their own attitudes towards them: as interested as these poets are in literary authenticity, in this case it is removed from the question. The linguistic difference that emerges regarding both poets' uses of the ideogram is more fundamental. The profound but subtle difference I have noted above colors both poets' interactions with translation and comes to differentiate these oeuvres unmatched in American letters: thus the twin moments of twentieth-century creative mistranslation, namely, Pound's *Homage to Sextus Propertius* (1919) and Zukofsky's *Catullus* (1969).

Notes

1. Stephen Fredman takes umbrage at these statements and posits a radical realignment of Objectivist influence away from a Kennerian Pound in "'And All Now Is War': George Oppen, Charles Olson, and the Problem of Literary Generations" (DuPlessis and Quartermain 286-93).

2. *I's (pronounced eyes)* was published by the Trobar Press, Deep Imagists George Economou and Robert Kelly's publishing off-shoot of their journal *Trobar*, in which various works by Zukofsky appeared during this period. Zukofsky's late interest in Zen should be read as having been conditioned by contact with such New American Orientalists as Economou, Kelly, Cid Corman and others. Corman's journal *Origin* and the Origin Press (publishers of the 1959 edition of *"A" 1-12*) were based in Kyoto for various periods and incorporated an Eastern aesthetic and sundry Zen influenced material while providing another important

early-1960s outlet for Zukofsky.

3. See   http://www.z-site.net/notes-to-poetry/Is-pronounced-eyes-1963.php.
Corman's account of this incident, and his reading of "(Ryokan's Scroll)" can be
found in his essay, "Ryokan's Scroll."

4. See Mortenson for a discussion of the various misinterpretations prevalent in
mid-century American verse of this "stillpoint."

5. 'Daruma' was written as a 'thank you' to Petersen, who had lent Zukofsky one
of his darumas in a repetition of Corman's loan of the Ryokan scroll. After hearing
of the object's delayed arrival in the U.S., Petersen wrote to Zukofsky relating the
story of how he had acquired it. Zukofsky's poem draws heavily on this material
and is in large part a collage of Petersen's letter, revealing 'Daruma' itself to be
a 'found object': lines 2-3, 11-14, and 17-32 are repeated almost verbatim from
Petersen (Petersen to Zukofsky, 19 October 1961, Louis Zukofsky Collection).

6. D.T. Suzuki writes: "The followers of Zen would say, A finger is needed to point
at the moon, but what a calamity it would be if one took the finger for the moon!
This seems improbable, but how many times we are committing this form of error
we do not know" (74).

Works Cited

Allen, Donald, ed. *The New American Poetry 1945-60*. New York: Grove Press,
    1960.

Corman, Cid. Letter to Louis Zukofsky. 13 December 1960. http://www.z-site.
    net/notes-to-poetry/Is-pronounced-eyes-1963.php

___. "Ryokan's Scroll," *Sagetrieb* 1.2 (Fall 1982).

Derrida, Jacques. *Of Grammatology*. Trans. Gayatri Chakravorty Spivak.
    Baltimore: Johns Hopkins UP, 1998.

Duncan, Robert. *Selected Prose*. Ed. Robert J. Bertholf. New York: New
    Directions, 1995.

DuPlessis, Rachel Blau and Peter Quartermain, eds. *The Objectivist Nexus*.
    Tuscaloosa: U of Alabama P, 1999.

Eliot, T.S. *The Complete Poems and Plays*. London: Faber, 1969.

Fenollosa, Ernest and Ezra Pound. Ed. Haun Saussy, Jonathan Stalling, and
    Lucas Klein. *The Chinese Written Character as a Medium for Poetry*. New
    York: Fordham UP, 2008.

Finkelstein, Norman. *The Utopian Moment in Contemporary American Poetry.* Lewisburg: Bucknell UP, 1988.

Fredman, Stephen. "'And All Now Is War': George Oppen, Charles Olson, and the Problem of Literary Generations." DuPlessis and Quartermain, eds. *The Objectivist Nexus.* Tuscaloosa: U of Alabama P, 1999. 286-93.

Hall, Donald. *Remembering Poets: Reminiscences and Opinions.* New York: Harper & Row, 1977.

Kenner, Hugh. *A Homemade World: The American Modernist Writers.* New York: Marion Boyars, 1977.

___. *The Pound Era.* Berkeley: U of California P, 1971.

Kerouac, Jack. *The Dharma Bums.* London: Penguin, 2007.

Leggott, Michele J. *Reading Zukofsky's 80 Flowers.* Baltimore: Johns Hopkins UP, 1989.

Middleton, Peter. *Distant Reading: Performance, Readership, and Consumption in Contemporary Poetry.* Tuscaloosa: U of Alabama P, 2006.

Mortenson, Erik. "Keeping the Vision Alive". *The Emergence of a Buddhist American Literature.* Albany: State U of New York P, 2009.

Petersen, Will. Letter to Louis Zukofsky. 19 Oct. 1961. Louis Zukofsky Collection. Box 26, Folder 2. Harry Ransom Humanities Research Center, U of Texas at Austin.

___. "Stone Garden." *Evergreen Review* 1.4 (1957). 127-37.

Pound, Ezra. *The Cantos.* 13th Printing. New York: New Directions, 1995.

___. *Poems & Translations.* Ed. Richard Sieburth. New York: Library of America, 2003.

___. *Selected Poems of Ezra Pound.* Ed. T.S. Eliot. London: Faber, 1961.

Pound, Ezra and Louis Zukofsky. *Selected Letters of Ezra Pound and Louis Zukofsky.* Ed. Barry Ahearn. London: Faber, 1987

Qian, Zhaoming. *Orientalism and Modernism: The Legacy of China in Pound and Williams.* Durham: Duke UP, 1995.

Snyder, Gary. *Earth House Hold.* New York: New Directions, 1969.

___. *The Gary Snyder Reader: Prose, Poetry, and Translations.* Berkeley: Counterpoint, 1999.

Suzuki, D.T. *An Introduction to Zen Buddhism.* London: Rider Press, 1991.

"Throngs of Vietnamese pilgrims visit pond of miraculous fish." http://www.z-site.net/notes-to-a/A-18.php

Twitchell Waas, Jeff. *The Z-Site: A Companion to the Work of Louis Zukofsky.* http://www.z-site.net

Whalen-Bridge, John and Gary Storhoff, eds. *The Emergence of a Buddhist American Literature.* Albany: State U of New York P, 2009.

Zukofsky, Louis. *"A" 1-12.* Ashland: Origin Press, 1959.

___. *"A."* Berkeley: U of California P, 1978.

___. *Complete Short Poetry.* Baltimore: Johns Hopkins UP, 1991.

___. *Found Objects 1962-1926.* Georgetown: H.B. Chapin (A Blue Grass Book), 1964.

___, ed. *An "Objectivists" Anthology.* Le Beausset: To, Publishers, 1932.

___, ed. *Poetry: Chicago.* February 1931.

___. *Prepositions +: The Collected Critical Essays.* Ed. Mark Scroggins. Middletown: Wesleyan UP, 2000.

The Orient in Later Modernist English Poetry

Tony Lopez

If Pound "invented" Chinese poetry for the West via Japanese at the beginning of modernism, then Chinese poetry, Japanese poetry, and the Orient have had another life among a whole range of later modernist English poets including Lee Harwood and Harry Guest.[1] In part this has to do with a specific strand of English poetry that uses invented new and free verse forms and allies itself to modern North American poetics, and in part it is a function of the radical difference and attraction of the East as a changing cultural phenomenon and source of spiritual insight for Westerners. It seems that Pound's version of the East, as it registers in *Cathay* and *Certain Noh Plays of Japan*, is an important constituent of literary modernism and the modernist aesthetic of less is more. An apparent streamlining of poetic effects and a foregrounding of the visual aspect in poetics seem to have been identified and elaborated through early twentieth-century contact with the art of China and Japan. Pound's representation of China and Confucius was substantially developed over many years and the visuality of this engagement was adapted via translation, ekphrasis, and direct insertion of Chinese characters into his *Cantos*. Modernist poets of the 1960s take up all three of these techniques in different ways, some connected and others not connected to the Orient.[2]

I want to focus on particular poems by two contemporary poets who began to be published in the 1960s and see how their allegiance to Pound and international modernism extended the literary representation of the Orient into a still developing late twentieth-century modernism. Of course the 1960s and 1970s cultural impact of the Orient was very different from that of 1900. Poems from the 1960s and 1970s use Chinese and Japanese reference partly as a mark of allegiance to what was at that time an uncertain tradition of Anglo-

American international modernism: to keep connections alive.

My first exhibit is a 1960s double poem by Harry Guest from his book *The Cutting-Room*, published by Anvil Press in 1970.[3]

Two Poems for O-Bon
(the Buddhist festival of the Dead; midsummer)

> *one*

Clean the altars.
                    Scour
the wood remembering
dead next of kin.
                    Their ashes
are gathering energy, emit to love
remembered presences.
                    Let
the temple-bell vibrate.

Clean the altars.
                    Prepare
the past, a welcome for the past.

And, waiting, pray.

                    The ghosts
enter the garden. Familiar
features take shape on the
lamplit leaves.

        A sad season (clean,
        the altars; longing so,
        the garden): chill
        inside drab heat.

                    Make
the whole house an expectation, greeting
the long-lost and the brief-loved.

Who, lightly, blur

the polished wood of the altars:
departing,
move like the faint
shadow of rain across the lanterns,
among us if they ever were
no more again.

          two
                    Half-seen
smiles unmet like mist,
maybe the touch of a hand
resembles dew,
their footprints tentative
cobwebs on the grass.

          Spectres
in air-conditioned
cinemas and, suddenly,
footless, shimmering on to the stage.
Tales of melancholy love,
revenge, the green flame
signifying presence.

          Phantoms
hiding behind peonies,
dissolving to hard
bones the further side
of tombstones at rendezvous.

The first poem begins by presenting ritual events in language: the phrases might be instructions to the reader or interior phrases addressed to the speaking self who is carrying out or watching what must be a well-known ceremony. This could be the memory of a familiar ceremony re-enacted in the imagination as it is remembered, and the meaning of the actions, both the emotional significance and the cultural significance, is explored by means of these stepped and carefully spaced lines in which the simple sentences are set out. "Clean the altars" feels like a straightforward instruction, whereas the next three lines, "Scour / the wood remembering / dead next of kin," already move from a physical task to the mental activity that accompanies it. The dead relatives are now reduced to ash, but that ash is imagined "gathering energy" as if in some sense active if not fully alive. Of course the altar wood, which is being scoured for the ceremony, is materially connected with firewood and thus with ash; there is a suggestion that the wood, as well as the person who scours it, remembers the "dead next of kin." The sentence that signals a particular, and for the reader, an imaginary sound (the vibrating temple-bell) has been separated into two parts by a line break after the verb. This pattern of isolating the initial verb is repeated as a structure throughout the poem: "scour," "let," "prepare," "make," are thus separated out as beginning verbs and "pray" is also isolated by the very particular eisthesis of long indentions after the line breaks. The indentions allow notional lines to be completed so that the *mise en page* is opened and spread out, similar in appearance to verse drama exchanges and many passages in Pound's later *Cantos*. The spacing is a set of implied reading instructions, incorporating pauses, adding emphasis to the verbs, and slowing down a performance of the poem.

The verse is managed and punctuated mainly by means of line breaks but the sentences are also reinforced as units, separated in every case by a long indent pause, sometimes extended by a clear line space. I think the verse shape is a sympathetic attempt to construct a re-enactment of the O-Bon ritual in language, to give the stages of the ceremony their due respect. The phrase "clean the altars" is repeated, twice used as a separate sentence with space around it, and once located within a bracketed aside that is itself within a blocked four-line indented sentence. But the third instance of the phrase is a variation, "clean, the altars," meaning the altars are now clean. The repeated and varied phrase within the pattern of instructions gives the poem its ritual quality. But the spacing pattern is not continued right through the poem. There is a turn after the line "And, waiting, pray." This is the point at which the poem becomes supernatural as "The ghosts / enter the garden."

In its second half the first poem's line breaks are hard returns to a steadier more solid left hand margin, and the long indention is used only once with the blocked indented passage (beginning "A sad season") interposed within the break. In this half the insubstantial presence of the familiar dead is tactfully imagined as a sequence of indefinite and uncertain images: as shapes seen among leaves, as a light blur on polished wood, as a shadow of rain across lanterns. They are ghosts; they are "the long-lost and the brief-loved" that are accommodated within that figure of opposition (long / brief – lost / loved) and in the imagined garden only on a temporary basis. This is not a Buddhist poem exactly—it certainly would not need its parenthetical subtitle if it were—but it is a respectfully thoughtful poem about a Buddhist custom, imaginatively working through the implications of the ceremony it describes.

The second poem is linked structurally to the second half of the first poem in that it presents images of the familiar dead within each of its three stanzas or verse paragraphs. Now the ghosts are imagined through insubstantial smiles, touch, footprints, compared in the first stanza with natural phenomena: mist, dew, and cobwebs on wet grass. In the second stanza, the scene changes to a cinema and the spectres seem to be made equivalent to ghosts. The reader will imagine ghosts on screen, as in a supernatural movie, or recognize that filmic characters are ghosts of a sort.

But in the heat of midsummer Japanese people like to go to the cinema to watch horror films of traditional ghost stories to cool down. And in the Kabuki theatre, ghost characters have no feet; they have long gowns that hide the actors' feet and move with short steps, appearing to glide. A green light is the theatrical signal whenever a ghost is on stage. In the third stanza "phantoms" are seen behind peonies, presumably identified with the lush beautiful heads of garden flowers, growing among tombstones and bones.

The ghosts are allowed to come provisionally and temporarily into a garden (and into a poem) set up for this ceremony that honors the dead. They are given space and time and then seen to be gone "among us if they ever were / no more again." In a sense the ceremony uses the superstition of the returning dead to be rid of them the rest of the time. The ceremony, at least as it is portrayed here, is a framework for the living to give proper respect to, and thus to be free of the dead and the associated fear, guilt and remorse, for the rest of each year.

I suppose that we should read this poem as a special kind of anthropological text, which takes a common Buddhist religious custom and makes it available to a Western readership. No one is going to deliberately seek out and use this text to find out about Buddhism. Poetry allows elements of the custom to be recomposed in a precision-made English text that encodes finely discriminated shades of insubstantial and ambiguous meaning. The equivocation over the presence of ghosts allows the possibility of a spiritual dimension, without any dogmatic statement of belief. This is tactful and delicate writing. Of course it is not intending to be anthropology in the sense of responsible social science but it is rather concerned with imaginative sympathy, with the representation of emotional and psychological being in its proper complexity. The poem does depend, however, on the O-Bon custom being unfamiliar to the reader, on the report coming from a faraway land, and it demonstrates the poet's understanding of the ritual and the Japanese way of life.

"Two Poems for O-Bon" appears in a book, *The Cutting Room*, whose wrap-around cover design is composed of Japanese characters set in long vertical lines printed in grey on off-white as a background to the author's name and title, also set vertically in red uppercase type. There is an outline square, type high, between the name and the beginning of the title. The English letters in Roman type, still legible running vertically down the page, but seen sideways on, relate in the design to the fainter vertical lines of Japanese characters, and the red outline square enhances this visual connection. The back cover copy tells us that "Harry Guest's second book contains his poems written in Japan during 1967-69" and explains that "the cover shows a detail of the Japanese translation by Eiji Yamazaki of 'A Bar in Lerici' by Harry Guest."

The whole design and presentation of the book relates Harry Guest's experience of Japan and writing about Japan with his originality as a poet. The use of Japanese characters on the cover incorporates a Japanese visual aesthetic into the book as a whole and has a similar effect to that of Pound incorporating Chinese characters into the *Cantos*. The cover concept incidentally informs us that Guest is an international figure whose poem about Italy translated by a Japanese poet is published in Japan. The first poem in the collection is "December in Kagoshima," set in a famous Japanese tourist spot that is being visited out of season. In the book there are family poems and various kinds of love poems, including the extended and ambitious sequence "Metamorphoses"

that is, in its sexual frankness, helping to establish the new freedoms
of that time. Some of this writing is located in, or contains descriptive
elements of, Japanese landscape and culture. The reader comes across
maples, banana trees, rice-fields, volcanoes, bamboos, palms, orange
trees, typhoons, and Japanese names such as Kagoshima and O-Bon.
But these are the incidental details of a cultural pluralism that is the
unifying idea of the book as a collection. "Two Poems for O-Bon," with
its generous and imaginative presentation of identity and difference,
and its openness to spiritual experience, is at the center of this theme.
Guest's poem, which takes up the Poundian method of clearing space
around carefully-placed images, seems also to manifest a similar
ambition to that of Pound writing *Cathay*, introducing us to another
world with a different aesthetic and a different framework of belief.

My second exhibit is a poem by Lee Harwood first published in 1974 in
a special Paul Blackburn memorial issue of the journal *Sixpack*.[4] This is
the first page of a serial poem in six pages:

Chên . 震

one of those

            rare

                        moments

            when

thoughts of death
strike

The desire to hang on

            to what
                        I have

to not   loose
sight

of

      what's held dear

the line of hills

      that edge

(the) coast

The poem begins with the reproduction of the handwritten word
"Chên" with circumflex accent over the "e," and this word is followed
by a double-spaced full stop and handwritten Chinese character. The
text below the offset title is printed in the standard sans serif type of the
journal and broken up by the layout into small fragments with plenty
of space around them. No line is more than five words long; and five
of the lines are only one word. The title "Chên" is the now obsolete
Wade-Giles Romanisation of the Chinese character 震 zhèn, shock or
shake, hexagram number 51 in the *Yi Jing*, the ancient Chinese book
of wisdom used for divination, widely known in the West in the Wade-
Giles form *I Ching*. With the Chinese character and transliteration,
and below that the widely spaced and fragmented text, we have a poem
that appears to depend formally on Pound's *Drafts and Fragments*. It
really looks like one of the late *Cantos*.

    The poem is simple in its way but not so simple as it first appears.
Punctuated by ample space, line breaks, one capital letter and one
pair of brackets, the poem seems to work confidently with reduced
means to express an intensity of feeling, a recognition coming from
the fear of death, about what is important to the speaker, who seems
to be identical with the poet. Though there are no full stops and thus
no indication of completed sentences, the use of a capital T for the
beginning of line 7 establishes a new sentence, at least the change of
voice that we would use for a new sentence, and thus the page becomes
in effect two sentences, even if they are only minimally marked in this
way. The following pages are similarly laid out, keeping the content
spare: the experience of fear, a wish for clarity, and how to carry on
with life in fear. The final section is on survival; it risks sentiment and
repeats the phrase "a long road," which is balanced against loss and
the consequences of loss. There is a shift in the formal structure of the

poem on the fourth page, which is a transcription from the *Yi Jing*

Chen / The Arousing   (51)

> When a man has learned within his
> heart what fear and trembling mean,
> he is safeguarded against any terror
> produced by outside influences.
>
> Six in the fifth place means :
> Shock goes hither and thither.
> Danger.
> However, nothing at all is lost.
> Yet there are things to be done.

This gendered but still very generalized text immediately shows why the *Yi Jing* works as a source for divination. It is abstracted to such a degree that it can be made to apply to a wide range of scenarios in just about any context we could imagine. But the language of the *Yi Jing* has been incorporated into the rest of the poem, both what precedes and what follows. The important vocabulary of the poem: *fear, death, loss, desire, survival*, is either identical to, or compatible with, the quoted material and, in its way, abstracted to the same degree. Thus on the first page, the thing "held dear" in the face of death is not a lover or family member but "the line of hills / that edge / (the) coast." The landscape feature is non-specific and cannot be located from within the poem. Coast is everywhere an edge between land and sea, here cutting off a line of hills, but there is nothing to specify what hills or what kind of cliffs must cut them off. The non-specific language of the *Yi Jing* has been incorporated thoroughly into the poem.

The fifth page in Harwood's poem is a quotation from an unnamed dictionary

> fear, v.i. & t. : to be afraid of,
> hesitate to do, shrink from doing ;
> revere

My first reaction as a reader to dictionary definitions is impatience. Does the audience for poetry really need the word "fear" to be glossed?

In my desk dictionary the entry for the noun "fear" is much longer than that for the verb – so why restrict this entry to the verb? Are we meant to notice that last word in the quotation, the fourth option, the odd one, the word "revere" separated on its own line? This is a special sense of the emotion of fear, something like the recognition of the sublime: a feeling that we need in order to access the spiritual or to be kept in our place by power and religion. I think that is why the dictionary quotation is included in the poem.

The subject of this poem is very traditional indeed, the convention of *memento mori*, a meditation on mortality and how the fear of death affects us, sharpening our sense of life and urgency. Where the poem differs from this convention in English poetics is formally in the cut-down spare free verse and in the serial form that incorporates carefully chosen alternative sources of textual authority. The *Yi Jing* was a commonplace of 1960s and 1970s counter culture in the U.S.A. and U.K. The book was on sale in bookshops and gift shops in major cities and university towns across the English-speaking world.[5] So the source is as unremarkable in itself as the unnamed dictionary. The direct use of the source in a poem, as the matter of poetry, however, is a precise cultural signal for poetry readers indicating an aspect of "open form" poetry such as Pound's *Cantos*, Williams' *Paterson*, or Olson's *Maximus*, all of which directly incorporate various kinds of text either as documentary evidence or authority within the poem.

The context in which I find this poem begins immediately to modify Harwood's spare and minimal-seeming poem. The special Paul Blackburn memorial issue of the journal *Sixpack* had two editors, one based in London and one in North Carolina, but it is an American production and the contributors are almost all American. The issue contains ninety pages of previously unpublished material by Paul Blackburn, followed by 150 pages of festschrift for Blackburn. Lee Harwood's contribution is the poem "Chên" preceded by a one-page tribute "A note on Paul Blackburn" (148). So the poem that meditates on the fear of death seems to be a direct response to Paul Blackburn's death. In Harwood's note, Blackburn is compared for his impact as a writer to Larry Eigner, Fielding Dawson, and John Ashbery. The comparison is followed, in a Poundian move, by a quotation from *Ta Hio* "Precise verbal definitions of their inarticulate thoughts (the tones

given off by the heart)" attributed to "Confucius / Kung" and a longer
quotation from a Blackburn poem, "Bluegrass."
    The note sets out a field of reference adding Blackburn's name to a
group of contemporary writers whom Harwood holds in high regard.
As a poet Blackburn was a committed Poundian open form writer who
dedicated most of his adult life to studying, collecting, and translating
Old Provençal poetry, taking Pound's interest in the Troubadours to
another level and fulfilling a Poundian ambition. Blackburn's 300-page
anthology of translated Troubadour poetry, *Proensa*, was published
posthumously in 1978. So Harwood's two-part tribute for Blackburn
sets out Harwood's own markers in contemporary English-language
writing: Pound, the Poundian Blackburn, and three other quite different
modernist Americans. The "note on Blackburn" is located and dated
"Brighton 23/24, ii, 74" so the coast in the poem "Chên" begins to be
located in this context, though it is not located in the poem. Harwood's
Poundian poem containing a Chinese character, text spliced in from
the *Yi Jing* and the dictionary, is about the fear of death and our grip
on the present, but it is also about allegiance to a range of modernist
tendencies in contemporary American poetry.[6]
    Harry Guest's and Lee Harwood's poems use the Orient in
different ways. Guest lived and worked in Japan from 1969-1973. He
taught in a Japanese university, translated and edited a collection of
Japanese poetry, and has since written a literary guide to Japan and
a language textbook, *Mastering Japanese*. "Two Poems for O-Bon"
has an anthropological motive but also explores spirituality and its
depiction in language. In "Chên" the Chinese title and hand drawn
Chinese character, the quotations from *Yi Jing* and Pound's *Confucius*,
show us that Harwood deliberately took on the Pound-Olson line in
American poetics; he also made his own extended open-form poems
such as "The Long Black Veil" and "Notes of a Post Office Clerk."[7]
Harwood's China seems to come via America as Pound's China came
originally via Japan. Both Guest and Harwood use the visual sign of
the Orient: Guest's book cover is made of Japanese printed characters,
and Harwood's poem includes a hand-drawn Chinese character. Guest
and Harwood have the international dimension in common, and this
is a contrast to the influential Movement poets who preceded them.
The Movement poets saw themselves as reconnecting with the sturdy

independence of the English tradition as exemplified by Hardy's poetry. They were attempting to undo modernism, which was seen as a suspect foreign import and responsible for English poetry losing its way in the 1940s.

Harwood translated the Dada poet Tzara who wrote in French, and Guest translated many French poets, including a volume of Victor Hugo. To make poetry with an international dimension in 1960s and 1970s England was to find an alternative to the antimodernist mainstream as defined in Philip Larkin's *Oxford Book of Twentieth-Century English Verse*. To write a spacious open-formed verse, which explored Eastern systems of ritual, belief and thought, was to keep alive a connection with the modernism of Pound, H.D., Eliot, and Olson, and to continue what is by now an established modernist tradition.

Notes

1. China and Japan are important themes in recent English poetry. I might well have chosen to discuss J. H. Prynne's *News of Warring Clans*, or his Chinese poem "Jie Ban Mi Shi Hu," or his essay "China Figures," or his edition of and afterword for *Original: Chinese Language-Poetry Group*, or Ralph Hawkins' sequence "China," or Wendy Mulford's "I China Am," or Carol Watts' "Found China" or the very widespread use, authentic or not, of Japanese verse forms translated into English, known as Haiku, Haibun, and more recently Renga which has been taken up as a process of collaborative working, both within day-long staged events and online. Alec Finlay has set up a series of Renga events, and James Kirkup and Peter Robinson are both English poets who lived in Japan and worked at universities there for some years.

2. Translation is an important part of both Guest's and Harwood's practice, and there are examples of ekphrasis in both poets' works; I'll have more to say about Chinese and Japanese characters later in this essay.

3. "Two Poems for O-Bon," copyright © Harry Guest 1970, is reprinted here by permission of the poet.

4. "Chên . 震" Copyright © Lee Harwood 1974, is reprinted here by permission of the poet; the poem was subsequently published in Lee Harwood's collection *Boston – Brighton*, 1977, a note on the contents page reads as follows: "The title *Chên*, and the Chinese ideogram accompanying it, were especially drawn for this edition by the author."

5. The journal *Sixpack* reflects this ubiquity, using an *Yi Jing* hexagram (number 43: Guài – displacement or breakthrough) as its punning logo.

6. When the poem "Chên" appears in the collection *Boston – Brighton* (1977), there is no mention of Paul Blackburn and no suggestion, therefore, that the poem was in any way an elegy for Blackburn. The coast in the poem "Chên," which seemed an unspecified and even abstract idea in the *Sixpack* printing, is surrounded by a mass of reference in other poems to the coast of South East England around Brighton.

7. "The Long Black Veil: A Notebook 1970-1972" (*HMS Little Fox*, 1975) is an extended open form love poem just short of 30 pages, which begins with an epigraph from Pound's "Canto 77" and includes the symbol for yin and yang (17) and a quotation from the *Yi Jing* (18), making it a patchwork of quotations from many authors. "Notes of a Post Office Clerk" (*Boston – Brighton*, 1977) is an Olsonian project of politics, local history, and coastal mapping, including hand drawn historical and geological maps and pasted-in shipping reports from Harwood's local Brighton paper.

Works Cited

Blackburn, Paul, trans. *Proensa: An Anthology of Troubadour Poetry*. Ed. George Economou. New York: Paragon House, 1986.

Guest, Harry. *The Cutting Room*. London: Anvil P, 1970.

___. *Post-War Japanese Poetry*. Ed. and trans. Harry and Lynn Guest and Kajima Shôzô. Harmondsworth: Penguin, 1972.

___, trans. *Victor Hugo: The Distance, The Shadows*. London: Anvil P, 1981.

___. *Mastering Japanese*. London: Palgrave Macmillan, 1989.

Harwood, Lee. "A note on Paul Blackburn / Chên." *Sixpack* 7/8 (1974). 148-154.

___. *HMS Little Fox*. London: Oasis Books, 1975.

___. *Boston – Brighton*. London: Oasis Books, 1977.

Hawkins, Ralph. "China." *Well, You Could Do*. London: Curiously Strong, 1979.

Larkin, Philip, ed. *The Oxford Book of Twentieth-CenturyEnglish Verse*. Oxford: Oxford UP, 1973.

Mulford, Wendy. "I China Am." *Infinite Difference: Other Poetries by UK*

Women Poets. Ed. Carrie Etter. Exeter: Shearsman Books, 2010.

Olson, Charles. *The Maximus Poems.* 2 vols. London: Cape Goliard P, 1960, 1968.

Pound, Ezra. *The Cantos.* 13th printing. New York: New Directions, 1995.

___, trans. *Cathay.* London: Elkin Mathews, 1915.

___, trans. *Certain Noh Plays of Japan.* Churchtown: Cuala P, 1916.

___, trans. *Confucius: The Great Digest, The Unwobbling Pivot, The Analects.* New York: New Directions, 1969.

Prynne, J. H. "China Figures." *New Songs from a Jade Terrace: An Anthology of Early Chinese Love Poetry.* Ed. and trans. Anne Birrell. Harmondsworth: Penguin, 1986.

___. *News of Warring Clans.* London: Trigram P, 1977.

___, ed. *Original: Chinese Language-Poetry Group.* Trans. Jeff Twitchell. Brighton: Parataxis, 1994.

___. *Poems.* Newcastle Upon Tyne: Bloodaxe Books, 1999.

Watts, Carol. "Found China." *Text 2.* Ed. Tony Trehy. Bury, Lancashire: Bury Metropolitan Borough Council, 2009. 57-59.

Wilhelm, Richard and Cary Baynes, ed. and trans. *The I Ching or Book of Changes.* Princeton N.J.: Princeton UP, 1950; 3rd edition with foreword by Carl Jung, 1967.

Williams, William Carlos. *Paterson.* Ed. Christopher MacGowan. New York: New Directions, 1992.

Notes on Contributors

DANIEL ALBRIGHT, Ernest Bernbaum Professor of Literature at Harvard University, writes on modernism in literature, music, painting, and philosophy, in such books as *Untwisting the Serpent* (2000), *Quantum Poetics* (1997), and *Representation and the Imagination* (1981). He has also edited a complete edition of Yeats' poems, and written books on Shakespeare and music, and on such nineteenth-century figures as Berlioz and Tennyson.

RONALD BUSH, Drue Heinz Professor of American Literature at Oxford University, is the author of *The Genesis of Ezra Pound's Cantos* (1976) and *T.S. Eliot: A Study in Character and Style* (1983). He has published widely on Pound, Eliot, Joyce, and other modernist topics and is at work on a two-volume genetic study and critical edition of the Pisan Cantos.

CHRISTINE FROULA, Professor of English, Comparative Literary Studies, and Gender Studies at Northwestern University, is the author of *To Write Paradise: Style and Error in Pound's "Cantos"* (1983), *Modernism's Body: Sex, Culture, and Joyce* (1996), and *Virginia Woolf and Bloomsbury Avant-garde: War, Civilization, Modernity* (2005).

FEN GAO, Professor of English at Zhejiang University, China, is the author of *Modernism, Roots and Trends* (2000). She has published on Woolf, Faulkner, and other modernist writers and is at work on Virginia Woolf's life poetics.

CHRISTIAN KLOECKNER teaches American Literature and Culture at the University of Bonn and has recently finished his dissertation, "Exploding Books: Contemporary American Fiction, Maurice

Blanchot, and the Writing of Terror(ism)." He has co-edited (with Sabine Sielke) *Orient and Orientalisms in US-American Poetry* and Poetics (2009) and (with Birte Christ, Elisabeth Schäfer-Wünsche, and Michael Butter) *American Studies/Shifting Gears* (2010).

TONY LOPEZ, Emeritus Professor of Poetry at the University of Plymouth, is an English poet best known for his book *False Memory* (1996, 2003, 2012), a poem that samples and satirizes the language of commodity culture in the west. His recent publications include *Meaning Performance: Essays on Poetry* (2006), *Only More So* (2011) and *Works on Paper* (2011). He now works on public art incorporating text.

IRA B. NADEL, Professor of English at the University of British Columbia, is the author of biographies of Leonard Cohen, Tom Stoppard, and David Mamet. He has also edited *The Cambridge Companion to Ezra Pound* (1999) and *Ezra Pound in Context* (2010). Published essays include work on Joyce, Brecht, and Stein. His current focus is Philip Roth.

RICHARD PARKER is an Assistant Professor of American Literature at the University of Gaziantep in Turkey. He received his D.Phil. from the University of Sussex for a dissertation on Ezra Pound and Louis Zukofsky. He has published in various journals on Pound and Zukofsky as well as on modernism, sports literature, and Victorian aestheticism. He is currently editing a collection of essays on Ezra Pound based on papers delivered at the London *Cantos* Reading Group

ZHAOMING QIAN, formerly Chancellor's Research Professor of English at the University of New Orleans, is Chair Professor of English and Comparative Literary Studies at Hangzhou Normal University. His books include *Orientalism and Modernism: The Legacy of China in Pound and Williams* (1995), *The Modernist Response to Chinese Art: Pound, Moore, Stevens* (2003), *Ezra Pound and China* (2003), and *Ezra Pound's Chinese Friends* (2008). His current project is *East/West Collaboration & Renewal of Modernism*.

SABINE SIELKE is Chair of North American Literature and Culture and Director of the North American Studies Program, the German-Canadian Centre, and the Forum Women and Gender Studies at the University of Bonn. She is the author of *Fashioning the Female Subject: The Intertextual Networking of Dickinson, Moore, and Rich* (1997) and *Reading Rape: The Rhetoric of Sexual Violence in American Literature and Culture, 1790-1990* (2002), as well as (co-)editor of more than ten essay collections. She has published widely on poetry and poetics, modern and post-modern literature and culture, literary and cultural theory, gender and African American studies, popular culture, and the interfaces of cultural studies and the sciences.

QIPING YIN, Professor of English at Hangzhou Normal University, is the author of *Debating the Discourse of Progress: A New Type of Novel in 19ᵗʰ Century England* (2009) and *A History of Criticism of English Fiction* (2001). He has published widely on the English novel and theories of the novel, and is at work on Raymond Williams.

ZHANG LONGXI, Chair Professor of Comparative Literature and Translation at the City University of Hong Kong, has published in both Chinese and English works in comparative literature and cross-cultural studies. His books in English include *The Tao and Logos: Literary Hermeneutics, East and West* (1992); *Mighty Opposites: From Dichotomies to Differences in the Comparative Study of China* (1998); *Allegoresis: Reading Canonical Literature East and West* (2005); and *Unexpected Affinities: Reading across Cultures* (2007).

Index

Also Available from

General Titles

Sometimes Courage Looks Like Crazy: A Journalist's Story by Kim Bondy, 978-1-60801-058-5 (2011)

Post-Katrina Brazucas: Brazilian Immigrants in New Orleans by Annie Gibson, 978-1-60801-070-7 (2011)

The Saratoga Collection, edited by Terrence Sanders, 978-1-60801-061-5 (2011)

The Garden Path: The Miseducation of a City, by Andre Perry, 978-1-60801-048-6 (2011)

Before (During) After: Louisiana Photographers Visual Reactions to Hurricane Katrina, edited by Elizabeth Kleinveld, 978-1-60801-023-3 (2010)

Beyond the Islands by Alicia Yánez Cossío, translated by Amalia Gladhart, 978-1-60801-043-1 (2010)

Writer in Residence: Memoir of a Literary Translator by Mark Spitzer, 978-1-60801-020-2 (2010)

The Fox's Window by Naoko Awa, translated by Toshiya Kamei, 978-1-60801-006-6 (2010)

Black Santa by Jamie Bernstein, 978-1-60801-022-6 (2010)

Dream-crowned (Traumgekrönt) by Rainer Maria Rilke, translated by Lorne Mook, 978-1-60801-041-7 (2010)

Voices Rising II: More Stories from the Katrina Narrative Project edited by Rebeca Antoine, 978-0-9706190-8-2 (2010)

Rowing to Sweden: Essays on Faith, Love, Politics, and Movies by Fredrick Barton, 978-1-60801-001-1 (2010)

Dogs in My Life: The New Orleans Photographs of John Tibule Mendes, 978-1-60801-005-9 (2010)

New Orleans: The Underground Guide by Michael Patrick Welch & Alison Fensterstock, 978-1-60801-019-6 (2010)

Understanding the Music Business: A Comprehensive View edited by Harmon Greenblatt & Irwin Steinberg, 978-1-60801-004-2 (2010)

The Gravedigger by Rob Magnuson Smith, 978-1-60801-010-3 (2010)

Portraits: Photographs in New Orleans 1998-2009 by Jonathan Traviesa, 978-0-9706190-5-1 (2009)

I hope it's not over, and good-by: Selected Poems of Everette Maddox by Everette Maddox, 978-1-60801-000-4 (2009)

Theoretical Killings: Essays & Accidents by Steven Church, 978-0-9706190-6-8 (2009)

Voices Rising: Stories from the Katrina Narrative Project edited by Rebeca Antoine, 978-0-9728143-6-2 (2008)

On Higher Ground: The University of New Orleans at Fifty by Dr. Robert Dupont, 978-0-9728143-5-5 (2008)

The Change Cycle Handbook by Will Lannes, 978-0-9728143-9-3 (2008)

Us Four Plus Four: Eight Russian Poets Conversing translated by Don Mager, 978-0-9706190-4-4 (2008)

The El Cholo Feeling Passes by Fredrick Barton, 978-0-9728143-2-4 (2003)

A House Divided by Fredrick Barton, 978-0-9728143-1-7 (2003)

William Christenberry: Art & Family by J. Richard Gruber, 978-0-9706190-0-6 (2000)

The Neighborhood Story Project

New Orleans in 19 Movements by Thurgood Marshall Early College High School, 978-1-60801-069-1 (2011)

The Combination by Ashley Nelson, 978-1-60801-055-4 (2010)

The House of Dance and Feathers: A Museum by Ronald W. Lewis by Rachel Breunlin & Ronald W. Lewis, 978-0-9706190-7-5 (2009)

Beyond the Bricks by Daron Crawford & Pernell Russell, 978-1-60801-016-5 (2010)

Aunt Alice Vs. Bob Marley by Kareem Kennedy, 978-1-60801-013-4 (2010)

Signed, The President by Kenneth Phillips, 978-1-60801-015-8 (2010)

Houses of Beauty: From Englishtown to the Seventh Ward by Susan Henry, 978-1-60801-014-1 (2010)

Coming Out the Door for the Ninth Ward edited by Rachel Breunlin, 978-0-9706190-9-9 (2006)

Cornerstones: Celebrating the Everyday Monuments & Gathering Places of New Orleans edited by Rachel Breunlin, 978-0-9706190-3-7 (2008)

The Engaged Writes Series

Medea and Her War Machines by Ioan Flora, translated by Adam J. Sorkin, 978-1-60801-067-7 (2011)

Together by Julius Chingono and John Eppel, 978-1-60801-049-3 (2011)

Vegetal Sex (O Sexo Vegetal) by Sergio Medeiros, translated by Raymond L.Bianchi, 978-1-60801-046-2 (2010)

*Wounded Days (Los Días Heridos) by Leticia Luna, translated by Toshiya Kamei, 978-1-60801-042-4 (2010)

When the Water Came: Evacuees of Hurricane Katrina by Cynthia Hogue & Rebecca Ross, 978-1-60801-012-7 (2010)

*A Passenger from the West by Nabile Farès, translated by Peter Thompson, 978-1-60801-008-0 (2010)

*Everybody Knows What Time It Is by Reginald Martin, 978-1-60801-011-0 (2010)

*Green Fields: Crime, Punishment, & a Boyhood Between by Bob Cowser, Jr., 978-1-60801-018-9 (2010)

*Open Correspondence: An Epistolary Dialogue by Abdelkébir Khatibi and Rita El Khayat, translated by Safoi Babana-Hampton, Valérie K. Orlando, Mary Vogl, 978-1-60801-021-9 (2010)

Gravestones (Lápidas) by Antonio Gamoneda, translated by Donald Wellman, 978-1-60801-002-8 (2009)

Hearing Your Story: Songs of History and Life for Sand Roses by Nabile Farès translated by Peter Thompson, 978-0-9728143-7-9 (2008)

The Katrina Papers: A Journal of Trauma and Recovery by Jerry W. Ward, Jr., 978-0-9728143-3-1 (2008)

Contemporary Poetry

California Redemption Values by Kevin Opstedal, 978-1-60801-066-0 (2011)

Atlanta Poets Group Anthology: The Lattice Inside by Atlanta Poets Group, 978-1-60801-064-6 (2011)

Makebelieve by Caitlin Scholl, 978-1-60801-056-1 (2011)

Dear Oxygen: New and Selected Poems by Lewis MacAdams, edited by Kevin Opstedal, 978-1-60801-059-2 (2011)

Only More So by Tony Lopez, 978-1-60801-057-8 (2011)

Enridged by Brian Richards, 978-1-60801-047-9 (2011)

A Gallery of Ghosts by John Gery, 978-0-9728143-4-8 (2008)

The Ezra Pound Center for Literature

The Poets of the Sala Capizucchi (I Poeti della Sala Capizucchi) edited by Caterina Ricciardi and John Gery, 978-1-60801-068-4 (2011)

Trespassing, by Patrizia de Rachewiltz, 978-1-60801-060-8 (2011)

*The Imagist Poem: Modern Poetry in Miniature edited by William Pratt, 978-0-9728143-8-6 (2008)

Contemporary Austrian Studies

Global Austria: Austria's Place in Europe and the World, Günter Bischof, Fritz Plasser (Eds.), Alexander Smith, Guest Editor, 978-1-60801-062-2 (2011)

From Empire to Republic: Post-World-War-I Austria Volume 19 edited by Günter Bischof, Fritz Plasser and Peter Berger, 978-1-60801-025-7 (2010)

The Schüssel Era in Austria Volume 18 edited by Günter Bischof & Fritz Plasser, 978-1-60801-009-7 (2009)

*Also available as E-book